Tackling Terrorism in Britain

In September 2001, the world witnessed the horrific events of 9/11. A great deal has happened on the counterterrorist front in the 20 years since. While the terrorist threat has greatly diminished in Northern Ireland, the events of 9/11 and their aftermath have ushered in a new phase for the rest of the UK with some familiar, but also many novel, characteristics.

This ambitious study takes stock of counterterrorism in Britain in this anniversary year. Assessing current challenges, and closely mirroring the 'four Ps' of the official CONTEST counterterrorist strategy – *Protect*, *Prepare*, *Prevent*, and *Pursue* – it seeks to summarize and grasp the essence of domestic law and policy, without being burdened by excessive technical detail. It also provides a rigorous, context-aware, illuminating, yet concise, accessible, and policy-relevant analysis of this important and controversial subject, grounded in relevant social science, policy studies, and legal scholarship.

This book will be an important resource for students and scholars in law and social science, as well as human rights, terrorism, counterterrorism, security, and conflict studies.

Steven Greer is Professor of Human Rights at the University of Bristol Law School, UK. He studied Law at the University of Oxford, UK, and Sociology at the London School of Economics and Political Science, UK. He also has a PhD in Law from Queen's University Belfast, UK. In a career spanning over 30 years he has taught and delivered numerous papers throughout the UK and abroad, including China and the United States. He is Fellow of the Academy of Social Sciences and of the Royal Society of Arts, has acted as consultant/ advisor to various organizations, and has published widely, particularly in the fields of criminal justice, human rights, and law and terrorism.

Routledge Research in Terrorism and the Law

Available titles in this series include:

The Impact, Legitimacy and Effectiveness of EU Counter-Terrorism
Fiona de Londras and Josephine Doody

Preventive Detention of Terror Suspects
A New Legal Framework
Diane Webber

Domestic Counter-Terrorism in a Global World
Post-9/11 Institutional Structures and Cultures in Canada and the UK
Daniel Alati

Anti-Terrorism Law and Foreign Terrorist Fighters
Edited By Jessie Blackbourn, Deniz Kayis, and Nicola McGarrity

Digital Privacy, Terrorism and Law Enforcement
The UK's Response to Terrorist Communication
Simon Hale-Ross

National Security, Personal Privacy and the Law
Surveying Electronic Surveillance and Data Acquisition
Sybil Sharpe

Law, Politics and Countering Violent Extremism
Mustafa Amin Farooq

Tackling Terrorism in Britain
Threats, Responses, and Challenges Twenty Years After 9/11
Steven Greer

For more information about this series, please visit: www.routledge.com/Routledge-Research-in-Terrorism-and-the-Law/book-series/TERRORISMLAW

Tackling Terrorism in Britain
Threats, Responses, and Challenges
Twenty Years After 9/11

Steven Greer

LONDON AND NEW YORK

First published 2022
by Routledge
2 Park Square, Milton Park, Abingdon, Oxon OX14 4RN

and by Routledge
605 Third Avenue, New York, NY 10158

Routledge is an imprint of the Taylor & Francis Group, an informa business

© 2022 Steven Greer

The right of Steven Greer to be identified as author of this work has been asserted by him in accordance with sections 77 and 78 of the Copyright, Designs and Patents Act 1988.

All rights reserved. No part of this book may be reprinted or reproduced or utilised in any form or by any electronic, mechanical, or other means, now known or hereafter invented, including photocopying and recording, or in any information storage or retrieval system, without permission in writing from the publishers.

Trademark notice: Product or corporate names may be trademarks or registered trademarks, and are used only for identification and explanation without intent to infringe.

British Library Cataloguing-in-Publication Data
A catalogue record for this book is available from the British Library

Library of Congress Cataloging-in-Publication Data
Names: Greer, Steven, 1956- author.
Title: Tackling terrorism in Britain: threats, responses, and challenges twenty years after 9/11/Steven Greer.
Description: Abingdon, Oxon [UK]; New York, NY: Routledge, 2021. |
Series: Routledge research in terrorism and the law |
Includes bibliographical references and index.
Identifiers: LCCN 2021021583 (print) | LCCN 2021021584 (ebook) | ISBN 9781032117027 (hardback) |
ISBN 9781032117003 (paperback) | ISBN 9781003221104 (ebook)
Subjects: LCSH: Terrorism–Prevention–Law and legislation–Great Britain. | Domestic terrorism–Law and legislation–Great Britain. |
War on Terrorism, 2001-2009–History.
Classification: LCC KD8039 .G74 2021 (print) |
LCC KD8039 (ebook) | DDC 344.4105/325–dc23
LC record available at https://lccn.loc.gov/2021021583
LC ebook record available at https://lccn.loc.gov/2021021584

ISBN: 978-1-032-11702-7 (hbk)
ISBN: 978-1-032-11700-3 (pbk)
ISBN: 978-1-003-22110-4 (ebk)

DOI: 10.4324/9781003221104

Typeset in Bembo
by Deanta Global Publishing Services, Chennai, India

To my little granddaughters, Aster and Penny

Contents

Preface	viii
1 Themes and trends	1
2 Global jihad	23
3 Domestic terrorism	49
4 *Protect* and *Prepare*	88
5 *Prevent*	112
6 *Pursue*	153
7 Threats, responses, and challenges	188
Appendix A: Fatal terrorist incidents in the UK, 2005–20	199
Appendix B: Chronology of key events, 1997–2020	201
Index	210

Preface

Twenty years ago, the world witnessed the horrific events of 9/11. A great deal has happened on the counterterrorist front since. For one thing, the term 'war on terror', which never had any official traction in the UK anyway, has all but disappeared from the serious debate. Nevertheless, the threat of terrorism, and the struggle against it, persist around the globe. The UK is no stranger to either, at home or abroad. In fact, taking various forms and manifesting in several phases, the British experience has spanned at least a century and a half rather than simply the past two decades. Today three distinct types of domestic terrorism – dissident Irish republican, far right, and particularly jihadi – predominate. A suite of counterterrorist laws and policies has been deployed to address the challenges they present.

Few systematic attempts have yet been made to take stock or to answer a key question – how *should* terrorism in Britain be tackled? Taking a bird's eye view which seeks to transcend technical detail, this study attempts to do just that. For the benefit of academic and professional readerships, and for the interested lay person, it seeks to describe, explain, and critically to appraise contemporary domestic British counterterrorism, and to challenge some pervasive myths. Chapter 1, *Themes and Trends*, provides a brief background and overview. Chapters 2 and 3, *Global Jihad* and *Domestic Terrorism* consider, respectively, the principal characteristics of current challenges in each of these contexts. Chapters 4–6, *Protect and Prepare*, *Prevent*, and *Pursue*, review the 'four Ps' of CONTEST, the official counterterrorist framework. Chapter 7, *Threats, Responses, and Challenges*, summarizes and develops the conclusions reached elsewhere in the text. But since it raises a host of complex questions requiring separate investigation, British counterterrorism abroad is not included. The Northern Irish experience, now a mere shadow of what it once was, is considered, but not in the depth found elsewhere in the extensive specialist literature. Hence the title of this book.

Jihadi terrorism, by far the most deadly and destructive of the three types, and the environment from which it has arisen and within which it is being tackled, are significantly different from anything experienced in Britain hitherto. Counterterrorist dilemmas have also arisen which cannot easily be referenced to the past, and which, in the present, may not be amenable to self-evidently correct resolution. As a result, responsible and humane people, equally well-informed and equally committed to the same goals and core values, may reasonably disagree about where the lines between legitimate and illegitimate responses should be drawn, and whether or not they have been crossed.

However, it is misleading to characterize domestic counterterrorism in Britain, as some do, in terms of 'the state versus the Muslims', or 'security versus liberty', where the latter of the two alleged protagonists in each of these antinomies is invariably and unjustifiably subordinated to the former. On the contrary, the central conclusion reached by this study is that, though imperfect, CONTEST is broadly compatible with human rights, democracy, the rule of law, and the legitimate interests of liberal cosmopolitan society. There is plenty of scope for debate about the details. But there is no convincing case for jettisoning any of its core components, much less the entire regime. For one thing, no viable alternative has yet been conceived, much less proposed.

This study would either not have been possible, or would have been much more difficult to accomplish, had it not been for the support and assistance of a number of individuals and institutions, to whom and to which I would like to express my profound gratitude. In particular, Professor Clive Walker provided invaluable expertise, advice, and encouragement at the project's inception and initial development. The imminent publication, by Oxford University Press, of the fourth edition of his magisterial study, *Blackstone's Guide to the Anti-Terrorism Legislation*, is eagerly anticipated. Until then, those interested in the finer details of the issues outlined in Chapter 6, *Pursue*, could do no better than consult the third edition which is appropriately cited. The University of Bristol Law School provided welcome research leave. The assistance of many colleagues and others, who either read and commented upon earlier drafts and/or provided various other kinds of assistance and support, is also gratefully acknowledged. These include Diego Acosta Arcarazo, Ardavan Arzandeh, Lindsey Bell, Pat Capps, Michael Ford, Sofia Galani, Clair Gammage, Roger George, Genevieve Lennon, Cian Murphy, Rachel Murray, Michael Naughton, Margherita Pieraccini, Devyani Prabhat, Julian Rivers, Roseanne Russell, Albert Sanchez Graells, Achilles Skordas, Phil Syrpis, Clare Torrible, Ian Turner, and Eleanor Zhao (who checked some of the statistics). The staff at Routledge also brought the project to fruition with professionalism and dedication.

In each of my previous books I have gratefully acknowledged the quiet background support and encouragement of my family. I repeat this here with one difference. Susan, Cara, Lucy, and Hope have already seen their names in print. It is now a considerable pleasure to add those of Aster and Penny, my two little granddaughters, neither of whom is old enough even to recognize theirs yet. The pursuit of a better future for them, and others, has been the most compelling motive for undertaking this project.

1 Themes and trends

Introduction

Subject to peaks and troughs, terrorism and counterterrorism in Britain have been locked in a deadly embrace for at least a century and a half. The contemporary landscape is dominated by three distinct threats – from a national offshoot of global jihadism, from dissident Irish republicans, and from the far right. Other much less prevalent risks also lurk in the shadows. Modern domestic counterterrorist law and policy have also evolved over the decades, particularly since 9/11 in 2001. This chapter seeks to identify the key themes and trends which the remainder of the study will explore more thoroughly. These include relevant concepts and definitions, types and phases of terrorism in Britain, continuities and discontinuities in domestic counterterrorism, risk and resilience, evaluations of relevant law and policy, and the implications of wider challenges including Brexit and Covid-19.

Concepts and definitions

The two key concepts at the core of this study are, of course, 'terrorism' and 'counterterrorism', particularly in the domestic British context.

Terrorism

In spite of a massive literature, there is no consensus amongst scholars, jurists, security analysts, and policy-makers about whether there is such a thing as 'terrorism' and, if so, how it should be characterised. The term first entered the modern political lexicon as a label for the policy adopted by the Jacobins in the 1790s to defend the French Revolution from its foreign enemies and their suspected domestic allies. The guillotining of many innocent people in the indiscriminate 'reign of terror' which unfolded leaves no room for doubt that the state itself is capable of 'terrorism'. However, the term 'terrorism' has since been more commonly applied to the activities of non-state actors using and threatening violence, particularly against soft civilian targets, in order to spread fear and insecurity in their conflict with the state, or in defending it from its adversaries.

Legal instruments in many states attempt to define non-state terrorism, and/or to list relevant crimes. Special processes to try such offences, and/or to deal with related issues, may also be provided. For instance, a schedule to the Northern Ireland (Emergency Provisions) Act 1973 provided a list of offences triable by Northern Ireland's, now effectively defunct, single-judge, non-jury 'Diplock' courts.

According to the current UK legal definition found in section 1 of the Terrorism Act 2000, as amended, 'terrorism' includes action or threats, in pursuit of a political, religious, racial, or ideological cause – designed to influence the government, or an international governmental organization, or to intimidate all or part of the public through serious life-threatening violence – which presents a serious risk to public health or safety, serious damage to property, or serious interference with, or disruption to, an electronic system. This can be criticized as over-inclusive, particularly because it could, in theory, potentially embrace certain kinds of public protest, including criminal damage to property, and mobilization in the UK in support of armed resistance against tyranny abroad. It has, nevertheless, been adopted by other jurisdictions, is broadly compliant with international law, and has not often be litigated.[1] There are, however, other approaches such as that found in the European Convention on the Prevention of Terrorism 2005 which, rather than attempting to define 'terrorism', instead provides an appendix citing 'terrorist offences' found in several other international conventions.

Social science also offers various approaches which differ from their legal equivalents in several respects. Typically they cover a wider range of issues and debates, including for example analysis of historic trends such as the so-called four 'waves' (anarchist, anti-colonialist, new left/right, and religious); the relationship between terrorism, war, and crime; the distinction between instrumental and symbolic manifestations; and whether the term 'terrorism' merely describes a type of observable, ideological, or 'grievance-motivated' violence or, because it almost invariably involves the deliberate targeting of non-combatants as a matter of strategy, is inherently pejorative.

Synthesizing the most illuminating insights from the widest range of sources, 'non-state terrorism' for the purposes of this study is taken to be violence, and the threat thereof, arising from conflict against, or in defence of, the state. This is conducted by militarily and politically weak, but ideologically committed, movements, organizations, and individuals, generally involving attacks on officials, public and private institutions, property, and civilian targets. For those struggling against the regime, these activities are intended to deliver a dramatic and highly visible message to the authorities, the public, and the world in

---

1 C. Walker, *Blackstone's Guide to the Anti-Terrorism Legislation*, 3rd edn. (Oxford University Press, 2014), p. 18.

general, about the intolerability of certain grievances, to create a climate of fear and insecurity, to undermine the credibility and legitimacy of public institutions, to provoke counter-productive official over-reaction, and to cause or aggravate social division. In the ensuing crisis, whatever opportunities might arise for the advancement of related goals – including destabilization, propaganda, and recruitment – are also likely to be exploited. The primary goal of non-state terrorists seeking to defend the status quo is typically to attack, not only organized armed adversaries, but also indiscriminately the communities from which they are deemed to emanate. However, in spite of valiant attempts by jurists and social scientists, no clear bright line has yet been found to distinguish terrorism from, in particular, violent resistance to tyranny, hate crime, and violent protest including riots where potentially lethal weapons such as firearms and bombs are used.

Counterterrorism

It follows that 'counterterrorism' is anything and everything, official and unofficial, lawful and unlawful, legitimate and illegitimate (including terrorism itself), intended to address, respond to, or tackle 'terrorism', thus conceived, from other sources. But things are not, of course, so straightforward. There is, for example, the familiar 'chicken-and-egg' or 'who-threw-the-first-stone?' problem. Those who resort to terrorism, including against liberal democracies, typically claim merely to be reacting against 'state terrorism' or oppression at home and/or abroad. For example, during the Troubles in Northern Ireland the IRA justified its 'armed struggle' as simply the most recent instalment in a centuries-old war of 'national liberation' beginning when the English crown invaded and colonized Ireland from the 12th century onwards.

Attempting to settle such claims, is, however, far beyond the remit of this study. It can, nevertheless, be observed that the relationship between 'non-state terrorism' and official 'counterterrorism' is essentially symbiotic and interactive: one side delivers a blow, the other responds, the former replies, and so on. But, as we shall see, both in this chapter and in the study more generally, for liberal democracies the suite of possible responses is limited, not only by what is logistically possible, but also by what is politically, constitutionally, and normatively acceptable.

Types and phases of British domestic terrorism

Various milestones could be taken as points of reference in the long experience of terrorism in the UK, and in Britain in particular. However, for present purposes the onset of 'the Troubles' in Northern Ireland in the early-1970s provides a particularly convenient one. Since then, the UK's domestic experience has fallen into three principal categories spanning two eras. 'Troubles-based' terrorism lasted from the early 1970s to 2003, the last year fatalities in this context reached double figures. Post-9/11 'British domestic jihadi' terrorism, which continues to present the most significant challenge, began with the 7/7 London bombings in July 2005 and shows no sign of ending. 'Miscellaneous terrorism', including particularly the violence of the far right, and to a much lesser extent the far left, has waxed and waned over the past few decades.[2]

Between 1970 and the end of 2020 there were just over 3,300 fatalities in the UK as a result of all kinds of terrorism.[3] The majority, between 1970 and 1990 (86 per cent), the period with the highest casualty rate, were in Northern Ireland. Amongst other things, Chapter 3 considers the threat posed by dissident Irish republicans, the only protagonist in the Northern Irish conflict with an enduring commitment to organized violence, including against targets in mainland Britain. Give or take a handful of incidents which could plausibly be regarded either as acts of terrorism or hate crimes, from the 7/7 London bombings to July 2020 there were 107 fatalities due to terrorism in mainland Britain, an annual average of 7.1.[4] The vast majority of these, 96 per cent, were perpetrated by jihadis, all but one of which, the Glasgow airport bombing of 2007, were in England. Jihadi terrorists also accounted for just short of 100 per cent of the non-fatal casualties. These figures are all significantly lower than the homicide rate for England and Wales (an annual average of 507 between April 2012 and March 2015),[5] for fatal stabbings (285 in England and Wales from March 2017 to March 2018),[6] and for deaths in road traffic accidents in Great Britain, just over 1,752 in 2019 alone.[7] Indeed, globally, more people die as a result of suicide than from terrorism, crime, and armed conflict combined.[8]

However, casualty figures do not tell the whole story. For one thing, it is said that since 2005, scores of terrorist plots, most of them jihadi, have been thwarted.[9] And, unlike many other hazards, terrorism not only poses risks to life and limb, but also damages property, public institutions, transport systems, the economy, the sense of safety in public places, and community relations. Its grim theatricality also tends to instil a sense of public fear wholly disproportionate to the risk, itself one of the core terrorist objectives. So, although

---

2 According to HM Government, *CONTEST: The United Kingdom's Strategy for Countering Terrorism*, June 2018, Cm 9608, no animal rights, extreme left wing, or environmental group is 'currently assessed as posing a security threat', para. 63.
3 G. Allen and N. Dempsey, *Terrorism in Great Britain: The Statistics*, House of Commons Library Briefing Paper CBP7613, 6 October 2017, 5. See also Appendix A.
4 See Appendix A.
5 Office for National Statistics, *Compendium: Homicide*, 'Expected Homicide Incidents per Day', available at: www.ons.gov.uk/peoplepopulationandcommunity/crimeandjustice/compendium/focusonviolentcrimeandsexualoffences/yearendingmarch2015/chapter2homicide.
6 A. Walker, 'Fatal Stabbings in England and Wales at Highest Level for More than 70 Years', *The Guardian*, 8 February 2019.
7 Department for Transport, *Statistical Release: Reported Road Casualties in Great Britain – 2019 Annual Report*, 30 September 2020.
8 S. Pinker, *Enlightenment Now: The Case for Reason, Science, Humanism and Progress* (Allen Lane, 2018), p. 192.
9 See Chapter 3.

jihadi terrorism may not pose an 'existential threat' to Britain or to the UK, it nevertheless presents a problem which neither government nor society can, or should, ignore.

Chapters 2 and 3 discuss the three types of terrorism to which the UK has been exposed since the 1970s, and their respective backgrounds. The main conclusion is that, although each is an instance of the same generic phenomenon – 'terrorism' – otherwise they could hardly be more different. In spite of some international dimensions, the Troubles were essentially a local conflict over whether Northern Ireland should remain part of the UK or become part of the Republic of Ireland. This effectively occurred within the parameters of modern European liberal democracy and was conducted by protagonists who, notwithstanding protestations to the contrary, share a great deal in common. Similarly, the terrorism of the British far left and far right, though not devoid of international dimensions, was and remains largely national in origin and focus. By contrast, British domestic jihadi terrorism is a national manifestation of a world-wide phenomenon motivated by the goal of establishing an ultimately global Islamic caliphate governed by a particularly uncompromising interpretation of Islamic law, the Sharia. Conducted by those from many races, ethnicities, languages, and nationalities, it is also compromised by multiple tribal, sectarian, and other rivalries which divide Muslims from each other as much as, if not more than, the jihadi cause unites and pits them against everyone else. In fact, 'Muslims remain the most numerous victims of terrorism, far outnumbering members of other faiths in many of the countries where terrorist-related activity is most prevalent'.[10]

Reflecting the background characteristics of the Troubles and jihadi conflicts, other differences explored more fully in Chapter 3, include grievances, ideologies, and goals; intended beneficiaries; modes of mobilization including types of movement and/or organization; targets, especially the willingness to cause mass civilian casualties; the weaponization of suicide; the role of freelancers and loners; and the contribution of existential and mental health crises to recruitment.

Continuity and discontinuity in British domestic counterterrorism

Over the past few decades, domestic counterterrorism in the UK has also exhibited a complex amalgam of continuity and discontinuity.[11] The central

---

10 M. Hill QC, *The Terrorism Acts in 2017: Report of the Independent Reviewer of Terrorism Legislation on the Operation of the Terrorism Acts 2000 and 2006, the Terrorism Prevention and Investigation Measures Act 2011, and the Terrorist Asset Freezing etc. Act 2010*, October 2018, pp. 3 and 18.
11 See S. Greer, 'Terrorism and Counter-Terrorism in the UK: From Northern Irish Troubles to Global Islamic Jihad' in G. Lennon, C. King, and C. McCartney (eds.), *Counter-Terrorism, Constitutionalism and Miscarriages of Justice: A Festschrift for Clive Walker* (Hart, 2019), pp. 45–62.

trends have included the 'growing profusion, scope and complexity' of counterterrorist law,[12] increasing emphasis upon protection and prevention, and a decisive shift in official policy from attempting to 'hold the ring', pending the negotiation of a political solution as during the Troubles,[13] to managing risk and increasing public resilience on the assumption that no viable off-the-peg solution to any of the current domestic terrorist threats can even be conceived let alone implemented. There are also significant differences in the extent to which everyday life was securitized in Northern Ireland at the height of the Troubles compared with that in mainland Britain today. Core issues concern the collection and processing of intelligence, the management and supervision of counterterrorist law and policy, how the tension between liberty and security is structured by the Human Rights Act, and the official counterterrorist framework, CONTEST.

Intelligence

The gathering and analysis of information, and deciding how to act upon it, have always been, and remain, central to tackling all types of domestic terrorism in Britain and elsewhere. The technology for obtaining and processing it has become vastly more sophisticated over the past 50 years or so. But the sources – places, people, their communications, and their belongings – and related normative challenges about how to collect it, and what to do with it once obtained, remain largely the same: prevention, pre-emption, or prosecution. While not clearly reflected in the official discourse, it is also useful to distinguish 'targeted' from 'general' responses, a distinction similar to that drawn in the wider criminal justice context between special and general deterrence where the former refers to specific individuals and the latter to society at large.

Although the modalities differ, targeted responses, familiar during the Troubles and in contemporary Britain, encompass attempts to pre-empt terrorist activities through disruption, interdiction, incapacitation, and restriction of identifiable individuals, activities, associations, plots, and conspiracies. As discussed more fully in Chapter 4, during the Troubles it was, for example, possible for specific individuals to be officially excluded from Great Britain, from Northern Ireland, and from the UK as a whole. Today, as Chapter 6 explains, designated people throughout the UK may be subject to tailor-made executive controls upon citizenship, entry from abroad, movement, residence, communication, and association. The deportation of foreign nationals suspected of terrorism, entirely absent from the Troubles, has also been a prominent feature of the post-9/11 landscape.

---

12 Walker, *Anti-Terrorism Legislation*, p. v.
13 P. Dixon, 'British Policy towards Northern Ireland 1969–2000: Continuity, Tactical Adjustment and Consistent "Inconsistencies"', *British Journal of Politics and International Relations*, (2001) 3, 340.

By contrast with the Troubles, in the jihadi context there have also been no allegations about the systematic abuse of suspects in police custody, no 'supergrass process' involving mass trials on the evidence of informers, and no notorious miscarriages of justice stimulating high-profile national and international campaigns resulting in quashed convictions. Unlike Northern Ireland, in the contemporary domestic British context, there have been no credible allegations about selective assassination either. The latter should not, however, be confused with 'shooting-to-kill' those suspected of posing a manifest and imminent risk of serious harm to others, from suicide bombing for example. Likely to hinge upon split second judgement on the part of those who pull the trigger, subject to more careful independent scrutiny later, this is lawful and human rights-compliant provided it results from the use of no more force than is absolutely necessary in the circumstances.

During the Troubles the general prevention of terrorism was sought largely through the deterrent effects of criminalization. By contrast, in the post-9/11 context, general prevention has, instead, been pursued through 'counter-radicalization' and 'de-radicalization', primarily because the prospect of punishment is unlikely to deter those intending to die as martyrs in jihadi incidents. However, apart from attempts to recruit informers, a universal feature of most if not all violent conflict and law enforcement, no formal de-radicalization programme was ever introduced in Northern Ireland. The institutional 'Prevent duty' – to 'have due regard to the need to prevent people from being drawn into terrorism', created by section 26 of the Counter-Terrorism and Security Act 2015 – does not formally apply there either, although the underlying principles do.[14] The absence of any formal counter-radicalization programme in Northern Ireland, either during the Troubles or since, may also be explained by the distinctive characteristics of this conflict considered more fully in Chapter 3.

Management and supervision

Post-9/11 domestic counterterrorism in Britain is also now much more tightly managed than its equivalent was during the Troubles. Relevant bureaucratic systems, much more sophisticated as a result of developments in IT, are subject to more effective regular independent scrutiny by a variety of institutions – including legislative, expert, and judicial bodies – within a framework defined by a formal commitment to legality, human rights, and democracy. For example, in December 2016, in his final annual report before handing over responsibility to Max Hill QC, the then Independent Reviewer of Terrorism Legislation, David Anderson QC, stated: 'the overall picture seems to me to be one of appropriately strong laws, responsibly implemented and keenly

14 See Chapter 5.

scrutinized by Parliament and by the courts'.[15] While warning of the constant need for vigilance with respect to civil liberties Mr Anderson also rejected 'the false narrative of power-hungry security services, police insensitivity to community concerns, and laws constantly being ratcheted up to new levels of oppression'.[16] Each of these conclusions is endorsed by this study.

Headed by the Counter Terrorism Command (CTC) of the Metropolitan Police, and managed by the Association of Chief Police Officer's Terrorism and Allied Matters unit (ACPO (TAM)), a complex, non-statutory police counterterrorism network has also emerged post-9/11, which straddles all 'four Ps' of CONTEST.[17] The chief of the CTC acts as Senior National Coordinator for Counter Terrorism, supported within the same organization by the National Co-ordinator of Terrorist Investigations. Outside London, there are four Counter Terrorism Units (CTUs) located in the North East, North West, West Midlands, and Thames Valley, plus four Counter Terrorism Intelligence Units (CTIUs) in Scotland, Wales, the South West, and East Midlands. Provincial Special Branches are increasingly regionalized and concentrate on borders and special protective duties. The work of the counterterrorism police network is coordinated by a Joint Counter Terrorism Oversight Group, overseen by a Police Counter Terrorism Board, chaired by the Home Secretary.[18] A specialist Counter Terrorism Policing National Digital Exploitation Service (NDES) was also established in 2016 to address the growing need for the police to provide the digital evidence required to convict the most dangerous terrorists.[19]

The dawning of the new millennium also coincided with three significant developments linking the Troubles and post-9/11 phases. Continuity has been provided by the Terrorism Act 2000 which consolidates the piecemeal UK-wide and Northern Ireland-specific legislation of the previous three decades. Amongst other things this includes provisions dealing with terrorist offences, property, finance, investigations, arrest, detention, stop, search, and seize, plus port and border controls. Having been temporarily retained, Northern Ireland's counterterrorist Diplock courts were phased out from August 2005. Subject to revival for exceptional cases, they were finally moth-balled as from July 2007.[20] However, the Human Rights Act 1998 (HRA), which came into force in 2000, and CONTEST – the part-legislative, part-administrative counterterrorist strategy developed by successive Labour, Coalition,

---

15 D. Anderson QC (Independent Reviewer of Terrorism Legislation), *The Terrorism Acts in 2015: Report of the Independent Reviewer on the Operation of the Terrorism Act 2000 and Part 1 of the Terrorism Act 2006*, Presented to Parliament pursuant to Section 36(5) of the Terrorism Act 2006, December 2016, para. 11.10.
16 Ibid., p. 2 and para. 11.14.
17 See A. Staniforth, C. Walker, and S. Osborne, *Blackstone's Counter-Terrorism Handbook*, 2nd edn. (Oxford University Press, 2011), Chapter 3.
18 See Home Office, *Pursue, Prevent, Protect, Prepare*, Cm.7547, 2009, para. 14.30.
19 Metropolitan Police Service (MPS), *Police Staff Information Pack Digital Specialist – Hardware*, 2018.
20 Justice and Security (Northern Ireland) Act 2007.

and Conservative governments in response to 9/11 and its aftermath – provide significant sources of discontinuity.

Liberty and security

The relationship between liberty and security is complex for three principal reasons: each is an abstract notion, no self-evident equilibrium between them can be found in liberal democracy, and in any given society, certain social groups may optimize their own liberty and security by restricting that of subordinate groups, and indeed often do. Benjamin Franklin's famous remark – 'Those who would give up essential Liberty, to purchase a little temporary Safety, deserve neither Liberty nor Safety' – is also typically misquoted with the qualifiers, *essential* liberty and *temporary* safety, ignored. But for present purposes it is sufficient to observe that it is impossible to counter terrorism or any other type of crime effectively without restricting somebody's liberty. Since the Human Rights Act 1998 ('HRA') incorporated the European Convention on Human Rights ('ECHR') into UK law, the relationship between liberty and security has been structured in the language of human rights and the restrictions which may legitimately be imposed upon the former in pursuit of the latter.

The Act has considerable implications for all branches of law, public administration, and policy in the UK. But the following elements are particularly important for the purposes of this study. The HRA makes it unlawful for 'public authorities', except Parliament, to 'act in a way which is incompatible' with a right found in the European Convention on Human Rights (ECHR).[21] Complaints that this statutory duty has been violated may be made in any legal proceedings, including appeals, and those brought expressly for this purpose in an 'appropriate court or tribunal'.[22] Section 2(1) requires courts and tribunals determining HRA-related issues to take relevant decisions and opinions of Council of Europe institutions (the parent body of the European Court of Human Rights, 'ECtHR') into account. This enhances the prospect of UK public policy, including in the counterterrorism field, being integrated into evolving pan-European human rights standards.

The HRA has also significantly increased the extent to which draft legislation is scrutinized to ensure compliance with the ECHR. Section 19 requires Ministers responsible for presenting bills to Parliament to make a written and published statement before the Second Reading, either to the effect that the proposed legislation is compatible with Convention rights ('a statement of compatibility'), or that the government wishes the House to proceed even though such an assurance cannot be given. This has added systematic Convention checking to the considerable bureaucratic effort already invested in legislative drafting. The presumption that legislation should be Convention-compliant

21 s. 6(1).
22 s. 7(1)(a).

has also given extra weight to the contribution NGOs and the Equality and Human Rights Commission make to the Whitehall and Parliamentary processes. Once bills have been presented to Parliament, the Joint Parliamentary Committee on Human Rights also plays an important scrutinizing and advisory role. Commentators agree that the significant reduction of Convention violations in the legislative drafting processes has been among the HRA's most notable achievements.[23]

Section 3 of the HRA also creates an obligation for primary and secondary legislation, whether enacted before or after the HRA came into force, to be read and given effect by the courts, 'so far as it is possible to do so', in a way which is compatible with Convention rights. Where this is not possible, the validity, continuing operation, and enforcement of the provision remain unaffected. However, while the courts have sometimes read words into statutes in order to avoid having to find a given provision incompatible with the ECHR, the vast majority of HRA cases since the Act came into force have concerned executive action rather than legislation.[24]

Finally, if, in any proceedings in the high court or any superior court, a provision of primary legislation is found to be incompatible with an ECHR right, the court may issue a 'declaration of incompatibility'.[25] These do not affect the validity, continuing operation, or enforcement of relevant provisions, are not binding on the parties, and as such are not regarded by the ECtHR as an effective domestic remedy. Where a domestic court, or the ECtHR, has declared specific statutory provisions incompatible with Convention rights, section 10 of the HRA enables them to be amended, subject to subsequent Parliamentary approval, by remedial order made by a Minister where he or she considers there are 'compelling reasons' for doing so.

A particularly important feature of the human rights-compliant delivery of domestic counterterrorist law and policy, provided by the ECHR and international human rights law generally, concerns the distinction between 'non-derogable' and 'derogable' rights. 'Derogation' is an official notice given by a state to a designated treaty body, that a specific human right provided by the international human rights regime in question, has been suspended. 'Non-derogable' rights are those that can never be lawfully suspended, including for the purposes of counterterrorism. Most are not subject to any express restriction for any reason, including counterterrorism, either. However, non-derogable rights comprise a very limited category. For example, there is only a

---

23 M. Hunt, 'The Impact of the Human Rights Act on the Legislature: A Diminution of Democracy or a New Voice for Parliament?', *European Human Rights Law Review*, (2010) 6, 601–8, 603; C. Gearty, 'The Human Rights Act: An Academic Sceptic Changes His Mind but Not His Heart', *European Human Rights Law Review*, (2010) 6, 582–8, 585; J. Straw, 'The Human Rights Act: Ten Years On', *European Human Rights Law Review*, (2010) 6, 576–81, 580.
24 R. Singh, 'The Human Rights Act and the Courts: A Practitioner's Perspective', *European Human Rights Law Review*, (2010) 6, 589–92, 589.
25 HRA, s. 4(1) & (2).

handful under Article 15 of the ECHR – the rights not to be: tortured, inhumanly or degradingly treated or punished; held in slavery or servitude; subject to the retrospective criminalization of conduct, or to a heavier sentence than that prescribed at the time; or killed, except as a result of lawful execution, lawful acts of war, or the use of force which was no more than absolutely necessary to defend someone from unlawful violence, in order to effect a lawful arrest or to prevent the escape of a person lawfully detained, or lawfully to quell a riot or insurrection. The right to life is, therefore, not absolute. Doubts have also been raised about how 'absolute' the other non-derogable rights are, especially when two instances of the same non-derogable right are in conflict.[26]

All other human rights are 'derogable'. This means they can be suspended across the board, providing this is no more than is strictly necessary in a war or public emergency threatening the life of the nation, including in a crisis presented by terrorism which fulfils this criterion. However, derogation may not be required because derogable rights are also typically subject to express limits including, for example, in the interests of national security and for the prevention of disorder or crime. But various tests, including compliance with the rule of law, democratic necessity, and proportionality, must be met. Therefore, a restriction or suspension of a derogable right in counterterrorist, or other, contexts will only amount to a violation if these requirements are not satisfied.

Contest

Since 9/11 successive British governments of every political stripe have sought to fashion a coherent part-legislative, part-administrative counterterrorist strategy known as CONTEST, defined by the 'four Ps' – Protect, Prepare, Prevent, and Pursue – discussed in Chapters 4, 5, and 6. The ultimate objective is to reduce the risk from, but not to eliminate, terrorism. *Protect* is intended to reduce vulnerability primarily as far as national border security, transport systems, national infrastructure, crowded places both public and private, and British interests overseas are concerned. The distinctive contribution of the *Prepare* stream is to mitigate the impact of terrorist attacks by bringing them to an end as swiftly and effectively as possible and by increasing capacity to recover in the aftermath ('resilience'). The *Prevent* strategy, by far the most controversial of the 'four Ps', aims to stop people from becoming involved in, or supporting, terrorism, by countering terrorist ideology and challenging those who promote it ('counter-radicalization'), steering vulnerable individuals away from it ('de-radicalization'), and working with sectors and institutions where these risks are considered high. The purpose of *Pursue* is to detect, disrupt, prosecute, punish, and/or control those who engage in terrorism both at home and abroad. The same generic challenges also arise in the context of each of the 'four Ps': risk assessment; effective

---

26 See, eg, S. Greer, 'Is the Prohibition against Torture, Inhuman and Degrading Treatment Really "Absolute" in International Human Rights Law?', *Human Rights Law Review*, (2015) 15, 101–37.

and efficient bureaucratization, management, and use of resources; compliance with legality, constitutionality, and rights; accountability and review; and sensitivity to actual and perceived impact upon different sectors of society.

While the 'four Ps' may be more memorable than other less alliterative alternatives, arguably, they do not clearly distinguish functions or objectives as clearly as they might. *Prepare* is, for example, the only one with no preventive element. Nor is it always obvious to which stream a specific counterterrorist law or policy, such as stop and search, belongs, particularly where it pre-dates the inauguration of CONTEST. Some elements of counterterrorist law and policy may indeed belong to more than one of the 'four Ps'. Although not so formally distinguished by Troubles-related counterterrorism, the core elements were and remain, nevertheless, covered in some shape or form in Northern Ireland.

Risk and resilience

In liberal democracies, such as the UK, counterterrorist law and policy must tread a fine line between, on the one hand, prevention, interdiction, and punishment and, on the other, building an effective state-society partnership to address real and perceived grievances, and to engage with ideologies which, though not themselves endorsing violence, share many of the assumptions and aspirations of those which do.

At its heart, this involves the delicate management of a twin set of risks. On the one hand, as already indicated, threats to life, limb, and public institutions and processes presented by terrorism must be tackled by the collection and use of information for the purpose of arrest, detention, search, seizure, prosecution, disruption, interdiction, and incapacitation. But, unless properly conceived and implemented, counterterrorism potentially threatens human rights, social cohesion, and public confidence in law and governance. The effective management of both elements needs to occur simultaneously on multiple dimensions: political, policing, criminal justice, social justice, ideological, cultural, educational, communal, and so on. This is not easy. But, in addition to the collection and analysis of information, the key is to be found in the involvement of, and communication with, all legitimate relevant parties, 'up stream' diversion before atrocities are committed, and active citizenship. The latter should include constructive engagement by all relevant sectors of civil society in debates about counterterrorist law and policy coupled with the discharge of the universal democratic responsibility to contribute, where possible, to the prevention of all forms of crime including terrorism. Focusing exclusively on only one type of risk to the total exclusion of the other – as the more strident critics of the UK's counterterrorist law and policy do – makes, at best, a simplistic, one-dimensional, and distorted contribution to resolving what is a complex and multidimensional problem.

Saving lives, reducing harm, and aiding recovery in the event of a terrorist attack have always been features of counterterrorism in Britain. However, cultivating 'resilience', in these senses is now a more formally specified element in the *Prepare* limb of CONTEST. Various programmes discussed in Chapter 4 seek to ensure that adequate facilities – including those for the management of mass casualty incidents, for the rapid restoration of key services such as power and transport, and for the immediate and longer term needs of victims and others – are available to achieve this result.

The domestic social impact of counterterrorism in Britain is arguably the most complex and fluid of all these dimensions. It has several elements, including effective communication between officialdom and citizens, public confidence in law and governance and between citizens and each other, plus understanding, mutual respect, and cohesion between all social groups. However, these aspects are not sharply differentiated, nor is it easy to assess much less to measure, effectiveness, success, or positive and negative outcomes on any, much less all, of these dimensions. Integral to the social impact of counterterrorism in Britain is the question of whether it is consistent, in whole or in part, with democracy, human rights, the rule of law, a commitment to the legitimate interests of a liberal state and cosmopolitan society, and the effective maintenance of community cohesion and confidence in relevant law and policy. This is considered in the following section.

Evaluating domestic counterterrorism

The question of how the UK should, or more commonly should not, tackle terrorism tends to be debated in two principal overlapping contexts – the 'official/technical' and the 'public'. In the former parliamentarians, civil servants, lawyers, judges, and jurists are concerned both with the big picture and with technical minutiae. By contrast, in the latter – which includes the same parties, plus journalists, NGOs, and a wider range of academics – only a fraction of the counterterrorist framework, and not necessarily the most significant, typically receives any attention. The public debate about CONTEST is, for example, overwhelming dominated by *Prevent*.

In their turn, critiques of British domestic counterterrorism lie along a continuum between two distinct poles. The 'reformist' tends to dominate the 'official/technical' debate. As the label suggests, aiming to improve the delivery of counterterrorist law and policy both in terms of efficacy and compliance with fundamental norms, it seeks to identify deliverable reforms. Although their remit does not include exercise of the Royal Prerogative (such as cancellation of, or refusal to issue, a passport), or the operation of non-statutory counterterrorist laws or powers including the operation of the *Prevent* programme, the annual reports of the Independent Reviewer of Terrorism Legislation provide particularly good examples. By contrast, 'rejectionist' positions, prominent in the 'public' debate, are characterized by condemnation, denunciation, and the rejection of specific features of counterterrorist law and policy or the whole package. These two evaluative perspectives also imply rival assumptions about relevant characteristics of state and society considered in the following sections.

Reform or rejection?

Both reform and rejection perspectives tend to invoke the same twin evaluative standards — legitimacy and efficacy — and the same values — principally democracy, human rights, the rule of law, and cosmopolitan social cohesion. However, reformism also tends to judge specific items of counterterrorist law and policy against deliverable 'second order' criteria, such as constitutionalism, accountability, review, and transparency, derived from the more fundamental ones. By contrast, 'rejectionist' critiques tend to denounce, condemn, and reject them as manifest and blatant violations of shadowy and implicit, rather than fully explicated, democratic and human rights principles. Typically, rejectionist approaches also decline to offer viable alternatives and fail to recognize that, as indicated above, the human rights paradigm permits the restriction of most human rights in the interests of counterterrorism providing relevant formal tests are observed. Once this has been acknowledged, a more complex issue than the simple matter of self-evident violation arises: have these tests been satisfied?

However, whatever evaluative perspective is applied, efficacy is very difficult to assess because discerning the relationship between cause and effect presents considerable challenges. Claims that any given proposal would improve it, therefore, tend to rest more on speculation than hard evidence. The dramatic escalation in the intensity of the conflict in Northern Ireland following the introduction of internment in 1971 provides a virtually unique example. As subsequent chapters will show, there is some evidence that the UK's participation in the US-led invasions of Afghanistan in 2001 and Iraq in 2003 have increased the risk of domestic jihadi terrorism in Britain. But it does not follow, as some suppose, that if the UK had not been involved, it would either not have been exposed to this risk at all or would have been vulnerable to a significantly lesser extent. Other countries, including Germany, Thailand, and Sri Lanka — which were not party to either intervention, and have not acted in any other way which could credibly be interpreted as 'hostile to the Muslim world' — have also suffered deadly jihadi attacks in the past few years.

Conflict or reflexivity?

Reform and rejection perspectives also tend to be underpinned by, or to imply, two competing theoretical models of liberal democratic states and societies. One, the 'conflict model', derived indirectly and loosely from Marxism, tends to assume that the state (the bad guy) is locked in a largely intractable, winner-takes-all conflict with the masses (the good guys) and especially with certain allegedly repressed minorities (the particularly good guys). It follows that, if this is true, counterterrorist law and policy in contemporary Britain will bear the hallmarks, particularly the illegitimate 'securitization' of society as a whole and specific minorities in particular.[27]

The other, let's call them 'reflexive social impact perspectives', embrace a range of other, more subtle, sociological outlooks which better capture the complex characteristics of late modernity in counterterrorist and other contexts. These include, for example, those approaches which focus on systems, fields, and communicative rationality, plus 'liquid' and 'reflexive' conceptions of modernity.[28] Although differing in many respects, they recognize, for example, that, in contemporary Western states and societies, power, wealth, benefits, burdens, authority, opportunity, meaning, identity, belonging, attachment, alienation, and so on, are constituted and distributed by fluid and reflexive interactions between a multiplicity of sites, social units, processes, and discourses, each with varying degrees of power, coherence, identity, and rigidity.

This has a number of implications for both the analysis and the effective management of counterterrorism in Britain. First, reflexive perspectives do not dispute the inevitability of 'securitization' in the sense of the state seeking to ensure 'security' for society at large and for certain vulnerable sectors in particular. Nor does it dispute that, in counterterrorist and other contexts, friction, conflict, controversy, abuses of power, security panics, and violations of human rights can and do arise. This is, not least, because the systems and processes that produce relevant law and policy are not in full control of consequences, including how they are received and perceived by minorities and other social, legal, and political units, systems, and subsystems. But, according to the reflexivity paradigm, these characteristics are not nearly so institutionalized, structured, rigid, or prejudiced as the conflict model claims. Rather, where disequilibrium arises, these perspectives tend to see late-modern liberal democratic societies as capable of resolving it 'reflexively'; that is to say through constructive and inclusive engagement, negotiation, and compromise, though not necessarily instantly nor in a manner that pleases everyone all the time.

Second, the reflexive approach also distinguishes between the effects of counterterrorist law and policy upon a wider range of constituencies than

---

27 See, eg, C. Pantazis and S. Pemberton, 'Resisting the Advance of the Security State: The Impact of Frameworks of Resistance on the UK's Securitization Agenda', *International Journal of Law, Crime and Justice*, (2013) 41, 1–17 and 'From the "Old" to the "New" Suspect Community: Examining the Impacts of Recent UK Counter-Terrorist Legislation', *British Journal of Criminology*, (2009) 49, 646–61; J. Cesari, 'Securitization of Islam in Europe' in J. Cesari (ed.), *Muslims in the West after 9/11* (Routledge, 2010).

28 See, eg, P. Bordieu, 'The Force of Law: Toward a Sociology of the Juridical Field', *Hastings Law Journal*, (1987) 38, 805–53; J. Habermas, *The Theory of Communicative Action Vols 1 & 2* (Heineman, 1984 & 1987); Z. Bauman, *Liquid Modernity* (Polity Press, 2000); N. Luhman, *Social Systems* (Stanford University Press, 1995).

'conflict/securitization' models. These include law, legal processes, public institutions, and those involved in them, on the one hand, and on the other, upon society in general. The latter may include such nebulous, but nonetheless important, elements, as social order, cohesion, integration, minorities, culture, religion, tradition, gender, ideologies, discourses, ideals, ideas, systems of meaning, identity, and belonging, media representations, and so on. These two categories are not, however, rigid or hermetically sealed. For example, politics – including how terrorism and counterterrorism are officially conceived, and debates about how the latter is and should be managed – arguably straddle both. Indeed, a key characteristic of reflexive models is their recognition of contingency, indeterminacy, permeability, reflexivity, and fluidity, to various extents at all levels.

Reflexive approaches are also capable of defining key concepts with greater precision than their conflict/securitization counterparts. Take, for example, the term 'social' or 'community cohesion', the sense in which communities effectively 'stick together'. This tends to apply to those at the 'horizontal', grass-roots level and may also suggest that interconnectedness may be realized without the constituent parts losing what makes them distinctive. 'Social integration', on the other hand, tends subtly to imply a loss of distinctiveness and may apply 'horizontally' between communities themselves, and 'vertically' between communities and public authorities including national ones. 'Cohesive' or 'integrated' communities can be described as those with a common vision and sense of belonging, which appreciate diversity, where there are similar life opportunities for all irrespective of difference, and where strong and positive relationships exist between people from different backgrounds in all public contexts especially workplaces, schools, and neighbourhoods. Reflexive social impact approaches are also better than the conflict/securitization perspective in recognizing that the relationships between cause and effect, direct, indirect, intended, and unintended consequences, positive and negative results, and perceived and 'objective' outcomes are unlikely to be straightforward, binary, and obvious, and much more likely to be complex, multidimensional, and difficult to discern. This is particularly the case where significant official discretion is involved.

As subsequent chapters will demonstrate more fully, reflexive approaches also seek to observe basic methodological axioms of social-scientific research more faithfully than their conflict/securitization counterparts. These include using the most appropriate, and optimally more than one, method to collect data, being aware that the limitations of data collection have significant implications for the reliability of the conclusions drawn from it, and recognizing that even where data have been reliably obtained, conclusions other than those which the evidence fully supports, should be avoided, particularly where there is a strong temptation to confirm a preconceived agenda. While evidence of levels of social and community cohesion and integration may be intangible and elusive, reflexive perspectives also make it possible to distinguish 'positive indicators', such as formal and informal cross-community dialogue and contact — including community festivals, active inter-faith groups, and inclusive civic participation — as well as 'negative' ones, such as the absence or low levels of such things as violence, anti-social behaviour, prejudiced conduct, hate crime, and impermeable forms of social segregation. By contrast, the opposite may be suggested by low levels of social and community cohesion and integration, for example, the absence of active inter-faith groups, high levels of hate crime, and ghettoization, etc. Sources of relevant data might include such things as crime rates and types (locally and nationally), opinion surveys conducted according to scientific polling methods, election results, and views expressed by local and national formal and informal associations and organizations.

Reflexive approaches also recognize more clearly that the central policy challenges raised by the social impact of counterterrorist strategy in Britain and elsewhere concern the effective management of 'double risk' to which reference has already been made. On the one hand, society should be protected from the terrorist threat whatever its source or ideology, without, on the other, exposing it to any avoidable adverse effects of counterterrorist law and policy. These are also matters of interpretation, reflexivity, fluidity, and negotiation. By contrast with the conflict/securitization approach, reflexive perspectives also much more readily accept that the social effects of counterterrorist law and policy are, and should be, managed by contingent and dynamic interactions between a wide range of systems, sub-systems, units, and sub-units of social organization. These typically, though not invariably, produce the kinds of negotiated, and sometimes uneasy, unstable, and evolving compromises, characteristic of functionally integrated and cohesive late-modern liberal democratic societies.

Unlike conflict/securitization approaches, reflexive alternatives also recognize that a particularly vital contribution to domestic counterterrorism can, and must, be made by Muslims in Britain themselves. This is not because they are collectively 'to blame' for jihadi terrorism, but because non-Muslims are much less well-placed to contest and to resist the distortion and debasement of the Islamic faith invoked by jihadis. This also implies that the principal contribution of non-Muslims and the state should be to support and encourage those interpretations of all faiths and ideologies which are life-affirming, tolerant, and non-violent, and to discourage those which are not. This is not, nor does it justify, interference in internal schisms or differences of opinion in any religion in the attempt to identify and defend the 'true faith'. But it does warrant supporting those interpretations which present the least danger to adherents and others. The kind of support which should be provided is, however, a matter for debate.

Amongst the most prominent claims made by the conflict/securitization perspective is that counterterrorism in Britain, particularly the *Prevent* strategy, is racist and/or Islamophobic and has turned Muslims into a 'securitized community' under pervasive and systematic official suspicion. Considered more systematically in Chapters 3–6 this is derived from three largely sound assumptions: society in Britain is permeated by racism and Islamophobia; criminal justice and law enforcement are not immune from these prejudices; counterterrorism impacts more upon Muslims, most of whom are non-white, than upon anyone else. However, not only do opinions differ about the extent to which any one or more of these facts is true, securitization perspectives entirely misconceive their implications for the matters under consideration. In spite of the considerable traction it has acquired in the campaigning and academic worlds, it is simply a non sequitur to infer from any of these observations that counterterrorism in Britain is racist and/or Islamophobic, or that it has turned Muslims into a securitized community. As the rest of this study will seek to demonstrate, there is, in fact, no credible systematic evidence for either allegation.

Brexit

In a referendum held on 23 June 2016, the UK voted to leave the European Union. A transition phase began on 31 January 2020 which ended on 31 December of the same year. Speculation about the immediate and longer term consequences for the UK has, not surprisingly, focused much more upon the economy, trade, migration, and constitutional issues than countering terrorism. While the most important contribution to the latter lies, in any case, with states themselves, the UK's departure from the EU will, nevertheless, disconnect it from the EU's relevant policy frameworks, databases, and networks. In order to assess this more fully, three core questions need to be addressed: what kind of counterterrorist relationship did the UK have with the EU before Brexit? How might this be affected by Brexit? And what kind of alternative arrangements, if any, might be provided instead?

The UK's pre-Brexit counterterrorist relationship with the EU had broadly two elements: the UK was party to relevant EU law, policy, and bureaucratic systems, and it also belonged to several bilateral and multilateral partnerships, especially regarding intelligence-sharing, with other EU states. Since the EU has no dedicated terrorism-related institutions of its own, such as a police force or intelligence services, it cannot contribute directly to counterterrorism itself. But both the EU, and other pan-European organizations – especially the 47-member Council of Europe to which all EU states but not the EU itself belong – have sought to develop transnational counterterrorist policy, particularly since 9/11. The Council of Europe led the field when, in 1977, it promulgated the European Convention on the Suppression of Terrorism which sought to establish a transcontinental 'prosecute or extradite' regime for offences contained in other relevant international conventions. The impact of this treaty has, however, been limited because it permits states to refuse to cooperate where there are substantial grounds for believing there is a risk of prejudice on the basis of race, religion, nationality, or political opinion on the part of any potential partner.

In 1992 the Treaty of Maastricht created the European Union by reconfiguring the existing European Community as one of three 'pillars' and adding two others, one on Common Foreign and Security Policy and another on Justice and Home Affairs. A commitment to Police and Judicial Cooperation in Criminal Matters followed later. All four elements have implications for counterterrorism, particularly concerning police and judicial cooperation, the development of Europol (the European Police Office), the EU's external activities, and the harmonization of criminal law and justice between member states. Although the three pillars were formally abolished by the Treaty of Lisbon on 1 December 2009 the existing commitments nevertheless remain.

The events and aftermath of 9/11 accelerated EU counterterrorist activity within an international environment framed by unanimous UN Security Council Resolution 1373 of 28 September 2001. This calls on states to prevent and suppress terrorist financing, to refrain from supporting terrorism, to prevent the movement of terrorists by improving border controls, and to cooperate with each other in counterterrorist activities including by sharing information. The post-9/11 environment finally prompted the EU to approve, in 2002, the European Arrest Warrant which requires a recipient member state to arrest and transfer to the issuing state, a criminal suspect or sentenced defendant for, respectively, trial or completion of a period of detention. The Council of Europe also added a Protocol to its 1977 convention and, in 2005, provided a treaty on the Prevention of Terrorism, to each of which reference has already been made. Another Council of Europe treaty, on Laundering, Search, Seizure and Confiscation of the Proceeds from Crime and on the Financing of Terrorism, was also opened for signature in 2005. Other EU law and policy developments include the criminalization of terrorism in EU law, and initiatives regarding money laundering, terrorist finances, targeted asset-freezing, and data surveillance. Most, if not all, EU states have also passed their own counterterrorist legislation.

The EU has, however, been relatively marginal to domestic counterterrorism in the UK which has developed its relevant domestic law and policy with little reference to this underdeveloped context. In any case, many aspects of the post-Brexit relationship between the UK and the EU, particularly in areas not related to trade, have yet to be finally settled. Therefore, the prospect of a close working relationship on security and counterterrorism, including continued UK membership of the European Arrest Warrant regime, cannot be ruled out. Nor is Brexit likely to affect the UK's existing bilateral and multilateral counterterrorist partnerships with specific EU states. The UK will also remain a member of the Council of Europe, including the ECHR system with which its counterterrorist, and other laws and policies, will still be required to comply.

It was not until the end of the transition period that the most serious threat Brexit posed for counterterrorism in the UK – the possible reconstruction of a 'hard border' on the island of Ireland which could potentially have unravelled the Good Friday/Belfast Agreement of 1998 – was finally resolved. One of the 1998 Agreement's most significant collateral achievements, welcomed on all sides, has been the creation of a pan-Ireland economy facilitated by a virtually invisible border between Northern Ireland and the Republic of Ireland across which goods, services, capital, and people can cross without bureaucratic interference or inconvenience. The most intractable of Brexit's many conundrums concerned how the UK, including Northern Ireland, could leave the EU yet avoid a hard border on the island of Ireland with physical manifestations such as customs posts which could have become easy targets for armed dissident republican groups.

However, these prospects have since largely, if not entirely, disappeared. A protocol to the Brexit deal came into force on 1 January 2021. This provides that Northern Ireland remains part of the EU's single market in goods, in spite of the fact that the rest of the UK has left it, effectively creating a border in the Irish Sea between the whole of Ireland, including Northern Ireland on one side, and Britain on the other. The result, which has greatly displeased Ulster unionists, is that trade between Britain and Northern Ireland is subject to customs checks not applicable to that between any other parts of the UK. In February 2021 officials implementing these arrangements were threatened by suspected loyalists. In April rioting, which broke out in predominantly loyalist areas and turned sectarian prompting nationalist involvement, was apparently inspired by several loyalist grievances, particularly hostility to the practical and symbolic implications of the protocol, police successes against organized crime, and a sense that nationalists and republicans benefited more from the Belfast Agreement of 1998 than unionists and loyalists. The decision of the police not to prosecute the Sinn Féin Deputy First Minister of Northern Ireland and others for breaching Covid restrictions by joining a large crowd of mourners at the funeral of a prominent republican in July 2020, was also cited as further evidence of the latter. However, according to the security forces, the reluctance of loyalist paramilitaries to enter the fray indicates that the peace process is not currently under serious threat.

The Covid-19 pandemic

The Covid-19 pandemic, and the official reaction to it, have impacted upon national life in Britain in numerous ways. As its gravity became apparent, and the rate of fatalities in many countries climbed, most governments, including the UK's, limited all but essential forms of face-to-face contact, and restricted the manner in which the latter could or should be conducted. Some outdoor, and most indoor, spaces, such as shops, schools, universities, pubs, restaurants, and places of work, were either closed or subject to various restrictions, typically in a series of phases. There were also significant limitations upon travel. The effects on virtually all spheres of normal life were substantial. In common with other states, the UK's national lockdown was relaxed in the summer of 2020. But, by the autumn fresh regimes of complex and localized restrictions were imposed in response to a resurgence of the virus. Only a few days into the new year a second national lockdown came into force.

One of the most obvious contrasts between terrorism and the pandemic has been the starkly different fatality rates. As already indicated, in the 20 years since 9/11, terrorism in Britain has claimed over 100 lives plus close to 1,000 other casualties. Yet, in the nine months between April and December 2020, the virus killed over 50,000 with hundreds of thousands experiencing no, mild, or severe though not fatal, symptoms. When the pandemic first began, the jihadi insurgent movement ISIS/DAESH announced that it was God's judgement upon the infidels, good Muslims would be immune, and that attacks should be stepped up against the weakened global enemy. However, it soon became clear that the virus was indifferent to matters of faith and ideology, and that Muslims were as much at risk as anyone else. The emptying of public spaces in Britain, and elsewhere, also reduced the opportunity for mass casualty attacks and made certain kinds of suspicious behaviour potentially more visible. Trials across the British criminal justice system, including counterterrorist ones, stalled or were postponed and restrictions upon association resulted in fewer referrals to the *Prevent* programme. Concerns have, nevertheless, been expressed that the risk of radicalization may have increased as a result of significantly greater unsupervised access to the internet by young people confined to their homes. It is also feared that jihadis may be planning a new global offensive, especially in weak states particularly badly hit by the pandemic, when the crisis abates.[29] The long-term impact of Covid-19 upon both terrorism and counterterrorism, therefore, remains to be seen.

Conclusion

The UK has been exposed to domestic terrorism of various kinds, not just for decades but, on and off, for a century and a half. However, with the violent element in the conflict in Northern Ireland now almost entirely resolved, the threat from this quarter, both there and in Britain as a whole, has been reduced to negligible, though still potentially deadly, proportions. Jihadis now present the principal terrorist threat in Britain followed, by a considerable margin, by that from the far right. There is currently no significant risk of terrorism from the far left, including from more militant elements in the environmental movement.

The key trends in counterterrorism in Britain over the past 50 years or so include the developing scale and bureaucratic complexity of relevant law and policy, increased emphasis upon protection and prevention, enhanced mechanisms of accountability, transparency, and review, and a decisive shift in official thinking from attempting to 'hold the ring' until a political solution is found (as during the Troubles), to managing risk and increasing public resilience on

---

29 J. Burke, 'Isis Plans to "Make News" with Wave of Violence – UN', *The Guardian*, 6 February 2021.

the assumption that no viable domestic political solutions to current challenges are available.

The characteristics of the various threats have also resulted in continuities and discontinuities in counterterrorist strategies. For example, during the Troubles, general prevention focused primarily upon the assumed deterrent effects of criminalization. Suicide attacks have undermined this in the post-9/11 era, prompting a more concerted policy of 'counter-radicalization' and 'de-radicalization'. Although there have been attempts in all domestic contexts to disrupt, interdict, incapacitate, and restrict the activities of specific individuals, these have taken different forms in each. By contrast with the Troubles, there has, for example, been no targeted assassination controversy in the contemporary domestic era. Nor did the, removal of foreign nationals suspected of terrorism and formal de-radicalization feature in the former although they do in the latter. Society is also much less visibly 'securitized' anywhere in the UK today than it was during the Troubles.

Conflict/securitization perspectives continue to dominate the British campaigning scene. But, for several reasons explored more fully in the remainder of this study, they lack credibility and have been increasingly discredited and marginalized in the more reflective analytical and policy debates. The most potent of their shortcomings include the narrowness and rigidity of their dated theoretical assumptions, their fatal methodological and interpretive flaws, and particularly the fact that rates of far-right referral to the *Prevent* programme, the prime target of accusations about racist and Islamophobic securitization, are now comparable to those relating to Islamist radicalization.

2 Global jihad

Introduction

As indicated in the previous chapter, domestic jihadi terrorism, the national characteristics of which will be considered in more detail in Chapter 3, currently presents the principal terrorist threat to Britain. However, the global dimension and, in particular, a key question – what is the relationship between jihadi terrorism and Islam? – will be considered here first.

Much about 'jihadi' or 'Islamist terrorism' is controversial. There is even little, if any consensus, about how it should be labelled. Terms currently employed include 'violent jihadism', 'jihadi terrorism', 'violent Islamism', 'violent Islamic extremism', 'Islamist terrorism', to name but a few. It is also worth noting that, in Islam, the term 'jihad' means striving or struggling for a worthy aim, including personal spiritual improvement, as well as violence in the name of the faith. Yet two characteristics of this type of terrorism cannot be denied: it is violent and Islam is invoked as the justification by those who resort to it.

However, that said, the precise nature of the relationship between Islam and jihadi terrorism is hotly disputed. Some claim that the connection is purely contingent and has no real significance because, while Islamic terminology is employed, the motives and goals of those involved have, in fact, little or nothing to do with the faith. Others, not least those who engage in it themselves, maintain that, on the contrary, it is nothing less than the inevitable and necessary expression of Islam given current conditions and developments. Yet others take the view that, although Islam is implicated in the activities in question, the conception invoked is debased and distorted, and at variance with its true, better, or best interpretations.

Matthew Wilkinson – former head boy at Eton College, Cambridge University graduate, convert from Christianity to Islam, and respected commentator on the latter and its adherents – claims that contemporary dilemmas and struggles facing Muslims, including about global jihad, are linked to debates and positions current in Islamic thought and culture for centuries.[1] The

---

1 M. Wilkinson, *The Genealogy of Terror: How to Distinguish between Islam, Islamism and Islamist Extremism* (Routledge, 2019), pp. 15, 48–9.

contemporary crisis, he maintains, stems from a double failure. One is on the part of governments to create effective long-term strategies that identify and disable terrorists without stigmatizing entire Muslim communities as a whole. The other concerns the failure of Muslims themselves to respond honestly and effectively to jihadi terrorism, not least because so many are in denial about its Islamic character.[2]

As we shall see in the following chapter, each type of terrorism the UK has faced over the past few decades has had at least one of two possible international dimensions: ideological and logistical. For example, both sides of the Northern Irish conflict were and remain motivated by competing, though now largely peaceful, forms of nationalism – a global, modern, political ideal. Throughout the Troubles Ulster loyalists also found some support from far-right movements in Britain and elsewhere. In their turn the IRA received arms supplies from Colonel Gaddafi's Libya, sought and constructed alliances with 'national liberation movements' abroad, and found a ready source of support from significant sections of Irish America. But this all ceased as the Good Friday Agreement of 1998 bedded down and deprived even the dissident rump of armed republicanism of all but the most insignificant international interest let alone assistance. In spite of the fact that far-right and far-left terrorists in Britain have also been motivated largely by nation-based goals, their ideals have also had international dimensions. They too have been, and some remain, connected by loose and fluid personal and internet networks to like-minded activists in other places.

However, as essentially a local manifestation of an international phenomenon, inspired by a global ideal though not expressed in any worldwide organization as such, for British domestic jihadi terrorism it is very much the other way around. Hence the devotion of this chapter to the global dimension. This includes brief reviews of Islamic history, the distinction between Islam and Islamism, Islamic holy and just war traditions, and the contemporary Salafi-Jihadi movement at the heart of contemporary global jihadi terrorism.

A brief history of Islam

Although the antecedents of contemporary jihadi terrorism can be traced to the very birth of the Islamic faith, this has always been a wayward and marginal tradition, shunned by the mainstream. But two things are clear: it is simply false to claim, as many do, that jihadi terrorism has 'nothing to do with Islam' or, at the other end of the continuum, that Islam is itself the problem. Focusing attention less upon religious doctrine and more upon the social, political, and military implications of the faith, this chapter seeks to explain why.

2 Ibid., p. xiv.

The word 'Islam' is Arabic for 'submission to the will of the one true God', while 'Muslim' means 'one who submits'.[3] The religion was established by the Prophet Mohammad (570–632 CE), an illiterate merchant from Mecca in Arabia. At the time, the peninsula was an anarchic region, dominated by an aggressive macho culture which venerated tribal loyalty, bravery in battle, wealth, generosity, fame, and a multiplicity of wives, concubines, and children.[4] It was, in fact, so afflicted by caravan-raiding, war, and vendetta that four sacred months were traditionally set aside each year for peace. From 610 CE to his death, Mohammad (which means 'highly praised') claimed to have received, through the medium of the Archangel Gabriel, a series of revelations from *al-lah* – literally 'the god', the creator deity of the traditional Arab pantheon – containing His final, flawless, and unalterable will for humanity. The Prophet also regarded this as the last instalment of the three monotheistic Abrahamic faiths. Jews and Christians, adherents to the other two, were seen as 'people of the book' following authentic, though less complete, religious truth and, therefore, entitled to special, though subordinate, status in what became 'Muslim lands'. Mohammad's revelations were delivered and initially received in an entirely piecemeal oral form.[5] Although, according to Muslim tradition, these had all been collected by 650 CE, the full 114-verse canon was not assembled in the 54 surahs (chapters) of the Qur'an (the 'recitation', 'lecture', 'discourse') until 933 CE.[6]

In a nutshell, Mohammad's initial revelations were that Allah is the one and only true God who will judge humanity at the end of time rewarding, with eternal paradise, those who obey Him and punishing those who defy Him with eternal torment in hell.[7] Opinion over their authenticity is said immediately to have divided his own tribe, the Quraysh. Some became believers. But most regarded Mohammad as a dangerous heretic, threatening traditional polytheistic Arab religion and values which had already been exposed to Judaic and Christian influences.[8] Over a 15-year period, without retaliating, the first Muslims endured harsh persecution from their own kith and kin in Mecca. Then, in 622 CE, having learned of a plot to kill him, it is said that Mohammad led his followers, in an event known as the Hijra, to Yathrib (later re-named Medina), a date-producing oasis occupied by other Arab tribes, 300km to the

---

3 Principal sources for this brief history include: M. Ruthven, *Islam: A Very Short Introduction*, 2nd edn. (Oxford University Press, 2012); P. Holt, A. Lambton, and B. Lewis (eds.), *The Cambridge History of Islam, Vol. 28B, Islamic Society and Civilization* (Cambridge University Press, 1970); J. Esposito and E. Shahin (eds.), *The Oxford Handbook of Islam and Politics* (Oxford University Press, 2013); J.-P. Platteau, *Islam Instrumentalized: Religion and Politics in Historical Perspective* (Cambridge University Press, 2017); J. Marozzi, *Islamic Empires: Fifteen Cities that Define a Civilization* (Allen Lane, 2019).
4 P. Hitti, *History of the Arabs: From the Earliest Times to the Present* (Palgrave Macmillan, revised 10th edn., 2002) Ch. VII; V. Parry, 'Warfare' in Holt et al. (eds.), *Islamic Society and Civilization*, p. 824.
5 M. Cook, *The Koran: A Very Short Introduction* (Oxford University Press, 2000), p. 127.
6 Ibid., p. 6, 119; Hitti, *History of the Arabs*, p. 123.
7 Cook, *The Koran*, p. 113.
8 Hitti, *History of the Arabs*, pp. 60–2, 89, 97–102, 107.

north. However, some commentators argue that this migration was, in fact, a strategic move to establish a military base from which to conduct hostilities against the Quraysh rather than simply to deliver the faithful from persecution.[9] Having previously arbitrated in a Medinan tribal dispute, Mohammad had little difficulty in forging an alliance with these new neighbours.

In order to survive, the nascent Muslim community resorted to two long-established Arab traditions – tribal warfare and caravan-raiding. Though frequent in Arabia, each had traditionally been conducted according to informal codes which sought to limit bloodshed.[10] But by engaging in them in this new environment Mohammad and his followers broke a core Arab taboo: the Muslims' targets were members of their own tribe. The Quraysh retaliated and a cycle of violence, with several consequences for the issues in this study, ensued. The war, which had begun primarily for material motives, became fiercely religious as the Quraysh attempted to exterminate rather than merely defeat the Muslims. In turn the Muslims, supported by their Medinan allies defended themselves ferociously, retaliated aggressively, and re-calibrated their identity in religious rather than kinship terms – as a community of believers known as the Ummah – while retaining a 'tribal mentality ... based on commerce and power'.[11] Mohammad also claimed to have received fresh revelations from God indicating, amongst other things, how the Muslims should deal with the violently hostile environment in which they found themselves. The distinction between the 'Meccan' and 'Medinan' revelations, with the latter marking a decisively more militant defence of the faith and the Ummah considered further below,[12] is universally acknowledged by Muslim and non-Muslim commentators.[13]

The Muslim counter-offensive against the Quraysh was hugely successful.[14] As Kelsay puts it, the result was nothing less than a cultural revolution in Arabia replacing tribal loyalties with a communal submissiveness to God. The traditional pantheon of patron deities, machismo and associated virtues, fame and reputation, plus heroic stories about ancestors, were replaced by the Qur'an, the example of the Prophet, piety, obedience to God and His Messenger, and the promise of resurrection, judgement, and eternal paradise.[15]

---

9 N. Sinai, *The Qur'an: A Historical-Critical Introduction* (Edinburgh University Press, 2017), p. 196.
10 Hitti, *History of the Arabs*, pp. 25, 87; Sinai, *The Qur'an*, p. 192.
11 Adonis, *Violence and Islam: Conversations with Houria Abdelouahed* (Polity Press, 2016), pp. 19, 28, 36, 61.
12 Sinai, *The Qur'an*, Ch. 8; R. Firestone, *The Origin of Holy War in Islam* (Oxford University Press, 1999); Adonis, *Violence and Islam*, p. 95.
13 Cook, *The Koran*, p. 130.
14 Hitti, *History of the Arabs*, pp. 117–18.
15 J. Kelsay, *Arguing the Just War in Islam* (Harvard University Press, 2007), p. 27; G. von Grunebaum, 'The Sources of Islamic Civilization' in Holt et al. (eds.), *Islamic Society and Civilization*.

By 630 CE the Muslims had completed their conquest of Mecca, its defeated inhabitants receiving magnanimous treatment unparalleled in the ancient world. In return for payment (*jizyah*), Christian and Jewish tribes in Arabia were also taken under Muslim protection.[16] Although it is likely that, by the time of Mohammad's death, fewer than a third of its inhabitants had converted to the new faith,[17] the entire peninsula, nevertheless, came under an uneasy *Pax Islamica*. But this did not last. The short reign of Mohammad's immediate successor, Abu Bakr (632–634 CE), was dominated by the so-called wars of succession/apostasy (*riddah*) in which those professing a different interpretation of Islam were ruthlessly crushed.

However, the faith not only weathered these early crises but flourished. Within a century of Mohammad's death the first Muslim empire extended from the Iberian peninsula to the Himalayas, the two regional superpowers, Byzantium and Persia, having been defeated in the process. This was achieved, in the first instance, as a result of war and conquest motivated primarily by the quest for booty and tribute rather than to spread divine revelation, and maintained by autocratic domination later cemented by trade, money, and conversion.[18] However, the Muslims themselves saw this not as an exercise in imperial expansion, but the liberation of people living in ignorance and subjugation by false religions and illegitimate political authorities. The success of the endeavour was also treated as clear evidence of divine favour and racial superiority.[19]

As 'Caliph' ('God's representative on earth' also later translated as 'Mohammad's successor'), the Prophet Mohammad exercised a distinct form of 'imperial absolutism' delegated by God on sacred trust for the welfare of all (especially Muslims) in the 'Caliphate', the territory governed by the Caliph, embracing religious, political, military, and judicial spheres of authority. Since there was no separation of religion from other public domains, there was also little room for a distinction between civil society and the state, and no scope for formal constitutional limits on the exercise of public power either.[20] In common with all traditional societies, the key normative concept in Islam was, and remains, 'obligation' rather than 'rights'.[21]

The power of the Caliph was, nevertheless, relatively rather than strictly absolute in several senses. First, as time passed, the authoritative interpretation of the faith was increasingly monopolized by the *ulama*, (literally 'the learned', or more loosely, 'Muslim clerics' or 'Islamic scholars'), to whom the Caliphs generally deferred. Second, since orthopraxy (orthodox practice) has always been valued more than orthodoxy (orthodox belief), Islam has historically

---

16 Hitti, *History of the Arabs*, pp. 60–2, 89, 119.
17 *Ibid.*, p. 141.
18 *Ibid.*, pp. 142–6; X. De Planhol, 'The Geographical Setting' in Holt et al. (eds.), *Islamic Society and Civilization*.
19 Kelsay, *Just War in Islam*, pp. 38–9; von Grunebaum, 'Sources of Islamic Civilization', pp. 472, 475.
20 Ruthven, *Islam*.
21 J. Schacht, 'Law and Justice' in Holt et al., *Islamic Society and Civilization*, p. 541.

been more tolerant of diverse interpretations of the faith than, for example, Christianity, with dissent generally only suppressed when posing a political threat.[22] Third, traditional Islamic societies have always been governed by a combination of the Sharia, the holy law discussed further below, political expediency, tribal and client-patron systems, and local law and custom, including power delegated to regional warlords (*emirs*).[23] Some of the latter became sufficiently powerful to challenge the Caliph himself, particularly when the latter was personally weak or beset by crisis. It did not take long for such power struggles to materialize. Indeed, three of the first four Caliphs to succeed Mohammad were assassinated, two at the hands of other Muslims.

Debate about the succession following Mohammad's death in 632 CE caused a rift between what became known as Sunnis and Shias and created 'a crisis of authority that has never been resolved'.[24] While the Sunnis favoured succession by acclamation, a form of 'charismatic' rather than democratic selection, the Shias (or 'party of Ali') favoured a hereditary alternative. Ali, Mohammad's son-in-law and the third Caliph after his death, was murdered in 661 CE by a Kharijite/Khawarij, the earliest Muslim sect to resort readily to violence in order to achieve political, religious, and personal objectives, and arguably, though not unproblematically, the first precursor of contemporary jihadi terrorism. The schism reached the point of no return when Husayn ibn Ali, son of Ali and also Mohammad's grandson, was killed in 680 CE by the forces of the Umayyed empire at the Battle of Karbala, as he travelled to Baghdad expecting to be installed as Caliph. Sunnis and Shias subsequently also later recognized different customary norms (*sunnah*) and each developed several different legal traditions. This historic and enduring split has not, however, been the only source of division in the Ummah. Islam, in common with Protestantism, Buddhism, and Hinduism, lacks any universally recognized ultimate authority to interpret the faith apart from the Caliph himself. As a consequence it has spawned many sects and traditions. Typically these have been, and continue to be, enunciated by charismatic preachers linking their insights with, or against, tribal leaders and/or warlords, often in pursuit of power and control over territory and people in complex and fluid political environments.

Sufism, followed by some Sunnis and Shias, is of particular relevance for present purposes. Although it originated at the very birth of the faith it did not fully crystallize until the 11th century.[25] According to Rahman, next to orthodoxy, Sufism has had the greatest influence upon Islam and has 'posed the biggest challenge to orthodoxy down to the dawn of modern times'.[26] 'Absorbing many elements from Christianity, Neo-Platonism, Gnosticism and

22 Holt et al., *Islamic Society and Civilization*, p. xv.
23 Hitti, *History of the Arabs*, p. 27; G. von Grunebaum, 'Sources of Islamic Civilization', p. 531.
24 Ruthven, *Islam*, pp. 59–60.
25 Hitti, *History of the Arabs*, pp. 433–9.
26 F. Rahman, 'Revival and Reform in Islam' in Holt (ed.), *Islamic Society and Civilization*, p. 633.

Buddhism, ... passing through mystical, theosophical and pantheistic stages',[27] Sufism is a peace-loving interpretation of the faith, more interested than other Islamic traditions in the subordination of the ego to the Will of God and the primacy of love and spiritual ecstasy over intellect, tradition, doctrine, and dogma as the preferred routes to authentic spirituality.[28] For the famous 'swirling Dervishes', bedecked with their conical hats, this is induced by slowly spinning in a white gown which gracefully opens like a parachute. Sufis also adopted liturgical forms of worship, diffused the use of the rosary among Muslims, and introduced the cult of saints whose graves became places of pilgrimage. Some also commemorate the Prophet's birthday. With its fraternal lodges, asceticism, and celebration of celibacy, Sufism is also the nearest Islam has come to developing a monastic movement. For these and other reasons it is regarded as heretical by many other Muslim traditions.

A series of Sunni and Shia Muslim empires followed the historic Sunni/Shia schism, the main ones being the Umayyad (capital – Damascus), mid-7th to mid-8th centuries; the Abbasid (capital – Baghdad), mid-8th to mid-13th centuries; the Seljuk (capitals – Nishapur, Merv, and Shahr-e-Rey), 11th–14th centuries; the Safavid (capitals – Tabriz, Qazvin, and Isfahan), 16th–18th centuries; and the Ottoman (capital – Istanbul), 1299–1922. In their heyday, many of these were the most advanced civilizations in the world, excelling in virtually every field of human endeavour including medicine, architecture, philosophy, science, astronomy, agriculture, engineering, mathematics, trade, technology, and philology. However, on account of their decadent and corrupt pursuit of wealth, power, and pleasure – including excesses of sex, drugs, alcohol, and luxurious living in preference to the stern austerities of the spiritual life – many Caliphs made unconvincing 'representatives of God on earth'. Abd al-Malik ibn Marwan, one of the Umayyad Caliphs, is, for example, reputed to have said at his coronation: 'I swear that I will behead anyone who expects me to be pious'.[29] Wilkinson maintains that the separation of the secular authority of Caliph/emirs/sultans, etc., from the spiritual authority of the ulama, coupled with the decline in legitimacy of the latter, deprived Muslim states of responsible Islamic constraints upon the exercise of public power and opened the door to self-appointed exponents with distorted interpretations of the faith as traditionally conceived.[30] It should also be noted that the influence of Islam also spread in non-imperial forms as far as western China and into what is now Malaysia, Indonesia, and the southern Philippines.

Today there are some 1.5 billion Muslims worldwide and Islam is the world's second largest religion, with 20 per cent of the world's population, after Christianity at 33 per cent. It is also the second largest religion in the

---

27 Hitti, *History of the Arabs*, p. 433.
28 See Rahman, 'Revival and Reform in Islam', pp. 633–5.
29 Adonis, *Violence and Islam*, p. 49.
30 Wilkinson, *Genealogy of Terror*, pp. 35–7.

UK and in many other European countries. Eighty-five per cent of Muslims are Sunnis and 15 per cent Shia, the majority of the latter in Iran and Iraq. Only 20 per cent of Muslims are Arabs.[31] Types of state with Muslim majorities also range from secular republics/democracies with no Sharia (eg Turkey, Algeria, Indonesia), to authoritarian modern Islamic republics (such as Iran) and traditional authoritarian monarchies with 'full' Sharia (eg Saudi Arabia). In between, with no or limited Sharia, are secular military or civilian dictatorships (such as Egypt, Iraq pre-2003, Syria, and Libya pre-2011), constitutional monarchies (such as Malaysia and Morocco), and 'hybrid republics/democracies' (such as the Islamic Republic of Pakistan).

Islam and Islamism

The heart of the Islamic faith is the Qur'an, a non-narrative, non-chronological, and non-systematic text, with no clear organization of themes, assembled according to the length of surahs, rendered in an allusive, rhythmic, rhetorical, and elliptical style, and addressed to people already familiar with its Abrahamic message.[32] As with any text, determining what it means involves interpreting what it says using standard exegetical and hermeneutic techniques – including, for example, reference to immediate and wider contexts – plus recourse to widely accepted traditional understandings. As with other canonical texts, the Qur'an has also generated a vast library of commentaries, to which more are constantly being added. Contributors to this literature face many challenges familiar to those encountered by commentators on other scriptures. These include distinguishing between the literal and metaphorical, and between those passages which are intended to be timeless and universal and those which are historically and context-specific. For an interested non-Muslim, knowledge of the wider social, political, economic, ideological, and relevant historical contexts in which the Qur'an was both delivered, and in which the standard interpretations later became institutionalized, are also important, as are reflections upon what it might mean for the contemporary world. But, for Muslims, these are likely to be subordinate to other considerations, particularly how the holy text governs daily life.

For Muslims, rules, norms, and guidelines about how to live the way God intends also derive from three other sources: the hadith, the sunnah, and the Sharia. The hadith are anecdotes about the life and sayings of the Prophet which do not necessarily create any obligation, religious or otherwise, but which are nevertheless respected as examples of worthy conduct and a source of inspiration. It is said, for example, that Mohammad spent more money on perfume than on food and mended his own clothes.[33] But neither has ever

---

31 Pew Research Center, *The Changing Global Religious Landscape*, 5 April 2017.
32 Cook, *The Koran*.
33 Hitti, *History of the Arabs*, p. 120.

been regarded as obligatory for all Muslims. The authenticity of some hadith is disputed by Muslims themselves, some Islamic traditions acknowledge some which others do not, and some hadith are unclear or difficult to reconcile with each other. The sunnah are rules or norms derived from those hadith which are regarded as creating obligations.[34] While there is consensus amongst Muslims over many, there is also some disagreement about those which have this effect and those which do not.

The Sharia ('path', 'way', 'well-trodden path', 'the way to a watering place', 'Islamic law'), derives from the Qur'an, the hadith, the sunnah, *ijma* (consensus amongst Muslims), and *qiyas* (reasoning by analogy).[35] Its fundamental purpose is to address and to cultivate a particular conception of human well-being. It applies not only to the familiar territory of modern 'law' – for example to social order, business, marriage, trial procedure, etc. – but also to personal religious observance, including food and drink, worship, and rites of passage. Rooted in pre-Islamic Arabian conceptions of patriarchy, personal status, family, inheritance, tribal blood feuds, and the discretionary application of custom by arbitrators (later state-appointed *qadis*)[36] rather than professional judges, it has been said that it 'represents the core and kernel of Islam itself and, certainly, religious law is incomparably more important in the religion of Islam than theology'.[37] However, while the Sharia retained these traditional pre-Islamic elements, it simultaneously transformed their content and function. For example, while the pre-Islamic structure of the family survived, ancient Bedouin tribal organization was dissolved. An attempt was also made to eliminate the blood feud, restrict private vengeance and retaliation, improve the position of women, orphans, the weak, and vulnerable, strengthen marriage, and control degeneracy by restricting sexual licence and banning alcohol and gambling.[38]

Whether it succeeded in these endeavours is a moot point. For example, although Islam is said to have improved the position of women in some respects, the encouragement of polygamy tended to undermine it.[39] Over time the sacred law became strongest in the fields of the family, inheritance, and the settling of endowments for public or private purposes, and weakest or nonexistent with respect to punishment, taxation, the exercise of public power, and the conduct of war. The law of contracts and obligations stands somewhere in between.[40] Uncompromisingly individualistic in its focus, there is no sense that corporate entities are, or should be, governed by the Sharia.[41] Nor is it entirely clear whether, or if so to what extent, it provides flexible principles

---

34 Schacht, 'Law and Justice', pp. 543–4.
35 K. Abou El Fadl, 'The Shari'ah' in Esposito and Shahin (eds.), *Islam and Politics*.
36 Schacht, 'Law and Justice', pp. 547–9, 556–9.
37 *Ibid.*, p. 539.
38 *Ibid.*, p. 542.
39 *Ibid.*, pp. 541, 545.
40 *Ibid.*, p. 565.
41 *Ibid.*, p. 563.

or inflexible rules. Of particular importance is the fact that its open texture, particularly as far as the sunnah are concerned, facilitated the formation of the ulama, a body of expert law makers, not just interpreters.[42] According to traditional Islam, the Qur'an and Sharia provide an exhaustive body of legislation. Although, in theory, the Caliph could not, therefore, legislate, he could, nevertheless, issue administrative regulations which both interpreted and subtly modified existing law.

In addition to the Qur'an, the hadith, the sunnah, and the Sharia, at the devotional core of the faith, are the so-called 'Five Pillars of Islam': the *shahadah*, the two testimonies that 'there is no God but Allah and Mohammad is his prophet', the sincere declaration of which is all that is required to become a Muslim; *salat*, praying five times a day; *zakat*, giving alms and paying taxes; *sawm*, fasting during Ramadan; and *hajj*, the pilgrimage to Mecca during the month of Dhu-al-Hijjah which all Muslims are expected to make at least once in their lifetime if they can afford it.

Like most other globally significant faiths and ideologies, contemporary Islam is complex and characterized by a multiplicity of interpretations, schools, traditions, and sects. According to Rahman, 'the germs of all the subsequent major developments ..., involving moral and spiritual issues, are traceable to ... (the) ... very early period in the history of the Muslim community after the death of the Prophet'.[43] Reflecting wider social and political conditions, Wilkinson distinguishes three principal methodological traditions which rose and fell over the centuries. 'Rationalism' ascribes primacy to reason, albeit within core Islamic assumptions about the existence and character of God, Prophethood, and Revelation.[44] This is represented in the modern era by, for example, Al Afghani (1838/9–97) who argued that gaps in the interpretative structure of the faith prevented it from adapting to modernity and needed to be filled by, amongst other things, positive engagement with non-Muslim thinking.[45] 'Traditionalism' is based upon the supremacy of Revelation as traditionally understood over other methods of interpreting authoritative Islamic sources and is represented in the modern era by, for example, the Deobandi and Barelwi movements prominent in Britain and discussed more fully in the following chapter.[46] 'Literalism' affirms that the Qur'an contains an easily accessible answer to every issue confronting Muslims and humanity and is represented in the modern world by, for example, Salafi elements in both mainstream Islam and Islamism.[47]

---

42 Ibid., p. 540.
43 Rahman, 'Revival and Reform in Islam', p. 632.
44 Ibid.; Wilkinson, *Genealogy of Terror*, pp. 37–42.
45 Wilkinson, *Genealogy of Terror*, p. 46.
46 Ibid., pp. 42–3, 47.
47 Ibid., pp. 43–5, 48.

According to Wilkinson, 'contemporary mainstream Islam' maintains that the faith is fundamentally about adhering to that which God requires, permits, forbids, and discourages.[48] Actively promoting these goals and objectives, 'activist traditional Islam' emphasizes the unity of all creation and all humankind and that the mission of the Ummah, united in diversity, is to guide humanity to God, without subjugating or oppressing other Muslims or non-Muslims in the process. According to this perspective, belief and practice should be integrated and a balance struck between God's right to worship and the right of humanity to well-being, respect, and just governance. For most Muslims living in the west this includes accepting the existing institutional and normative framework of liberal democracy. Contemporary mainstream Islam also seeks to specify the ethical and legal conditions for peace as a basic premise for a just and godly human life. While it sanctions self-defence and openly declared and properly regulated warfare, this is subject to strict limits considered more fully below, and is justified only as a temporary rupture of tranquillity to allow a just peace to be established or re-established.

'Islamism' by contrast, rejects all systems of governance, including those based on democracy, human rights, and the rule of 'man-made' law, except an Islamic state anchored exclusively in the Sharia and Qur'an.[49] Assuming a fundamental difference and antagonism between 'true' Muslims, 'partial' Muslims, and non-Muslims, Islamists seek a world in which Muslims are in charge, ideally realized in a Sharia-governed global Islamic state.[50] Its contemporary manifestations are increasingly individualized and decreasingly connected to a concrete, physical, mass movement.[51] According to Wilkinson, Islamism is a combination of what, for Muslims, are both 'noxious absences' and 'vicious presences'.[52] The former include the lack, to various extents in the west and elsewhere, of employment status and wealth commensurate with talent, qualifications, and aspirations; civic belonging and empowerment; effective Islamic education and educational attainment which has given rise to 'us v them' ideologies; and engaged parenting which has increased the risk of recruitment to the more extreme interpretations of the faith. The 'vicious presences' include political oppression and corruption in 'Muslim lands'; anti-Muslim prejudice in the west coupled with discrimination in employment, etc.; prejudice on the part of 'significant pockets' of Muslims against non-Muslims; wealthy Muslim funders of terrorism plus abundant supplies of arms; western intervention in 'Muslim lands'; and distorted Islamic narratives on social media, the internet, etc.[53]

48 *Ibid.*, plate 3 and p. 201.
49 *Ibid.*, plates 2–4, pp. 15, 202.
50 *Ibid.*, pp. 66, 67–70, 201.
51 *Ibid.*, pp. 15, 202.
52 *Ibid.*, pp. 204–5.
53 *Ibid.*, p. 207.

'Non-violent Islamist extremism' shares the foundational assumptions of Islamism, including the rejection of all other religions and ideologies and an absolute and enduring antagonism between 'true' Muslims and everyone else.[54] But, apart from exceptional circumstances, it stops short of advocating violence, particularly terrorism. By contrast, 'violent Islamist extremism', or 'jihadism', considered more fully in the last section of this chapter, advocates the use of whatever violence, including terrorism, is deemed necessary to achieve Islamist objectives. Wilkinson maintains that, as far as issues pertaining to law, governance, social transformation, war, and other forms of violence are concerned, 'contemporary mainstream Islam', 'Islamism', and 'Islamist extremism' (both violent and non-violent), have now become fundamentally different bodies of belief and practice.[55]

Friction between rival interpretations of the political implications of Islam has been increasingly fuelled, at least since the 18th century, by the slow and inexorable decline of the great Muslim empires of the Middle East and northern India as a result of modernization, western colonialism, and postcolonial nation and state building. Broadly speaking the various types of Islam distinguished by Wilkinson and others now lie along a spectrum of reactions to these developments. At one pole are those who advocate the modernization of the faith in order to enable it better to accommodate those features of western civilization – such as mass education, science, technology, the emancipation of women, and greater public participation in modern political life – which to them seem to have contributed most significantly to the success and dominance the west has achieved. However, at the other end, are those who argue that the decline of Islamic civilization, and its vulnerability to external interference, are divine punishments for impiety in response to which a 'back to basics' alternative, coupled with offensive and defensive armed resistance to the colonial interloper, are required. Adherents to this view despise the alleged decadence, pleasure-seeking, and materialism of western consumerist society and the atheism and class-based ideology of what was Soviet-style communism. They also repudiate western notions of national sovereignty, liberalism, democracy, pluralism, and human rights, and reject the post-Second World War and post-Cold War international orders. But there are also significant differences of opinion over methods and tactics, particularly regarding participation in democratic processes, the use of violence and terrorism, and the profile and characteristics of Sharia in the envisaged new world.[56]

In the 17th, 18th, and 19th centuries various movements sought to remedy the perceived social degeneration of the Islamic faith, and to arrest its retreat in the face of increasing western global ascendancy, by returning to the imagined

---

54 Ibid., p. 201.
55 Ibid., pp. 51–2.
56 Esposito and Shahin, 'Introduction' in Esposito and Shahin (eds.), Islam and Politics, p. 1.

pristine religion of the first Muslims.⁵⁷ For example, in the 18th century, followers of Shah Wali Allah of Delhi (1703–62) and, in the 19th century, admirers of al-Afghani, advocated violent opposition to British rule in northern India and Afghanistan.⁵⁸ A particularly influential movement to which reference has already been made, Salafism – from the Arabic term *salaf* ('predecessors') – has also sought to return the faithful to the beliefs and lifestyles of the 'pious predecessors', the Prophet Mohammad, and the first three generations of his disciples. Its connection with jihadism is explored further below. Also known as Wahhabism after its founder, Salafism began in Arabia in the mid-18th century when Mohammad ibn Abd al-Wahhab (1703–91) sought to purge the faith of the many distortions and lapses from orthodoxy to which it had allegedly succumbed over the previous millennium.⁵⁹ A return to the Qur'an and the sunnah as the only authentic guides to godly personal conduct, law, and public policy – with respectful but not blind adherence to the scholarship and tradition accrued over centuries – was recommended. This produced a particularly austere interpretation of Islam – a philosophy of 'progression through regression'.⁶⁰

Amongst other things, Salafism abjures mysticism and any whiff of compromise with the oneness of God (*tawid*), such as the cult of saints found in Sufi traditions, insists upon strict doctrinal purity (*aqida*), generally favours the veiling of women in the public sphere, and disparages music, television, photographs of living things, and in order to avoid the sin of pride, men's trousers and robes which cover the ankles. In 1744 Ibn Abd al-Wahhab forged an alliance with local tribal leader, Mohammad ibn Saud, according to which the latter recognized the former and his successors as imam (religious leader) and the former recognized the latter and his successors as emir (political leader). Threatening other Muslims in the peninsula with punishment enforced by arms if they resisted, this alliance was a great success, enduring to this day in what is now known as Saudi Arabia.

A decade after the suppression of what is known, amongst other things, as the 1857 'Sepoy Mutiny' or the 'First War of Independence',⁶¹ which brought the Mughal empire of northern India to an end, a centre for Islamic Studies was established in Deoband, 150km from Delhi. Two very different movements with enduring relevance emerged from it. Tabligh Jamaat aims to revive Islamic influence through the cultivation of spirituality, while the other, the Taliban, which governed Afghanistan in the late 1990s, briefly hosted Al Qaeda and facilitated the 9/11 attacks on the United States. From the 18th

---

57 Rahman, 'Revival and Reform in Islam', p. 640.
58 *Ibid.*, pp. 638–9, 642–3.
59 R. Leiken, *Europe's Angry Muslims: The Revolt of the Second Generation* (Oxford University Press, 2012), p. 70.
60 S. Maher, *Salafi-Jihadism: The History of an Idea* (Penguin, 2016), p. 6; Leiken, *Angry Muslims*, pp. 66–9.
61 Other terms include, the 'Indian Mutiny', the 'Great Rebellion', the 'Revolt of 1857', and the 'Indian Insurrection'.

century onwards Shia scholars in Iran also began to urge their Qajar rulers to use military force against Russian imperial expansion, and in the 1890s al-Afghani emerged as a key player in Iranian resistance to British rule.[62]

The 20th century saw further developments, including significant contributions from, amongst others, Hassan al Banna (1906–49),[63] founder of the Muslim Brotherhood in Egypt, Mawlana al-Mawdudi (1903–79),[64] and Sayyid Qutb (1906–66),[65] the intellectual forbearer of Al Qaeda. A number of issues dominated the debate between these, and similar, thinkers and their acolytes. One concerns the implications of the view that Islam is not only a comprehensive faith and ideology, but a complete way of life for both personal matters and those of law, state, and politics, for which the Qur'an and Sunnah provide an inexhaustible and infallible guide. Another relates to the characteristics of Islamic states, governed by virtuous rulers, motivated by the goal of purifying society, who seek to realize this vision on earth. Amongst other things, this has included such issues as how Islamic states should be established – including the role of violence in their creation, extension, and defence – the conditions for political participation by non-Muslims in them, and the relationship between Islam and the west, typically presented in binary terms between the godliness of the former and its utter negation in the latter.

Although hostile to western notions of democracy, these thinkers were, nevertheless, generally in favour of consultative decision-making, underpinned by the belief that professional Muslims not members of the traditional ulama had a right to seek to understand and to apply the Sharia, an idea with a particular appeal to the rising Muslim middle classes. A significant exception was Iran where, inspired by Ayatollah Khomeini (1902–89),[66] the Iranian revolution of 1979–82 demonstrated the popular appeal of Islamization directed and governed by mullahs, imams, and the ulama. Modern Islamist liberation movements have also sought to oppose and expel foreign interlopers, while also, nevertheless, incorporating some of their key characteristics – for example, nationalism, scientific thinking, and improvements in both political representation and the position of women.[67] However, they nevertheless remain 'essentially a continuation of the pre-Modernist reform movements' whose roadmap to the future lies in invoking an imagined pristine past.[68]

---

62 Kelsay, *Just War in Islam*, pp. 75–80.
63 A. Moussalli, 'Hassan Al-Banna' in Esposito and Shahin (eds.), *Islam and Politics*; Wilkinson, *Genealogy of Terror*, pp. 158–61; Leiken, *Angry Muslims*, pp. 83–4.
64 J. White and N. Siddiqui, 'Mawlana Mawdudi' in Esposito and Shahin (eds.), *Islam and Politics*; Wilkinson, *Genealogy of Terror*, pp. 155–8.
65 S. Akhavi, 'Sayyid Qutb' in Esposito and Shahin (eds.), *Islam and Politics*; Wilkinson, *Genealogy of Terror*, pp. 162–70; Leiken, *Angry Muslims*, pp. 84–5.
66 M. Mahdavi, 'Ayatollah Khomeini' in Esposito and Shahin (eds.), *Islam and Politics*.
67 Rahman, 'Revival and Reform in Islam', pp. 641–56.
68 Ibid., pp. 641–2.

A key development in the early 20th century was the dismemberment of the Ottoman empire and the distribution of its component parts to the victorious allied powers under the League of Nations' mandate system. While this was welcomed by some Muslims it was also deeply resented by others. The most thorough-going version of the view that the Islamic world needed secularization and modernization was Kemal Ataturk's conception of a secular, democratic, nationalist, modern Turkey, in military and other alliances with the west.[69] This seemed to have been successfully institutionalized until the increasingly Islamist authoritarianism of the Erdogan presidency from the mid-2010s onwards. The regime's response to a botched Kemalist coup in July 2016 – which it blamed on the pro-western, pro-democracy, Sufi-inspired Gülen movement – and the thorough purge of alleged participants from public institutions, seemed to confirm this trend. However, a victory for secularism in the mayoral elections in Istanbul in June 2019 suggests a cross current, the wider significance of which is, as yet, difficult to discern.

The discovery of oil in Iran in 1908 also greatly increased western interest there and led to support for the pro-western secular Pahlavi dynasty installed by coup d'état in 1921.[70] The emergence of communism and fascism in the early and mid-20th century also offered Islamists an alluring way of achieving their vision by mobilizing small, militant, highly disciplined, and ideologically committed activists. The decolonization and partition of India in 1946 added a further ingredient to the mix. Islamists were divided over the creation of Pakistan, not least concerning its Islamic character,[71] and a substantial Muslim minority remained in the new Indian state.

Added to these developments, three further complications followed in the Cold War aftermath of the Second World War: the discovery of oil throughout the Middle East, the establishment of the state of Israel, and the ensuing demands for Palestinian freedom and statehood, widely supported throughout the Arab and Muslim worlds. To begin with, the Palestinian cause was pursued politically and also by various secular and religious armed groups and their allies. Those engaging in violence embarked upon hostage-taking, plane hijacking, rioting, stabbing, shooting, rocket attacks, and suicide bombing, both inside and outside Israel and directed against Israelis and the citizens of other, including Arab, countries.[72] Since the violent schism between the secular Fatah and Hamas wings of the Palestine Liberation Organization in 2007, Hamas has emerged as another key violent Islamist player in the region.

Another experiment with secularism and modernization in the Muslim world, pan-Arab national socialism, has however conspicuously failed. Popularized in

---

69 B. Lewis, *The History of Modern Turkey*, 3rd edn. (Oxford University Press, 2001).
70 E. Abrahamian, *A History of Iran: Revised and Updated*, 2nd edn. (Cambridge University Press, 2018), ch. 3.
71 I. Talbot and G. Singh, *The Partition of India* (Cambridge University Press, 2009).
72 M. Qumsiyeh, *Popular Resistance in Palestine: A History of Hope and Empowerment* (Pluto Press, 2010).

the 1950s and 1960s, particularly by Nasser's Egypt and Ba'athism in Syria and Iraq, this maintained that each Arab country, acting in a spirit of pan-Arab solidarity and cooperation, should develop its own socialist economy, state, and society ultimately leading to a single Arab state straddling north Africa and the Middle East, which would oppose western intervention, cultivate close relations with the Soviet bloc, and adopt the technological achievements of both sides in the Cold War.[73] However, regimes based on this model failed to generate prosperity and also limited, and/or dissolved, legislatures whenever they chose. In Egypt, for example, Islam was recognized as the official religion and, the Sharia, though effectively circumscribed in the context of marriage and divorce, became the primary source of legislation. Certain forms of Islamic practice were also relegated to private associations outside officially sanctioned public institutions. In spite of being officially acknowledged as equal under the law, Coptic Christians and other minorities were also, nevertheless, subject to restrictions upon both religious observance and material opportunity. The appeal of the pan-Arab nationalist vision and the strongman-dominated military regimes it produced, was fatally discredited by the victory of Israel over Egypt, Jordan, and Syria in the Six Day War of 1967.

Holy and just war traditions in Islam

The vast majority of Muslims today are likely to regard their faith as inherently peaceful, life-affirming, universally valid for all human kind, and promising not only personal peace between the believer and the Almighty, but concord between individuals and peoples. Indeed, the Arabic salutation, *As-salāmu 'alaykum* ('peace be upon you'), has been adopted as an every-day greeting by Muslims in many parts of the non-Arab world. However, as Holt et al. maintain two of Islam's principal institutions, Holy Law (*Sharia*) and Holy War (*jihad*), are intertwined because the latter is waged to defend the former from its internal and external enemies.[74] With this in mind, this chapter proceeds to consider what the Qur'an says and means about these issues. It also examines the profile the resort to arms has had, and continues to have, in Islam, including at the inception of the faith.

The words 'peace' and 'tranquillity' feature some 30 times in the Qur'an, with 'violence', 'kill', 'fight', and 'war' twice as often. But, of themselves, this tells us very little about the relationship between Islam, armed conflict, and terrorism.[75] The dozen or so better-known Qur'anic verses about violence and killing, rendered during the Medinan period, include the following.

---

73 Y. Choueiri, *Arab Nationalism – A History: Nation and State in the Arab World* (Blackwell, 2000).
74 Holt et al., *Islamic Society and Civilization*, p. xiv.
75 The verb 'to fight', and the corresponding verbal noun, appear almost 70 times in the Qur'an, and the verb 'to struggle', with associative participle and noun, more than 30 times. Sinai, *The Qur'an*, p. 189.

Fight for the cause of God, those who fight you, but do not transgress, for God does not love the transgressors.[76]

Jihad (holy fighting in Allah's Cause) is ordained for you (Muslims) though you dislike it, and it may be that you dislike a thing which is good for you and that you like a thing which is bad for you. Allah knows but you do not know.[77]

When the sacred months are over, slay the pagans wherever you find them. Capture, besiege, and ambush them. If they repent, perform prayers and pay the religious tax, set them free. God is All-forgiving and All-merciful.[78]

Fight those who do not believe in Allah, nor in the latter day, nor do they prohibit what Allah and His Messenger have prohibited, nor follow the religion of truth, out of those who have been given the Book, until they pay the tax in acknowledgment of superiority and they are in a state of subjection.[79]

A famous lengthy sunnah also contains the following commands from Mohammad himself: 'Fight in the name of God and in the path of God … Do not cheat or commit treachery and do not mutilate anyone or kill children'.[80]

Several observations can be made about these and related texts. First, they clearly endorse violence, fighting, warfare, and killing. But Islam is by no means unique as a faith in this respect. Second, they do so upon certain, not entirely clear, conditions. Interpretation is, therefore, required in order to determine what they imply for Muslims in the contemporary world. Together with appeals to deeper and wider features of the Islamic faith, this involves such techniques as *ijtihad* (the expenditure of effort and application on the relevant sources, especially the sunnah), *ijma* (recourse to precedents which command consensus among Muslims), *qiyas* (reasoning by analogy), *shabah* ('similitude'), *'illa* (appeal to a common principle), *maslaha* (the attempt to discern that which is conducive to the public interest), *taqlid* (imitation), and *kalam* (a form of dialectical doctrinal reasoning). For Muslims, the most persuasive opinions are those which command consensus among believers.[81]

Given the Muslim conviction that Islam commands right and forbids wrong, and also permits, recommends, or discourages certain things that are neither commanded nor forbidden, it is not surprising that reflection upon the legitimacy of the resort to, and conduct of, armed conflict, including armed

---

76 *Holy Qur'an*, 2:190, https://corpus.quran.com/.
77 *Ibid.*, 2:216.
78 *Ibid.*, 9:5.
79 *Ibid.*, 9.29. See also *ibid.*, 4:74; 5:33–4; 9:12; 9:36; 22:39.
80 Kelsay, *Just War in Islam*, pp. 100–1.
81 *Ibid.*, p. 125.

rebellion, began very early in the history of the faith. Indeed, the notion of a just war is part of its foundational narrative.[82] Although most of the standard authoritative judgements pertaining to it (*ahkam al-jihad*) originated in the period between 750 and 1400 CE, when Muslim political power was at its height, these nevertheless continue to provide the key point of reference for a distinctive Islamic doctrine of 'just (or holy) war', including in debates about jihadi terrorism today.[83] As already indicated, although the interpretation of Islamic doctrines of all kinds, including those relating to violence, was traditionally practised only by the ulama, as the level of literacy and education has improved in the Muslim world, non-experts have increasingly engaged in reasoning based on the Sharia.[84] Although there is a distinctive Islamic conception of legitimate resort to violence, there is, however, a lack of consensus, not unlike that in its Christian and secular counterparts, about what constitutes fulfilment. This, in turn, reflects a crisis of legitimacy in the Ummah about legitimate political authority, also integral to the process of reasoning based on the Sharia itself. According to Kelsay 'the history of Sharia reasoning is a history of conflict, in which argument is often connected with violence'.[85]

In common with the *jus ad bellum* (resort to arms) limb of the western just war tradition, the relevant Islamic doctrine endorses the principles of legitimate authority, just cause, right intention, and last resort, but differs from it over what constitutes their satisfaction. Reasonable hope of success and proportionate cause are not included.[86] However, since the Prophet stipulated that an invitation to fight is essential – with the possibility of avoiding it by conversion, migration, or the payment of tribute – a distinctive aspect of the Muslim *jus ad bellum* doctrine is a prohibition upon preemptive attack.[87] As far as *jus in bello* (the conduct of hostilities) is concerned, Muslim thinkers have been willing to grant a wide discretion to commanders in the determination of appropriate means but with, for example, no concept of prohibited weaponry. Advising that care be taken to avoid Muslim casualties on enemy territory, it has also been argued that children, slaves, women, old, blind, lame, and hopelessly insane people should generally be immune from direct and deliberate attack.[88] But those in these categories forfeit this protection if they themselves participate in hostilities.[89] As in the western tradition, unintended yet unavoidable damage, collateral to that which is otherwise legitimately required for a military objective, has also been deemed acceptable. Although ill-defined, the notion of limits to hostilities and legitimate targets reflects historic constraints

---

82 Ibid., p. 97.
83 Ibid.
84 Ibid., ch. 2.
85 Ibid., p. 75.
86 Ibid., pp. 101, 102.
87 Ibid., pp. 101, 102, 105, 113.
88 Ibid., pp. 106, 104, 108, 114.
89 Ibid., p. 114; Maher, *Salafi-Jihadism*, pp. 46–9.

upon pre-Islamic tribal conflict in Arabia. These included the prohibition of fighting in the traditional sacred months, and the virtue of magnanimity in response to the submission of, and repentance by, adversaries.

According to Sinai, violent militancy has also been regarded as 'an integral component of the Medinan vision of piety … not just a circumstantially necessary measure of defence'.[90] Some commentators also argue that the Medinan endorsement of holy war was a response to the unexpected delay in the dawning of the Day of Judgement with the result that, since the Almighty had seen fit to defer the final reckoning, Muslims had to bridge the gap themselves. There is evidence that this conclusion might also have been influenced by the contemporaneous development of militant piety in Christianity in late antiquity which also invoked a 'narrative of victimhood', framed violent conflict in religious terms, and also promised heavenly reward for the martyred. This was, however, generally confined to personal assault and intercommunal rioting.[91]

Needless to say, other sacred texts, not least the Bible (particularly the Old Testament), also contain blood-curdling endorsements of violence, including, for example: 'And when the Lord thy God shall deliver them before thee; thou shalt smite them, and utterly destroy them; thou shalt make no covenant with them, nor shew mercy unto them';[92] 'Thou shalt surely smite the inhabitants of that city with the edge of the sword, destroying it utterly, and all that is therein, and the cattle thereof, with the edge of the sword'.[93] And even Jesus once said: 'Think not that I am come to bring peace on earth: I came not to bring peace, but a sword'.[94]

However, at least two significant differences regarding holy and just war between the Christian and post-Christian west on the one hand, and the Islamic world, on the other, shed some light on contemporary jihadi terrorism. First, for three centuries Christianity was a marginal and then a persecuted faith with no aspirations for worldly power, whose adherents endured rather than resisted the torments inflicted upon them by the Romans and others. By contrast, as we have already seen, from not long after the inception of the Islamic faith, the Ummah resolved to defend itself violently from persecution by other Arabs. As already indicated, this not only proved to be extremely effective, but rapidly developed into remarkably successful wars of conquest and imperial expansion, themselves taken by the faithful as indicators of divine favour. Some Muslims also advocated a deliberate policy of organized violence against other Muslims. For example, as already indicated, only a few decades after the death of the Prophet, the Kharijites/Khawarij embarked upon a centuries-long campaign of assassination and murder against successive Caliphs and their supporters as

90 Sinai, *The Qur'an*, p. 191.
91 Ibid., pp. 192–4.
92 *Deuteronomy*, 7:2.
93 Ibid., 13:15.
94 *The Gospel According to Matthew*, 10:34.

retribution for their departure from what they considered the true path. Later the Assassins, who bequeathed a new word to several European languages, did the same although it is said they never targeted civilians.[95]

Second, by contrast with the Islamic world, in the past few hundred years the west has undergone first the Reformation and then the Enlightenment, with the result that, a minority of Christian fundamentalists aside, the Bible has been largely downgraded from the status of a divinely dictated, to at most, a divinely inspired text, the meaning of which for the contemporary world requires, at best, considerable deliberation and contemplation. By contrast, for some Muslims it is but a short step from regarding the Qur'an as divinely dictated truth, to the identification of simple putatively universal injunctions, extracted without regard to context or meaning which a few have taken to justify holy terrorism.

It can, therefore, be concluded that, while there is a distinct but not unique conception of just war in Islam, only the most marginal and wayward interpretations of the faith advocate or justify terrorism, the leading contender in the world today being Salafi-Jihadism, the subject of the following section.

Salafi-Jihadism

The movement and ideology at the heart of the contemporary jihadi terrorism, Salafi-Jihadism, link otherwise disparate groups such as Al Qaeda, Boko Haram, Al Shabaab, and ISIS/DAESH. As already indicated, expressing a distinctive, though controversial and marginal, interpretation of most of the issues considered in the previous section, it arguably continues a tradition dating to the very birth of the faith – the Kharijites/Khawarij and their legacy.[96] However, several, not entirely discrete, branches of the Salafist tradition, not all of which are violent, can be distinguished: 'pietists' are interested only in personal salvation through faith, religious ritual, and strict adherence to the Qur'an and sunnah; 'political Salafis' seek to establish Islamic states in Muslim-majority countries; while 'Salafi-Jihadis' advocate taking up arms to further Salafi objectives.[97] Within the latter category a further distinction can be drawn between those who confine themselves to attempting to overthrow, through violent revolution, what they regard as un-Islamic regimes in Muslim lands, and those who pursue this objective together with terrorist attacks in the west and elsewhere.

The core characteristics of Salafi-Jihadism are: violent jihad; excommunication of apostates and heretics (*bara'a*)[98] including the killing of other Muslims

---

95 Hitti, *History of the Arabs*, pp. 446–8.
96 Maher, *Salafi-Jihadism*, 6; Wilkinson, *Genealogy of Terror*, pp. 28–9.
97 I. Bowen, *Medina in Birmingham, Najaf in Brent* (Hurst & Co., 2014), p. 59; A. Saeed, 'Salafiya, Modernism and Revival' in Esposito and Shahin (eds.), *Islam and Politics*.
98 A core Kharijite doctrine, Schacht, 'Law and Justice', p. 543.

deemed to have become bandits, rebels, apostates, and/or to be involved in decadent and corrupt pro-western Muslim governments (*takfir*);[99] loyalty to and love for God and all that which pertains to Him plus hatred and disavowal for that which does not (*al-wala'wa-l-bara*); strict monotheism (*tawhid*); Islamic governance (*hakimiyya*);[100] tit-for-tat retaliation – 'as you kill our women and children, we kill yours' (*qisas*); and collaterally damaging 'human shields' allegedly used by the enemy (*tatarrus*). Allied to these is the novel doctrine of vicarious and collective liability, which expands the category of legitimate targets to include the citizens of western democracies held responsible for the alleged crimes perpetrated by their governments against the faithful across the globe. This also includes as 'enemies of Islam', international systems and institutions regarded as western instruments of domination, against which armed action is considered legitimate and necessary.

Articulated by several figures over the past few decades – including Muhammad Abd al-Salam Faraj (1954–82),[101] Abdullah Azzam (1941–89),[102] Osama bin Laden (1957–2011),[103] Anwar Al-Awlaki (1971–2011),[104] Ayman Al-Zawahiri (1951–),[105] Abu Musab Az-Zarqawi (1966–2006),[106] Abu Bakr Al-Baghdadi (1971–2019),[107] and Abu Muhammad Al-Adnani (1977–2016)[108] – Salafi-Jihadi ideology can be found in various documents including *The Neglected Duty* (1981), the so-called testament of the Islamist assassins of Egyptian President Sadat, and the *Charter of Hamas* (1988). But on 23 February 1998, *Al-Quds al-Arabi*, an Arabic newspaper published in London, printed the text of a *Declaration of the World Islamic Front for Jihad against the Jews and the Crusaders*, signed by Osama bin Laden and the leaders of four other militant groups. This has become an iconic testament of Salafi-Jihadi grievances and aspirations.[109]

Quoting from the Qur'an and from Mohammad who is said to have declared – 'I have been sent with the sword between my hands to ensure that no one but God is worshipped' – the Declaration claims that other nations are attacking Muslims, 'like people fighting over a plate of food'. It also makes three other key allegations. First, it maintains that for over seven years the United States has been occupying the holiest sites of Islam, plundering the Arabian Peninsula, dictating to its rulers, humiliating its people, terrorizing its

---

99 R. Pantucci, *'We Love Death as You Love Life': Britain's Suburban Terrorists* (Hurst, 2015), p. 10.
100 Maher, *Salafi-Jihadism*.
101 Wilkinson, *Genealogy of Terror*, pp. 174–6; Leiken, *Angry Muslims*, p. 86.
102 Wilkinson, *Genealogy of Terror*, pp. 176–9.
103 Ibid., pp. 179–84.
104 Ibid., pp. 184–7.
105 Ibid., pp. 187–8; Leiken, *Angry Muslims*, p. 86.
106 Wilkinson, *Genealogy of Terror*, pp. 189–91.
107 Ibid., pp. 193–4.
108 Ibid., pp. 197–8.
109 www.mideastweb.org/osamabinladen2.htm.

neighbours, and preparing its bases to launch attacks on neighbouring Muslim peoples. Second, despite the great devastation already inflicted on Iraq 'by the crusader-Zionist alliance', the Americans are said to be intent on repeating it. Third, it claims that, while the aims of this aggression are largely religious and economic, the interests of Israel, including the occupation of Jerusalem, are also being promoted and attention diverted from Israeli murder of Muslims. All these 'crimes and sins' are said to be a 'clear declaration of war on God, his messenger, and Muslims'. The authors maintain that, throughout Islamic history, the ulama has unanimously agreed that, where an enemy destroys Muslim countries, jihad is an individual duty and that, apart from belief in Islam itself, nothing is more sacred than repulsing an enemy attacking the faith and its adherents.

On this basis, and 'in compliance with God's order', the following *fatwas* ('instructions') were issued. In order to liberate the al-Aqsa Mosque in Jerusalem and the holy mosque in Mecca from the grip of the infidels, and to drive their armies out of all Muslim lands, each and every Muslim has an individual duty to kill Americans and their allies, civilians, and military, wherever possible. This obligation is allegedly in accordance with the words of Almighty God who commands: 'fight the pagans altogether as they fight you altogether', and 'fight them until there is no more tumult or oppression, and there prevail justice and faith in God'. Every Muslim who believes in God and wishes to be rewarded, is, therefore, called upon to comply with this divine order, and with God's help, to kill the Americans and plunder their property wherever and whenever they are found. The ulama, Muslim leaders, youths, and soldiers are also urged to 'teach them a lesson' by launching raids on 'Satan's US troops' and 'the devil's supporters allying with them', and to displace their supporters.

Several observations can be made about this statement. First, it invokes the Sharia in an attempt to justify jihadi terrorism, including attacks upon civilians. Second, authority to do so is claimed by those outside the traditional ulama. Third, as the previous section showed and contrary to the statement's claims, the historical precedents provide no support whatever for the kind of activities advocated. Not only do they have to be stretched to arrive at this result, virtually the entire centuries-old tradition of interpreting the Sharia in order to identify the principles justifying the resort to, and conduct of, armed conflict is ignored.

Needless to say, Salafi-Jihadism is a highly contentious doctrine, not least amongst Salafis themselves. Some of the latter have argued that the deliberate targeting of women and particularly children is strictly forbidden by the Sharia unless they themselves are active combatants, that retaliation for its own sake is only permissible against specific individuals found culpable by a court of law, and that scrupulous attention should be paid to the fact that, although the Sharia sanctioned certain types of violent conduct in the early history of Islam, this was later retracted or limited.[110]

---

110 Maher, *Salafi-Jihadism*, pp. 54–6.

In spite of these challenges the Salafi-Jihadi ideology has, however, gained currency as a result of a series of international events, particularly in the post-Cold War era. One of the first was the Soviet invasion of Afghanistan in 1979 in support of a fraternal communist regime which had come to power in a revolutionary coup the year before. This plunged the country into civil war. The west regarded the *mujahideen* ('those engaged in jihad'), who took up arms against the infidel invader, as natural allies. Together with Arab nations and other parts of the Muslim world, the United States and others provided substantial material and other support. Between 1979 and 1989 between half a million and two million Afghans were killed, around two million were displaced, and just under 14,500 Soviet troops died, nearly 54,000 were wounded, and nearly half a million fell ill. The human impact and the costs to the USSR, both in terms of resources and international reputation, contributed significantly to the demise of the Soviet system itself.[111] In 1989 the Berlin Wall fell and the USSR withdrew from Afghanistan leaving competing factions – particularly the Taliban and the secular, western-sponsored Northern Alliance – to continue the struggle.

The breakup of the Soviet Union also revived dormant ethnic and religious conflicts involving Muslims in various parts of the former Soviet-influenced world, including Bosnia, Kosovo, and Chechnya. Islamists have not been slow to capitalize on the opportunities this has created. Meanwhile, between 1980 and 1988 Iraq and Iran fought a vicious, bloody, and inconclusive war, resulting in over a million fatalities, and a deepening of the pre-existing hostility (*fitna* – discord particularly amongst Muslims) between Sunni Arabs and Iranian Shia and their respective allies.

There were several other developments in the 1990s. In secular post-colonial Algeria, the prospect of the Islamic Salvation Front winning the 1991 general election on a 'one person, one vote, once only' platform, provoked a military coup and catapulted the country into almost a decade of civil war between the regime and Islamist rebels. This claimed between 40,000 and 200,000 lives and ended with the defeat and 'repentance' of the latter.[112] Also in 1990 Saddam Hussein's Iraq invaded neighbouring Kuwait prompting the deployment of a massive US-led international coalition to Saudi Arabia. Kuwait was liberated in the swift and, for the allies, remarkably blood-free Gulf War which followed. But Saddam's regime was left in power. The terms of surrender included a 'no fly zone' over the northern Kurdish and southern Shia regions, ostensibly intended to prevent Iraqi forces from continuing the massacres and other brutalities which followed their withdrawal from Kuwait. The United States and its allies also maintained a military presence in the region, including in Saudi Arabia, to ensure, amongst other things, that these and other conditions were

---

111 A. Saikal, W. Maley, and A. Saikal, *The Soviet Withdrawal from Afghanistan* (Cambridge University Press, 2009).
112 P. Nesser, *Islamist Terrorism in Europe: A History* (Hurst & Co., 2015), ch. 3.

met. Meanwhile, in 1995 the Taliban, now the enemy of the west on account of its Islamist programme, entered Kabul and declared the Islamic Emirate of Afghanistan. Amongst other things, this established a safe haven for Al Qaeda which, together with its affiliates, had already launched several attacks on US targets around the world including a fatal bomb attack on the World Trade Center in New York in 1993. The stage was, therefore, set for 9/11.

In response to the events of 9/11 the United States led an invasion of Afghanistan and President George W. Bush announced an ill-defined 'war on terror', a term never officially endorsed by other states including the UK. Indeed, even the Pentagon referred to the 'long war' instead.[113] Since then Salafi-Jihadi groups such as the Taliban, ISIS/DAESH, and Boko Haram in west Africa, supported by at least 45,000 foreign fighters, have increasingly made their presence felt.[114] Amongst other things, this has included attempts to institutionalize particularly brutal and uncompromising forms of Islamic law involving routinized torture and execution and the systematic violation of a whole raft of other human rights, such as the enslavement of non-Muslim women and girls, and, at best, intolerance of other minorities and other Muslim traditions.[115] As already indicated, the pursuit of these goals has also often been complicated, and compromised, by tribal and sectarian rivalries in regional or national contexts and conflicts, including the wars in Syria, Iraq, and Yemen, global friction between Sunnis and Shia, and competition between Sunni Saudi Arabia and Shia Iran for regional domination.[116] A complex mixture of antagonism, rivalry, and collaboration also surfaced between Islamists and the anti-authoritarian movements during the short-lived Arab Spring which began in 2011 and flourished for a few years before, in most cases, being overwhelmed by tyranny or anarchy.

Salafi-Jihadism has also caused significantly more Muslim than non-Muslim casualties around the world. Global fatalities due to terrorism rose from 6,000 in 2005, the year of the London bombings, to 33,000 in 2014.[117] Over this period more fatalities occurred in Nigeria, Syria, Iraq, Afghanistan, and Pakistan than in the rest of the world combined. Four of these countries are

---

113 D. Staunton, 'Pentagon Says "Long War" Could Last Decades', *Irish Times*, 4 February 2006.
114 K. Willsher 'Europe Faces New Wave of Terrorism as Jihadis Return, Says Interpol Head', *The Guardian*, 20 December 2018.
115 S. Khan with T. MacMahon, *The Battle for British Islam: Reclaiming Muslim Identity from Extremism* (Saqi Books, 2016), pp. 51–86, 177–8; J. Stern and J. Berger, *ISIS: The State of Terror* (William Collins, 2015); H. Solomon, *Terrorism and Counter-Terrorism in Africa: Fighting Insurgency from Al Shabaab, Ansar Dine and Boko Haram* (Palgrave Macmillan, Basingstoke, 2015); R. Meijer (ed.), *Global Salafism: Islam's New Religious Movement*, (Hurst & Co., 2009); B. Tibi, *Political Islam, World Politics and Europe: Democratic Peace and Euro-Islam versus Global Jihad* (Routledge, 2008); P. Sookhdeo (ed.), *Global Jihad: The Future in the Face of Militant Islam* (Issac Publishing, 2007).
116 Leiken, *Angry Muslims*, pp. 87–8.
117 University of Maryland National Consortium for the Study of Terrorism and Responses to Terrorism, *Patterns of Islamic State-Related Terrorism, 2002–2015*. www.start.umd.edu/pubs/START_IslamicStateTerrorismPatterns_BackgroundReport_Aug2016.pdf.

overwhelmingly Muslim, and in the fifth, Nigeria, Muslims account for about 40 per cent of the population. However, since 2014 terrorism has declined globally. While attacks between 2012 and 2017 took place in more than 140 countries, 60 per cent occurred in five states (Afghanistan, India, Iraq, Nigeria, and Pakistan). Seventy-five per cent of deaths due to terrorism were in five countries (Afghanistan, Iraq, Nigeria, Pakistan, and Syria).[118] Yet, no country is entirely safe. In addition to the UK, attacks have occurred in places as diverse as Australia, Belgium, China, Egypt, France, Kenya, Spain, Sweden, Russia, and the United States.

As these, and other developments have unfolded, several differences between Al Qaeda and ISIS/DAESH, the most prominent and notorious jihadi movements, have been noted by observers.[119] Prior to 9/11, Al Qaeda was primarily a 'company headquarters'[120] for a predominantly anti-western-imperialism organization, offering funding and training for its highly autonomous franchises throughout the Middle East and elsewhere. Its attention was focused upon attacking the 'far enemy', namely the United States and its allies at home and abroad. Occasionally this involved cooperating with Shi'ite Iran which other Salafists regard as heretical. By contrast, ISIS/DAESH has been primarily interested in establishing, defending, and extending a territorial caliphate and destroying the 'near enemy', the allegedly apostate regimes of, in particular, Egypt, Jordan, Iraq, Lebanon, Iran, and Saudi Arabia. While it has not prioritized attacks upon the west, it has, nevertheless, encouraged freelancers, wherever they have the opportunity, to do so. Unlike Al Qaeda, ISIS/DAESH also embraces *takfir*, denouncing other Muslims as apostates, with all this implies about the brutal treatment they are then deemed to deserve. Unlike Al Qaeda, ISIS/DAESH also believes the prophesied millennium is at hand with the imminent return of the *Mahdi* (Messiah) and the final segregation of the righteous ('true Muslims') from everybody else including other Muslims.

Conclusion

By contrast with all other forms of terrorism to which Britain is currently exposed, the Salafi-Jihadi variety is a national manifestation of a global phenomenon, afflicting many very different countries, but especially those in the west and in the 'arc of chaos' from west through north Africa and the Middle East, to the borders of India and China. Motivated by the goal of establishing a global Islamic caliphate, governed by a particularly uncompromising interpretation of the Sharia, jihadi terrorism is conducted by Muslims from many races,

---

118 University of Maryland National Consortium for the Study of Terrorism and Responses to Terrorism, *Country Reports on Terrorism – Statistical Annex*, www.start.umd.edu/research-projects/country-reports-terrorism-statistical-annex.
119 Leiken, *Angry Muslims*, pp. xv–xvii.
120 *Ibid.*, p. xv.

ethnicities, languages, and nationalities. Coupled with many tribal, doctrinal, and other differences it has divided Muslims from each other as much, if not more than, it has united them against everyone else.

There can, however, be no doubt that Islam itself is not the core problem. While it celebrates peace, the faith is not passivist. But, it is not unique in that. Like the Bible, the Qur'an contains many verses justifying violence and warfare. But, since the earliest days, the mainstream interpretations of the Sharia have sought to subject the resort to, and use of, arms to certain conditions not so different from those in the western just war tradition. While this has produced some consensus with respect to abstract principles, several core issues, particularly what constitutes their fulfilment, remain unresolved. Other religious and secular traditions are similar and all the relevant canonical texts in each context require interpretation guided by factors both internal and external to the specific faith or ideology itself.

But there are, however, two crucial differences between the Qur'an and other scriptures including the Bible, in this respect. First, unlike the Islamic world, the west has undergone the Reformation, the Enlightenment, secularization, and modernization. One important result is that, even in countries such as England, Norway, and Greece, where different branches of Christianity are recognized as effectively the state religion, the Bible has largely lost whatever official political status it once had. Even many Christians regard it as, at most, a divinely inspired source of insight, rather than a blueprint for public policy dictated, word-for-word, by God Himself. Second, unlike Christianity, the Islamic faith was born in armed self-defence which developed rapidly into territorial expansion and empire-building, initially propelled more by material than by ideological or spiritual motives.

It is not surprising, therefore, that since the founding of their faith, Muslims have struggled with the question of what constitutes 'just' and 'holy' war, often disagreeing violently with each other about how, and against whom, it should be conducted. For them, as for adherents to most other religions and ideologies, the legitimacy of the resort to arms and the conduct of armed conflict have never been easy to separate from the pursuit of worldly power. Nor has it been easy to find effective ways of ensuring that unnecessary savagery is avoided. But the fact that atrocities, including the deliberate killing of non-combatants, have been committed in the name of Islam – as they have also been in the name of every other faith and ideology the world has ever seen – does not mean they are sanctioned by any credible interpretation of the Islamic faith itself. This is especially true of jihadi terrorism which can only be justified by a particularly warped version of Islam, radically out of step with mainstream and more reflective interpretations. But, because the current jihadi threat to Britain stems principally from a particular post-Caliphate vision, it cannot be effectively addressed, either by state or society, unless this dimension is both acknowledged and tackled head-on both by Muslims and others. What this has entailed, and should entail, will be the subject of the remainder of this book.

3 Domestic terrorism

Introduction

This chapter seeks to answer two core questions: what are the key characteristics of the three principal types of domestic terrorism Britain currently faces – dissident Irish republican, far right, and jihadi – and why is it exposed to the threats they present? Adopting a framework developed particularly by scholars in the jihadi context, three key clusters of factors are explored with respect to each: background; grievance and ideology; mobilization and modus operandi.[1] While no bright line separates them from each other, 'background' refers to relevant social contexts. 'Grievance' concerns a sense of resentment about being in an environment perceived to be hostile, not being able to progress in life, and/or some other real or perceived injustice, together with the conviction that another identifiable party is to blame. 'Ideology' refers to the way in which this experience is explained and justified from a particular perspective, and how those at the receiving end should respond. 'Mobilization' concerns organization and recruitment to the specific cause, while 'modus operandi' refers to action taken and recommended to redress grievances and implement ideology.

It should not be forgotten, however, that Britain has experienced other forms of terrorism over the past few decades, including, for example, the violence of the far left, militant Welsh nationalists burning English-owned holiday homes in Wales, Palestinians, Sikhs, and others pursuing foreign conflicts on British soil but with no particular animus against the UK or its inhabitants, and the nerve agent attack in 2018 attributed to the Russian state.[2] Although very

---

1 See R. Pantucci, *'We Love Death as You Love Life': Britain's Suburban Terrorists* (Hurst, 2015), pp. 6–17. Other commentators use slightly different labels. See, eg, A. Kruglanski, M. Gelfand, and R. Gunaratna, 'Aspects of Deradicalization' in R. Gunaratna and L. Rubin (eds.), *Terrorist Rehabilitation and Counter-Radicalization: New Approaches to Counter-Terrorism* (Routledge, 2011), pp. 135–6.
2 Pantucci, *Britain's Suburban Terrorists*, pp. 31–49.

few casualties and few other harms have emanated from these threats so far, the risk some pose remains dormant rather than extinct.[3]

The violence of the 'far left', for example, resembles that of the 'far right' in several respects, albeit reflecting a radically and viscerally antagonistic global outlook. This includes type of organization – typically loose, amorphous movements with little or no electoral support, a few self-initiating cells involving handfuls of militants, and little if any obvious leadership – an aggressive internet profile, hate-filled rhetoric, public protest with a particular fondness for street confrontations with political adversaries and the police, and loose connections with like-minded militants abroad typically sustained by social media. However, not everyone on the far left advocates violence and not all who do endorse 'terrorism' as such. Indeed, the 'far left' is a catch-all term which embraces positions, movements, organizations, and perspectives with a variety of priorities and ideologies sharing only a vague common commitment to 'universal human emancipation', and an antipathy of variable intensity and coherence to 'the establishment', 'the state', 'the rich', 'the status quo', or 'the system'.

Dominated by anarchists and extreme animal rights, environmental, and anti-globalization activists, far-left violence in Britain has caused significant damage to property and minor injuries but has not yet resulted in any fatalities. For example, from 1970–1, targeting banks, embassies, the homes of several Conservative MPs, and a BBC Outside Broadcast vehicle earmarked for use in TV coverage of the Miss World competition, an anarchist group calling itself the Angry Brigade launched a bombing campaign in England which slightly injured one individual. Over the past few decades there have also been sporadic attacks by animal rights militants against scientists and sites involved in animal research. In January and February 2007 seven letter bombs were, for example, sent to various companies and agencies causing minor injuries to eight people. And on 27 August 2013 a Police Firearms Training Centre under construction in Portishead near Bristol was burned to the ground in an arson attack claimed by the anarchist group Angry Foxes Cell.[4] It is debatable whether these activities are frequent, widespread, and serious enough to put even a section of the public in fear or to threaten the stability of the state, public institutions, or systems. Whether they meet the threshold criteria for 'terrorism' specified by the Terrorism Act 2000, discussed in Chapters 1 and 6, or any other credible conception, is, therefore, debatable.[5]

---

3 C. Walker, *Blackstone's Guide to the Anti-Terrorism Legislation*, 3rd edn. (Oxford University Press, 2014), pp. 2–4.
4 'Anarchists Say They Started Fire at Portishead Police Gun Centre', www.bbc.co.uk/news/uk-england-somerset-23861098.
5 Walker, *Anti-Terrorism Legislation*, pp. 10–11, 14–15.

Dissident Irish republican terrorism

Dissident Irish republican terrorism represents the smouldering embers of a once blazing violent feature of Irish politics which, until the Belfast/Good Friday agreement of 1998, was one of the key elements in the Northern Irish Troubles.[6] While some commentators prefer 'radical republican movement', the term 'dissident' is nevertheless useful since it highlights one of its key features – dissent from the contemporary mainstream post-1998 formerly armed Irish republican tradition.

Background

There are differences of opinion in the extensive literature about the character and origins of the Northern Irish conflict. But there is little doubt that the following were and are among its core features. In the early 17th century the English Crown, which had had an imperial toe hold in Ireland since the 12th century, attempted to colonize the entire Catholic island with English and Scottish Protestants in order to prevent it becoming a bridgehead for an invasion of Britain by France or Spain, hostile Catholic powers. But, in the event, this policy succeeded only in the north-east where there was already a long and deep, historic connection with Scotland. In the early 1920s, as a result of a British-brokered compromise between (mostly Catholic) Irish nationalists who wanted the whole country to be independent, and (mostly northern Protestant) Unionists who wanted it all to remain part of the UK, Ireland was partitioned, creating two confessional states.

Contrary to what the British hoped, there was little rapprochement between the two parts as time progressed. For various reasons, including electoral constituencies gerrymandered by the Unionist authorities, coupled with nationalist/republican abstentionism, the substantial Catholic minority in Northern Ireland, some 40 per cent, was not successfully incorporated into the Northern 'statelet'.[7] Other forms of active official discrimination against Catholics, including in jobs and the allocation of public housing, compounded Catholic/nationalist grievances. As a result of post-Second World War prosperity and the expansion of educational opportunities, a Northern Irish Catholic/nationalist middle class emerged. Modelling itself on the US civil rights movement, it substituted 'end discrimination' for the traditional demand

---

6 M. McGlinchy, *Unfinished Business: The Politics of 'Dissident' Irish Republicanism* (Manchester University Press, 2019), p. 195; J. Morrison, *The Origins and Rise of Dissident Irish Republicanism: The Role and Impact of Organizational Splits* (Bloomsbury Academic, 2014); M. Taylor (ed.), *Dissident Irish Republicanism,* (Continuum, 2011); A. Sanders, *Inside the IRA: Dissident Republicans and the War for Legitimacy* (Edinburgh University Press, 2011).

7 D. McKittrick and D. McVea, *Making Sense of the Troubles: A History of the Northern Ireland Conflict* (Penguin, 2012), chs. 1 and 2; M. Mulholland, *Northern Ireland: A Very Short Introduction* (Oxford University Press), chs. 1 and 2.

to 'end partition' to redress its complaints. This created a reform-or-repression dilemma for Unionism.

Responsibility for dealing with the public order crisis which spiralled out of civil rights mobilization and Unionist obduracy, lay primarily with the devolved government at Stormont. The Civil Authorities (Special Powers) Act (Northern Ireland) 1922 (the 'Special Powers Act'), provided a ready-to-hand battery of draconian measures including the banning of associations, assemblies, and publications, curbing the display of the Irish tricolour and, most controversially of all, imposing indefinite internment without trial. However, the local administration proved ineffective both in managing the sectarian street disturbances, which rapidly degenerated into armed conflict from 1969 onwards, and in addressing the nationalist grievances which had sparked them in the first place. The introduction of internment in 1971 demonstrably exacerbated the problem. So, in 1972, the UK parliament prorogued the Stormont regime and took direct control of the affairs of Northern Ireland.

A counterterrorist policy characterized particularly by 'Ulsterization', 'police primacy', 'criminalization', and 'normalization' was then rolled out.[8] This included reduced reliance on the army (deployed in August 1969) in favour of a higher profile for the police and the locally recruited Ulster Defence Regiment. Internment was also phased out in favour of prosecuting those suspected of involvement in terrorism in special, single-judge, no-jury, 'Diplock' courts, named after the British judge who recommended them. These were serviced by extended police and army powers of stop, search, seizure, arrest, and detention. A fourth combatant in the violent conflict, now between Irish republicans, the British state, and provincial authorities, was the loyalist paramilitaries, particularly the Ulster Defence Association and Ulster Volunteer Force. Vehemently committed to Northern Ireland remaining part of the UK, these terrorist organizations pitched themselves not only against republican paramilitaries but also law enforcement agencies and did not shrink from indiscriminate murder of Northern Irish Catholics and deadly attacks south of the border.

It should not be forgotten, however, that in addition to violence and sectarian polarization, the Troubles also produced a vibrant and enduring civil society 'reconciliation movement'. Spearheaded by those members of the laity and clergy on both sides of the sectarian divide, this emphasized shared elements of the respective faiths rather than their doctrinal and other differences.[9] However, the problem with this and other movements of a similar kind as constraints upon intercommunal conflict, is that they are inevitably pioneered and sustained by those already committed to improving mutual understanding. The extent to which they succeed in diverting others from violence is impossible to

---

8 T. Hadden, K. Boyle, and C. Campbell, 'Emergency Law in Northern Ireland: The Context' in A. Jennings (ed.), *Justice under Fire: The Abuse of Civil Liberties in Northern Ireland*, 2nd edn. (Pluto Press, 1992).
9 M. Scull, 'The Churches, the Peace Process and Reconciliation', *Irish Times*, 6 April 2018.

measure. But in Northern Ireland they at least asserted non-antagonistic interpretations of relevant faiths and ideologies and continue to do so. In the recent past this may have constituted a form of 'counter-radicalization', constraining what might otherwise have been an even more vicious conflict, while in the present it offers one of several pillars of support for the peace process.

Nevertheless, in the wake of the Belfast Agreement, both shared and divergent identities continue to be affirmed in Northern Ireland. By global standards, nationalist/republican and unionist/loyalist communities largely mirror each other in a common ideological and socio-political environment. Each assumes, for example, the framework of secular, European nation-state liberal democracy. Ethnically they are also rooted in the same thousand-year-old mix of white, northern European Celt, ancient Briton, Anglo-Saxon, Danish, Norse, and Norman. English is the mother tongue of all but a tiny minority who nevertheless speak it fluently. Each acknowledges, nominally or devoutly, the same Christian heritage, the schism of the 16th century Reformation partially softened by 20th century ecumenism. Both communities also proudly proclaim their own culture. Catholics/nationalists tend, for example, to embrace more enthusiastically the Irish language plus traditional Irish music and dance than Protestants/unionists, notwithstanding a few aficionados amongst the latter. However, many other cultural artefacts – including cuisine, colloquialisms, humour, marching bands, pipers, and gable wall murals – transcend the sectarian divide, though some more in structure than content. The Catholic minority currently constitutes about 41 per cent of the population of Northern Ireland.[10] And, although opinion polls disclose much more complex attitudes towards the 'national question' than the electoral arithmetic suggests,[11] the combined republican/nationalist (Sinn Féin/SDLP) vote in the 2017 Assembly elections was 43.4 per cent.[12] In the 2019 UK general election the Democratic Unionist Party (DUP) obtained 30.6 per cent of the vote, Sinn Féin (SF), 22.8 per cent, the Alliance Party (AP), 16.8 per cent, the Social Democratic and Labour Party (SDLP), 14.9 per cent, the Ulster Unionist Party (UUP), 11.7 per cent, and other parties, 1.2 per cent, making a combined pro-Union vote (DUP, UUP, and AP) of 59.1 per cent and a combined Nationalist vote (SF and SDLP) of 37.7 per cent.[13] By contrast, in the general election in the Republic of Ireland in 2020, Sinn Féin emerged with 37 seats, the second highest number in the legislature. Fianna Fáil gained the most, 38, and Fine Gael, 35. The remaining

---

10 Northern Ireland Statistics and Research Agency, *Census 2011: Key Statistics*, December 2012, www.nisra.gov.uk/sites/nisra.gov.uk/files/publications/2011-census-results-key-statistics-press-release-11-december-2012.pdf.

11 J. Tonge, 'A Campaign without End? Dissident Republican Violence in Northern Ireland', *Political Insight*, (2014) 5, 14–17.

12 N. Dempsey, *Northern Ireland Assembly Elections: 2017*, House of Commons Library Briefing Paper, Number CBP7920, 9 March 2017, p. 3, http://researchbriefings.files.parliament.uk/documents/CBP-7920/CBP-7920.pdf.

13 www.bbc.co.uk/news/election/2019/results/northern_ireland.

50 seats were won by several smaller parties and independents, of which the Green Party obtained most, 12.[14]

Grievances and ideology

In essence, the grievances and ideology of Irish republicanism are very clear: there will be no enduring peace or justice in Ireland, especially for the nationalist/republican community in the six north-eastern counties, until the last vestiges of the British presence are finally removed from the whole island, and an independent 32-county, socialist republic established instead. While this remains the goal for the entire modern republican movement, by the beginning of the 21st century the mainstream, represented by Sinn Féin–IRA, had renounced violence and accepted the 1998 Belfast/Good Friday agreement as a stepping-stone towards the peaceful achievement of these objectives.

By contrast, the dissident republican movement, which nevertheless accepts that discrimination against northern Catholics has decreased, rejects the 1998 agreement as normalizing partition and derailing, rather than peacefully delivering, the Irish republican vision. Some, but not all dissident elements, remain committed to terrorism. Those who do, denounce Sinn Féin–IRA as authoritarians – intolerant of any dissent from the allegedly rigidly imposed post-1998 mainstream party line – and traitors to the militant Irish republican cause for abandoning the 'armed struggle' in favour of constitutionalism and the pursuit of electoral mandates.[15]

Mobilization and modus operandi

Both loyalist and republican Troubles-based terrorism had some international links, particularly between the IRA and Irish Americans. But their respective campaigns were intended primarily to benefit one or other of the two main communities in Northern Ireland, and were deeply anchored in tightly knit, highly segregated, and viscerally antagonistic republican and loyalist, mostly working class, communities.

A few terrible mass casualty atrocities aside, the Troubles were also characterized by a relentless series of almost daily incidents, each typically involving a few victims. Arguably suicide was 'weaponized' in the early 1980s by the hunger strikes of republican prisoners in the ultimately unsuccessful quest for political status which, nevertheless, contributed significantly to the electoral rise of Sinn Féin. However, intentional suicide bombing was never a feature of the conflict. Troubles-based terrorist organizations were also hierarchical and self-consciously military in structure. Each eventually spawned, or already had, political wings which contested elections. Sinn Féin, the political branch of the

---

14 www.bbc.co.uk/news/world-europe-51441410.
15 McGlinchy, 'Dissident' Irish Republicanism, p. 196.

IRA, has been significantly more successful than any of its loyalist counterparts, particularly since the IRA disbanded in 2005. As already indicated, the party received, for example, 22.8 per cent of the Northern Irish vote in the 2019 UK general election.

Freelancers and loners were also a rare, though not entirely unknown, feature of Troubles-based terrorism. Mental ill-health, existential, and other life crises may have been exploited by the various paramilitaries, including for maintaining control over territory and people, and also by the security forces to recruit and manage informers. But there is little evidence that these factors had a high profile in terrorist mobilization itself. The primary motive for participation lay mostly in an ideologically channelled communal loyalty. Information technology and social media – including for cyber war, recruitment, propaganda, motivation, and organization – had no significance in the Troubles, not least because the relevant technology was not then available. Finally, because Troubles-based terrorism was highly instrumental in character and conducted largely by more-or-less disciplined, ruthless, paramilitary organizations with political wings, it has always in principle been amenable to a negotiated resolution because all the key protagonists, and their goals, could readily be identified. The challenge was 'merely' to find a viable compromise.

Notwithstanding the Belfast Agreement, problems with organized crime deriving from moribund or redundant paramilitary organizations, which also engage in punishment shooting and beating for 'anti-social elements', also persist on both sides of the sectarian divide. Between 2013–17, or example, the number of such incidents rose from 64 to 101, an increase of almost 60 per cent, with those on the republican side responsible for 24 of the 27 shootings. It has also been reported that, having plied them with drugs and/or alcohol to ease the pain, parents take their children to pre-arranged appointments in an attempt to secure less severe retribution from these brutal, self-appointed, dispensers of rough justice.[16]

Only a tiny handful of small, fluid, and often mutually hostile armed dissident republican organizations – for example, the Real IRA, Continuity IRA, the Irish National Liberation Army, the Irish Volunteers, the New IRA, Republican Action Against Drugs, and Óglaigh na hÉireann – continued the 'armed struggle' after the Provisional IRA disbanded. Some have also since renounced it. These organizations have also been responsible for virtually all Troubles-related terrorism since the 1998 agreement.[17] This has involved over 50 killings, the most horrific being the bombing of Omagh by the Real IRA

---

16 H. McDonald, 'Northern Ireland Punishment Attacks up 60% in Four Years', *The Guardian*, 13 March 2018.
17 See BBC, 'Timeline of Dissident Republican Activity', 26 July 2017, www.bbc.co.uk/news/uk-northern-ireland-10866072; Tonge, 'Campaign without End?', pp. 14–17; M. Frampton, 'Dissident Irish Republican Violence: A Resurgent Threat?', *Political Quarterly*, (2012) 83, 227–37; Morrison, *Origins and Rise of Dissident Irish Republicanism*.

on 15 August 1998 which resulted in 29 fatalities (including a woman pregnant with twins) and over 220 injured. Using firearms, explosives of various kinds including letter bombs, and implements such as cudgels for punishment beatings, the targets in Northern Ireland have included alleged 'delinquents', soldiers, police (particularly Catholic officers), prison staff, government employees and premises, and other buildings. However, in spite of at least one thwarted attempt, a significant attack has yet to be launched in Britain.

Since 2007 the official UK-wide threat level from armed dissident republicanism has been judged 'severe', meaning that an attack is 'highly likely'. Commentators agree, however, that, while such groups have the will to launch deadly attacks, their resources are seriously depleted by comparison with their immediate forebears, they have virtually no support from republicans more widely,[18] their ranks are deeply penetrated by informants (though not so thoroughly that all their activities can be confidently predicted), and that the threat they currently pose both in Northern Ireland and Britain is unlikely to undermine the current political settlement.

By contrast with jihadi terrorism, a key question with respect to these organizations is less about mobilization and more about the absence of demobilization. Although sharing common grievances and ideology, the disparate and factionalized dissident republican movement lacks a 'coherent policy or strategy regarding a way forward',[19] particularly with respect to persuading northern unionists to embrace Irish reunification.[20] However, it is also generally agreed that it is too early to tell whether violent dissident republicanism represents the last gasp of the centuries-old 'physical force' tradition in Irish nationalism, or whether, consistent with a recurrent historic pattern, the latter remains alive though largely dormant, ready to present a more substantial threat at some future point.

Far-right terrorism

Far-right terrorism has claimed less than a handful of fatalities and just under a dozen other casualties in Britain over the past few decades. The threat it poses is, nevertheless, said to be growing.[21] It has recently been estimated, for example, that between 50 and 100 people may be involved.[22] While this is considerably fewer than the estimated number of British domestic jihadis (see

18 McGlinchey, *'Dissident' Irish Republicanism*, p. 202.
19 Ibid., p. 200.
20 Ibid., p. 206.
21 Appendix A.
22 D. Gayle, 'The Far-Right Threat – Modelled on Jihad', *The Guardian*, 3 February 2018; V. Dodd and K. Rawlinson, 'Review of Far-Right Threat after Mosque Attack', *The Guardian*, 2 February 2018; See also R. Lambert, 'Anti-Muslim Violence in the UK: Extreme Nationalist Involvement and Influence' in M. Taylor, D. Holbrook, and P. Curie (eds.), *Extreme Right Wing Political Violence and Terrorism* (Bloomsbury Academic, 2013), pp. 51–3.

below), it is still more than enough to cause death, injury, and destruction on a significant scale. Those responsible for several potentially lethal, though thwarted, right-wing plots have also been tried and sentenced.[23] The horrific mass casualty attacks by lone right-wing terrorists in Norway on 22 July 2011 and New Zealand on 15 March 2019 also indicate that there are no grounds for complacency in Britain or elsewhere. In 2016, National Action, a white supremacist, neo-Nazi organization, became the first extreme right-wing movement to be banned as a terrorist organization in the UK. However, as the remainder of this section shows, the relationship between right-wing terrorism and far-right political agitation is not straightforward.

Background

Echoing recent European trends, over the past few decades, the far right in Britain has shifted from the quest for electoral mandates to more aggressive street-based anti-Islam politics. This has resulted in an increase in both online and offline criminal activity, in competition between rival movements and ideologies, and in direct action activities as a means both of mobilization and articulating grievances.[24]

The 'far' or 'extreme' right in Britain is, in fact, less homogenous than the terms suggest.[25] A distinction can be drawn, for example, between, on the one hand, 'old school' neo-Nazi and neo-fascist movements, directly descended from their 20th century antecedents, and on the other, the relatively new extreme populists. The former, which are of declining significance in contemporary Europe as a whole, tend to be elitist, disciplined, hierarchical, anti-democratic, and have either paramilitary wings or are organized along paramilitary lines. By contrast, the latter tend to define themselves in reaction to 9/11 and its aftermath and are principally concerned with defending western civilization from the existential threat they believe Islam poses. Their enemies also include the political left, multiculturalists, and liberal elites for allegedly having contributed to causing this putative problem or for failing to address it. However, unlike the neo-Nazis and neo-fascists of the past, the extreme populists do not expressly challenge the foundational assumptions and institutions of constitutional democracy, nor have they spawned paramilitary organizations. Indeed, one of the most prominent British far-right protest movements, the English Defence League (EDL), styles itself as a 'human rights organization' dedicated to protecting 'the inalienable rights of all people to protest against

---

23 See, eg, D. Gayle and agency, 'Britain's Youngest Terrorist Given Rehabilitation Order', *The Guardian*, 9 February 2021.
24 W. Allchorn, *Anti-Islamic Protest in the UK: Policy Responses to the Far Right* (Routledge, 2019), pp. 18–19.
25 *Ibid.*, ch. 1.

radical Islam's encroachment into the lives of non-Muslims'.[26] Other core liberal concerns, such as feminist critiques of the Islamic headscarf and animal rights objections to halal meat, have also been co-opted.[27]

Nazism and fascism never gained anything like the foothold in Britain they had in other parts of 20th century Europe. But this is arguably less true of the extreme populists such as the EDL and Britain First whose internet profiles appear to far outstrip the relatively small numbers attracted to their rallies and street protests. The contemporary organized far right in Britain has sought to defend itself from the charge of anti-Muslim prejudice by distinguishing between jihadis and law-abiding Muslims. It claims to have no quarrel whatever with the latter provided they refrain from 'threatening the British way of life' by demanding public recognition and the accommodation of their 'alien' cultural and religious practices. The Facebook page of Britain First had over two million 'likes', nearly twice as many as that of the Labour party, the mainstream political party with the most, until it was closed, in March 2018, by the platform on the grounds that it 'repeatedly posted content designed to incite animosity and hatred against minority groups'.[28] This is said to have included claims by activists that they were proud Islamophobes, derogatory comparisons between Muslim immigrants and animals, and videos which included hate-laden anti-Islamic comments. Attempts by such groups to obtain democratic legitimacy have always resoundingly failed. For example, Jayda Fransen – who together with Paul Golding, leader of Britain First, received short jail sentences in March 2018 for religiously aggravated harassment – obtained only 56 votes and lost her deposit in a parliamentary byelection in 2014.[29]

Grievances and ideology

Prominent features of British far-right grievances, shared with fellow activists around the world, include xenophobia, ultra-nationalism, prejudice against Muslims and LGBT+ people, racism, hostility to immigrants, anti-multiculturalism, anti-Semitism, and neo-Nazism.[30] The corresponding ideologies advocate states with strong, macho leaders, and uncompromising policies to deal with perceived threats. However, not every far-right movement includes all these ingredients. Although some are anti-Semitic, others express their hostility to Islam by supporting the state of Israel. While the EDL is a secular organization, Britain First expressly invokes a Christian identity.[31] It is also

---

26 EDL website 2013, quoted in *ibid.*, p. 2.
27 *Ibid.*, p. 12.
28 A. Hern and K. Rawlinson, 'Britain First "Could Fold" as Hate Speech Leads to Facebook Ban', *The Guardian*, 15 March 2018.
29 K. Rawlinson, 'Britain First Leaders Jailed for Anti-Muslim Hate Crimes', *The Guardian*, 8 March 2018.
30 Walker, *Anti-Terrorism Legislation*, pp. 2–4.
31 Allchorn, *Anti-Islamic Protest*, p. 2.

worth observing that, while domestic jihadi terrorism is a local manifestation of a global anti-nationalist phenomenon, for the British far right it is much more the other way around. In other words, although sharing ideologies and grievances, and emulating, identifying, and cooperating with far-right movements in other countries, the British far right is primarily focused upon its own national preoccupations.

Mobilization and modus operandi

Elements associated with both 'old' and 'new' schools have been involved in violence of various kinds across Europe, including against the general public and public institutions. However, according to some commentators the contemporary British far right is more marginalized, fragmented, extreme, and violent than at any time in the past 20 years.[32] Although far-right violence in Britain has focused to date upon members of minority communities, and associated symbolic targets such as mosques and synagogues, deadly, less discriminate, though sporadic, attacks have also, nevertheless, occurred over the past few decades.

However, not all far-right violence in Britain and elsewhere is perpetrated by 'card-carrying members' of identifiable movements. A significant contribution has, for example, been made by lone actors – often with personality disorders and/or mental health/behavioural problems – 'self-radicalized' by, amongst other things, extreme material on the internet. Between 2000 and 2014, for example, 80 per cent of deaths caused by lone, non-jihadi terrorists in the west were at the hands of right-wing extremists, nationalists, anti-government militants, and others, almost half of whom expressed extreme views or an intention to attack, including divulging some details of their plans in advance.[33] In Britain, both Thomas Mair, who murdered Labour MP Jo Cox in 2016, and Darren Osborne, who used a van to mow down a group of worshippers outside Finsbury Park mosque in London in June 2017, fit this profile. Moreover, the distinction between far-right terrorism and hate crime is not clear cut. At least some of the violence from this quarter, particularly when not intended to be fatal and not obviously involving a committed right-wing militant, could just as credibly be regarded as either. Nevertheless, there can be little doubt that the disturbance, conflict, and agitation provoked by far-right street protests and internet propaganda have intimidated and frightened many Muslims and others.

Patterns of far-right recruitment, strikingly similar to those of jihadis, suggest 'reciprocal' or 'vicious circle' radicalization. As with the latter, the far right

---

32 *Ibid.*, p. 13.
33 C. Ellis, R. Pantucci, J. de Roy van Zuijdewjin, E. Bakker, B. Gomis, S. Palombi, and M. Smith, *Lone Actor Terrorism: Analysis Paper* (RUSI, 2016), p. vi: https://rusi.org/publication/occasional-papers/lone-actor-terrorism-analysis-paper.

seeks recruits through the internet, social media, and also amongst university students whose technical and other skills make them particularly desirable. Extreme populism is, for example, especially appealing to frustrated, unfulfilled young white non-Muslims, rebelling against the perceived injustices of state and society, and searching for meaning, belonging, friendship, and a connection with others experiencing similar challenges. Common factors in recruitment include problems at home, mistrust of authority including the police, prejudices often stemming from having been the victim of violence from members of other ethnic groups, the desire for revenge, and binary 'us v them' thinking. However, these tend to precede rather than follow ideological commitments and also generally increase the attraction of violence which, in turn, serves to underscore aggressive masculinity and to boost credibility amongst peers. But not all far-right sympathizers are violent and there is some debate about whether exclusionary or inclusionary responses from the political mainstream are more effective in neutralizing or diminishing the threat they pose.[34] Some research suggests, for example, that it may be lower in countries where relatively strong right-wing political parties are included in the mainstream democratic process.[35]

Delivering the annual Colin Cramphorn memorial lecture in February 2018 at the end of a 31-year career, the outgoing head of counterterrorist policing in the UK, Mark Rowley warned that the threat from right-wing terrorism is 'significant' and that the public should be 'gravely concerned' about National Action in particular.[36] Mr Rowley said that, while, hitherto, the risk posed by this kind of terrorism had come entirely from lone individuals influenced by extreme right-wing rhetoric, increasingly it is being organized in ways strikingly similar to its Islamist counterpart. Each of these types of terrorist movement seeks to increase communal tensions and to undermine the values of tolerance and diversity in western liberal democracies by offering 'warped parallel alternatives', using sophisticated propaganda, exploiting the vulnerable, manipulating grievances, and fostering intolerance, isolation, and hostility towards the state. Mr Rowley also claimed that, though their goals are radically different, the former EDL leader Tommy Robinson and the jailed Islamist preacher, Anjem Choudary, otherwise shared a lot in common. He advised the media not to give them the kind of exposure they had hitherto received which, he said, was wholly disproportionate to the tiny sectors of the public whose views they articulate and represent.

---

34 Allchorn, *Anti-Islamic Protest*, pp. 4–5.
35 Taylor, Holbrook, and Currie (eds.), *Extreme Right Wing Political Violence and Terrorism*.
36 J. Grierson, 'Four Far-Right Plots Foiled in 2017, Says Anti-Terror Chief', *The Guardian*, 27 February 2018.

Jihadi terrorism

Having killed over 100 people and injured over 1,000 in Britain since 2005 – over 70 per cent of the fatalities in the London bombings of July 2005 and the Manchester Arena attack of May 2017[37] – jihadi terrorism is not only the deadliest of the three principal domestic terrorist threats, it also presents much greater risks of significant damage to the institutions of government, transport, other social systems, and to the national economy than the other two combined. As already indicated, it is also fundamentally a national manifestation of a global phenomenon, the domestic grievances, ideology, mobilization, and modus operandi of which closely follow those at the international level. In common with its global counterparts, British domestic jihadi terrorism is Islamist by nature and self-definition and not by Islamophobic social or official designation.

Background

The experience of Muslims in Britain, and Britain's experience of Muslims, are each increasingly well documented and debated in an expanding literature.[38] Archaeological evidence indicates that the British and Irish Isles have been in contact with Islam since the eighth century, not long after the birth of the faith itself. However, for nearly a thousand years thereafter this was largely indirect and occurred through trade, art, literature, diplomacy, pirate and slaving raids by barbary corsairs, foreign wars of conquest and defence (particularly the Crusades), and curiosity about the religion and its adherents often coloured and/or distorted by Christian prejudice. The 16th and 17th centuries witnessed the first known conversions of Britons to Islam, the first translations of the Qur'an into English, and the establishment of the first small Muslim communities, largely of seafarers, in a few British coastal towns and cities.

Muslim immigration

By the 19th century Muslim communities had grown in size – particularly in Tyneside, South Shields, Liverpool, Hull, Glasgow, and Cardiff – populated, not only by sailors but also by traders and university students. Tension with the indigenous inhabitants, typically expressed in terms of race and national origins rather than religion, was not uncommon. In the years between the two World Wars the distribution of Muslims in Britain, by this stage mostly from Pakistan

---

37 Appendix A.
38 W. Ahmed and Z. Sardar (eds.), *Muslims in Britain: Making Social and Political Space* (Routledge, 2012); S. Gilliat-Ray, *Muslims in Britain: An Introduction* (Cambridge University Press, 2010); P. Hopkins and R. Gale, *Muslims in Britain: Race, Place and Identities* (Edinburgh University Press, 2009); S. Saggar, *Pariah Politics: Understanding Western Radical Islamism and What Should Be Done* (Oxford University Press, 2009).

and Bangladesh, shifted to the growing industrial cities of northern England and the midlands, especially Oldham, Bradford, and Birmingham. This was further fuelled by the post-Second World War economic boom. However, the original expectation on the part of both migrants and hosts was that the sojourn would be temporary and that, when the menfolk had earned enough money, they would go back to the 'sender villages' from which they had come (the 'myth of return').[39]

By the 1960s when families started to arrive, wages for labouring jobs in Britain were more than thirty times those in Pakistan.[40] A close relationship was typically established, and has been maintained, between villages of origin, such as Mirpur in Pakistan-administered Kashmir, and 'daughter communities', such as Beeston Hill in Leeds, home to four of the 7/7 bombers. Wherever the migrants settled, the languages, culture, religion, clan allegiances (*baradari*), and sense of honour, reputation, and status (*izzat*) of the homeland were maintained.[41] Rather than severing the elaborate social bonds of birth, marriage, family, death, creed, and the 'gift economy' (the expectation of benefits on the part of those left behind), Pakistani immigration to Britain has, on the contrary, extended them – a 'home away from home' (*desh pardesh*). To cut any of these threads, such as by refusing to marry the cousin in Pakistan, tears the delicate social fabric and may constitute, as in the case of 7/7 bomber Siddique Khan, a significant step on the road to jihad.[42]

According to Leiken, from 1948 to 1962 'Britain ran one of the most generous immigration schemes on earth, granting citizenship to hundreds of thousands of its colonial subjects across the globe', a policy not then even subject to any serious public debate.[43] This changed with the passage of a series of Commonwealth Immigration Acts from 1968 onwards which provided, amongst other things, that only individuals with a parent or grandparent born in the UK could enter freely. The offspring of the overwhelmingly white emigrants to British overseas colonies, such as Canada, New Zealand, and Australia, were thereby favoured over those mostly non-whites with no such connection.[44] Yet, by 2000, 91,000 of the total of 122,000 immigrants were from Africa or Asia and 70 per cent of residence permits were being issued to those from the Indian subcontinent.[45]

From the 1970s the Muslim population of Britain diversified further with the arrival of wealthy Arabs, mostly in London, and others from elsewhere in the Middle East, Turkey, South Asia, Uganda, Algeria, Bosnia, and Somalia.

---

39 R. Leiken, *Europe's Angry Muslims: The Revolt of the Second Generation* (Oxford University Press, 2012), p. 263.
40 Ibid., p. 94.
41 Ibid., pp. 94, 119–20, 129.
42 Ibid., pp. 131–5, 137–50, 193.
43 Ibid., pp. 96–7.
44 Ibid., pp. 98.
45 Ibid., pp. 101.

However, the 2011 census indicates that these new groups together account for only about 10 per cent of the total Muslim population.[46] The English Channel has also ensured that – by contrast with other European countries, particularly Turkey, Greece, Italy, and Germany – the UK has not received significant numbers of Muslim, or other, refugees or asylum-seekers from North Africa and the Middle East as a result of the mass migrations of the mid-to-late 2010s.

Demographics

Although Muslims constitute a distinctive social group in Britain, they are divided at least as much by class, sect, national origins, race, gender, language, and so on, as they are united by a common faith. The term 'diverse and distinctive Muslim communities in Britain' is, therefore, a much more accurate descriptor than 'the Muslim community of Britain'.[47] Religious, social, and political identities have also been shaped largely by Islamic movements in countries of origin and by international events considered more fully in the previous chapter and also later in this one.[48]

As with any social group, the demographics of Britain's Muslim communities are difficult to determine with precision, particularly since the most reliable source, the 2011 census, is now a decade old. However, subject to this proviso, figures and trends can, nevertheless, be established with reasonable accuracy from this and other sources.[49] The census recorded 2,786,866 Muslims in the UK as a whole, an increase from 1.5 million a decade before, around 5 per cent of the total UK population and some 0.2 per cent of the Ummah worldwide. Of these there were 2,706,066 in England and Wales (97 per cent), 77,000 in Scotland (2.8 per cent), and 3,800 in Northern Ireland (0.4 per cent). Islam is now the country's second largest religion after Christianity, the latter accounting for just under 60 per cent of the population. There are also more Muslims in Britain than members of all other non-Christian faiths combined.

As with any religion, devotion to Islam varies along a spectrum from 'nominal' to 'devout'. Studies, nevertheless, show that typically over 70 per cent of Muslims in the UK say their faith is 'very important' to them.[50] Around two-thirds of Muslims in the UK (68 per cent) come from Asian backgrounds, with Pakistanis constituting 38 per cent and Bangladeshis 12 per cent of the total. In spite of the fact that, by 2011, the number of Muslims in the UK born elsewhere had almost doubled to 53 per cent – from 828,000 in 2001 – some 73 per cent nevertheless state that their only national identity is British or

---

46 Muslim Council of Britain, *British Muslims in Numbers: A Demographic, Socio-economic and Health Profile of Muslims in Britain Drawing on the 2011 Census* (Muslim Council of Britain, 2015), Table 4, p. 25.
47 S. Gilliat-Ray, *Muslims in Britain*, p. xii.
48 Pantucci, *Britain's Suburban Terrorists*, pp. 35, 63; Gilliat-Ray, *Muslims in Britain*, p. 2.
49 Muslim Council of Britain, *British Muslims in Numbers*.
50 T. Modood, R. Berthould, J. Lakey, J. Nazroo, P. Smith, S. Virdee, and S. Beishon, *Ethnic Minorities in Britain: Diversity and Challenge* (Policy Studies Institute, 1997).

other-UK. As a result of the historic pattern of employment-seeking migration, some 76 per cent of Muslims continue to live in the inner-city conurbations of Greater London (some 12 per cent of its population), the West Midlands, the North West, Yorkshire, and Humberside. The age profile of Muslims is also younger than that of the general population: 33 per cent aged 15 or under as compared with 19 per cent.

The dominant Muslim sects in Britain – the Deobandis and Barelwis, plus some followers of the Ahl-i Hadith sect, all conservative Sufi branches of Sunni Islam – hail from the Indian subcontinent. They share a great deal in common including a fusion of universal Islam, mysticism, and a distinctive regional folk culture.[51] Sufi-oriented groups are said to control nearly 40 per cent of Britain's 1,700 mosques[52] and, in 2005, were seen by the government as a potentially influential ally in countering Islamist extremism.[53]

Deobandis take their name from the northern Indian village of Deoband. Inspired by the anti-western ideas of Shah Waliullah Dehlawi (1703–62) – who sought to purge Islam of the alleged errors and distortions accrued over the centuries and to restore it to its foundational pristine purity – a theological training centre was founded there in 1867 in the wake of the failed mutiny/war of independence a decade earlier. The Deobandis, who have a reputation for scholarship, self-discipline, puritanism, austerity, aloofness, and an unwillingness to integrate, overwhelmingly dominate Islamic education in Britain and control over half its mosques.[54] Some commentators, however, claim it is a more heterogenous movement than a sect as such.[55]

The Barelwis were originally established in the late 19th century to defend their distinctive Sufi practices from the Deobandis. They take their name from the birthplace, Bareilly, of their founder, Ahmed Raza Khan Barelvi (1856–1921), an Islamic scholar, jurist, theologian, Sufi, ascetic, and reformer who, amongst other things, regarded the Shia and Wahhabis as heretics.[56] Although originally opposed to Gandhi's independence movement, on the grounds that it was led by a non-Muslim and that Islam was already freely practised under British rule, the Barelwis, nevertheless, became enthusiastic supporters of Pakistan following partition in 1948. In common with the wider Sufi tradition, they also embrace mysticism, celebrate the Prophet's birthday, and occasionally use music and dance in worship, all of which the Deobandis and Ahl-i Hadith deplore.

---

51 Pantucci, *Britain's Suburban Terrorists*, pp. 36–8; J. Fergusson, *Al-Britannia, My Country: A Journey through Muslim Britain* (Banthan Press, 2017), pp. 139–40; I. Bowen, *Medina in Birmingham, Najaf in Brent: Inside British Islam* (Hurst and Co., 2014), 3, chs. 1 and 6; Leiken, *Angry Muslims*, pp. 61–2, 80–3.
52 Bowen, *Inside British Islam*, p. 115.
53 Ibid., p. 124.
54 Ibid., p. 34.
55 Fergusson, *Journey through Muslim Britain*, p. 155.
56 See ch. 2.

The Ahl-i Hadith (people of the *hadith*), a Salafist branch of Islam which also emerged in northern India in the mid-19th century, claims fidelity to the pristine original conception of the faith and rejects all later modifications and interpretations. Although said to resemble Wahhabism, the movement itself affirms its distinctiveness.[57] In 2013 it accounted for fewer than 100 of the UK's 1,700 mosques. However, since this constituted a 50 per cent increase in only four years, it is the fastest growing of Britain's major Islamic movements.[58]

A key feature of the debate about Muslims in Britain – with potentially significant implications for how jihadi terrorism can be explained and should be tackled – concerns material disadvantage, discrimination, and Islamophobia. While these are all linked, it is, however, important to distinguish between them.

Muslim material disadvantage

A 'material disadvantage' is an objectively measurable, and by comparison with others, a less favourable, differential in access to material benefits, such as income, employment, education, qualifications, health care, other opportunities, and life chances. While evidence from the 2011 census also shows that, on some socio-economic indicators, the position of Muslims in Britain is comparable to that of the rest of the population, it also reveals disadvantage on others.[59] Examples of the former include those Muslims self-declaring 'bad or very bad' health (5.5 per cent compared with 5.4 per cent of the general population), those with qualifications at degree level and above (24 per cent as compared with 27 per cent), and those in business as small employers and self-employed (9.7 per cent as compared with 9.3 per cent). Other figures show wider differences, such as those in higher professional occupations (5.5 per cent as compared with 7.6 per cent).

However, examples of disadvantage, particularly acute with respect to employment and housing include (with figures in brackets for non-Muslims), 19.8 per cent in full-time employment (34.9 per cent), 7.2 per cent unemployed (4.0 per cent), 29 per cent of women between the ages of 16–24 in paid employment (50 per cent), and 18 per cent of women between 16–74 looking after home or family (6 per cent). Forty-six per cent of Muslims also live in the 10 per cent most deprived, and 1.7 per cent in the 10 per cent least deprived, local authority districts in England compared with, respectively 36.9 per cent and 2.9 per cent of the general population.[60] According to the 2011 census,

---

57 Bowen, *Inside British Islam*, p. 60–81.
58 *Ibid.*, p. 80.
59 Muslim Council of Britain, *British Muslims in Numbers*.
60 Department for Communities and Local Government, *The English Indices of Deprivation 2015 – Statistical Release 2015*, Chart 9, p. 20, https://assets.publishing.service.gov.uk/government/uploads/system/uploads/attachment_data/file/465791/English_Indices_of_Deprivation_2015_-_Statistical_Release.pdf.

43 per cent of Muslim households were owner-occupied, 30 per cent rented, and 28 per cent lived in social housing. Comparable figures for the general UK population in 2016 were 65 per cent, 17 per cent, and 18 per cent, respectively.[61] The 2011 census also revealed that 5.1 per cent of Muslims live in hostels and temporary shelters compared with 2.2 per cent of the UK population as a whole.

Data collected by the UK Longitudinal Household Panel Study and published in 2014 – linked to the earlier British Household Panel Study and involving just under 61,000 valid responses to questions about religion – revealed that 50 per cent of Muslims live in poverty by contrast with 27 per cent of Sikhs, 22 per cent of Hindus, 19 per cent of Catholics, 18 per cent of people with no religious affiliation, 14 per cent of Anglicans, and 13 per cent of Jews.[62] The report explains these differentials in terms of historically contingent factors reflecting a given community's migration history which, it claims, are likely to be mitigated across time. Relevant factors producing these results are said to include the absence of good qualifications, lack of fluency in the English language, and traditional family values (possibly more prevalent in some religions than others), which may, for example, encourage women to look after children or care for other family members rather than engaging in paid employment outside the home. Prejudice and discrimination on the part of wider society, considered more fully below, may also result in increased incidence of unemployment or low pay.

Measurable predictors of poverty – such as lack of fluency in English, number of dependent children, economic inactivity, and low pay – do not fully account for higher levels of poverty among Muslims by comparison with adherents to other minority religions. Muslims, Sikhs, and Hindus are, however, less likely than Christians to participate in a range of voluntary and civic organizations which build 'social capital' – including ties with people outside immediate social circles, improved information flows, personal support, and professional development – and typically lead to greater success in the labour market. The report claims that, while it is not possible to measure the effect of each cluster of factors precisely, 'statistical analysis of the available data suggests that all three play substantial roles'.[63] Yet, assuming this is true, the relative effects of each remain unclear.

---

61 House of Commons Library, *Home Ownership and Renting – Demographics*, 9 June 2017, https://researchbriefings.parliament.uk/ResearchBriefing/Summary/CBP-7706#fullreport.
62 A. Heath and Y. Li, *Reducing Poverty in the UK: A Collection of Evidence Reviews* (Joseph Rowntree Trust, 2014), p. 34.
63 Ibid., p. 35.

Anti-Muslim discrimination

Not every disadvantage suffered by Muslims, or any other minority, is necessarily the result of discrimination − the allocation of goods or benefits on a differential basis without adequate justification by reference to the rights and freedoms of others and/or to legitimate public interests. The difference between 'disadvantage' and 'discrimination' is that disadvantage can occur without discrimination, while discrimination is a type of disadvantage occasioned by avoidable and unjustified conduct on the part of others.

Several further distinctions should be drawn. One is between direct and indirect discrimination. The former is deliberate and intentional while the latter is the result of unintended consequences. A second is between discrimination on the part of the state and on the part of society at large. A third is between, on the one hand, 'systemic' or 'systematic' discrimination − which occurs on a wide social scale though possibly varying from sector to sector and may include that which is 'institutionalized' − and, on the other, 'casual' or 'contingent discrimination' which occurs sporadically and randomly. It is also important to distinguish between 'objective' discrimination, typically very hard to prove, with the 'perception of discrimination' which is, in principle, much easier to document, but may not be a reliable indicator of the former.

Official discrimination can occur in several ways. A law or public policy is 'directly discriminatory' or 'discriminatory by design' if, without justification, it expressly targets a specific social group. However, even if not open to this accusation, it may, nevertheless, be indirectly discriminatory for other reasons. For example, in *DH v Czech Republic*, the European Court of Human Rights (ECtHR) found that the relevant test for diagnosing children with learning difficulties in the Czech Republic was indirectly, though unintentionally, discriminatory because it resulted in a disproportionate number of Roma children being allocated to special schools.[64]

Alternatively, a law or policy, otherwise blind to minority identity, may be implemented in a systematically discriminatory manner as a result of deliberate 'institutional discrimination' on the part of particular agencies involved in its administration and/or enforcement. Examples from another context might include how accusations of rape by black complainants against white rapists are likely to have been managed by the criminal justice system in certain parts of the southern states of the United States during the segregation era. Although the relevant law would have been formally 'race blind', it is unlikely that many, if any, such rapists would ever have been convicted. Third, a law or policy indifferent to minority identity may be applied on isolated occasions in a discriminatory manner as a result of deliberately discriminatory conduct on the part of the specific official(s) concerned, but not the agency as a whole ('contingent' or 'random' individual discrimination).

---

64 (GC), 13 November 2007, paras. 175–6, 189, and 195.

There is no clear answer to the question – to what extent is Muslim material disadvantage in Britain the result of any or all of these kinds of discrimination? According to the 2011 census, 92 per cent of Muslims in England and Wales are non-white and 31 per cent of non-whites are Muslim.[65] This means that a law or policy which discriminates against Muslims in England and Wales is also likely to be indirectly racially discriminatory.[66] The UK has an obligation under Article 14 of the European Convention on Human Rights to ensure that the rights and freedoms it contains are enjoyed 'without discrimination on any ground such as sex, race, colour, language, religion, political or other opinion, national or social origin, association with a national minority, property, birth or other status'. A number of anti-discrimination laws have also been passed, including the Equality Act 2010, to which reference has already been made, which, amongst other things, seek to increase equality of opportunity and to outlaw discrimination and harassment relating to certain personal characteristics. However, while the existence of laws outlawing discrimination is to be welcomed this does not necessarily ensure their effective enforcement.

Attitude surveys, anecdotal evidence, journalistic and qualitative studies suggest that at least some forms of Muslim disadvantage, for example in employment, may be socially discriminatory.[67] However, data from such sources have complex relationships with the objective social reality. For example, attitude surveys record *opinions about*, rather than the *fact of*, discrimination. And even when they might indicate a genuine social problem, anecdotal evidence cannot provide authoritative information about its scale, distribution, etc. The conclusions of qualitative studies also typically suffer from methodological limitations, sometimes even acknowledged by their authors. For example, recent academic research into the perceptions of young Muslims in Britain about social mobility found widespread concerns about possible obstacles and difficulties, including harassment, racism, Islamophobia, negative stereotyping, low expectations on the part of teachers and others, and various self-limiting factors such as low confidence and self-esteem stemming from being members of minority communities.[68] Yet, the fact that no white British Muslim or white European Muslim respondents were included makes it impossible to distinguish between discrimination on racial and religious grounds in this context. Disarmingly the authors also admit that 'the data contained in this report reflect only the experiences of those who participated' and that 'such an approach does not, of course, lend itself to statistical generalizability'.[69] This did not, however,

---

65 Muslim Council of Britain, *British Muslims in Numbers*, p. 40.
66 *JH Walker v Hussain* (1996) ICR 291.
67 A. Heath and Y. Li, *Review of the Relationship between Religion and Poverty: An Analysis for the Joseph Rowntree Foundation*, CSI Working Paper 2015-01, http://csi.nuff.ox.ac.uk/wp-content/uploads/2015/03/religion-and-poverty-working-paper.pdf.
68 J. Stevenson, S. Demack, B. Stiell, M. Abdi, L. Clarkson, F. Ghaffar, and S. Hassan, *The Social Mobility Challenges Faced by Young Muslims* (Social Mobility Commission, 2017).
69 Ibid., p. 8.

discourage them from choosing the misleading title – *Social Mobility Challenges Faced by Young Muslims* – which suggests young Muslims face similar *objective* challenges, when the research in question is, in fact, confined to the challenges *perceived* by a very small sample, the representativeness of which is in doubt. Nevertheless, one of the most important facts to emerge from studies such as this is that a 'striking majority of people in the UK acknowledge the fact of religious discrimination and accept that it is wrong'.[70]

Those who believe they have been the victim of direct discrimination of any kind in a job application may also simply be mistaken, for example about, or misinterpret the reasons for, the outcome. Some may, for instance, seek to find something or someone to blame other than weak credentials or poor interview performance. Alternatively, some may believe that, in the game of life, the dice are unfairly loaded against people from their background even if this is untrue, or not as true as they think. Where discrimination has in fact occurred, the victim may also fail to attribute it correctly to the operative feature of their identity. So, for example, if an appropriately qualified, black Muslim woman fails, as a result of direct discrimination, to get the job for which she has applied, she may conclude that this was because of anti-Muslim prejudice or misogyny, when it may have been on account of her race, or various combinations of the other variables including all three. And even widespread perceptions of discrimination do not necessarily confirm that there is a genuine systemic, structural, or institutional problem. They may be based upon, or influenced by, self-validating, but false or not wholly reliable, perceptions. Nevertheless, widespread perceptions of discrimination should be taken seriously not least because, whether or not they correspond with the 'objective' reality, the perception is itself a social phenomenon, potentially damaging social cohesion.

Anti-Muslim 'racism', prejudice, and Islamophobia

Prima facie, anti-Muslim prejudice and Islamophobia are wider than either Muslim material disadvantage or discrimination because they embrace a much broader class of negative experiences, ranging from, for example, 'micro aggressions' such as 'bad taste' jokes or muttered insults at one end of the continuum, to murder at the other end. As above, it is also worth considering some relevant working definitions. In the popular sense, 'race'/'ethnicity' involves shared physical identity (particularly skin colour, facial features, and possibly accent), plus assumptions about kinship and origins more often imagined than real. Standard components of 'racism', typically based on myth, caricature, and stereotype, generally include the belief that 'races' possess distinct and inherent characteristics including social practices, the sense that one's own race is superior to most if not all others, and express or implicit prejudice

---

70 S. Saggar, *Understanding Western Radical Islam*, p. 175.

against people of races apart from one's own.[71] 'Islamophobia' generally refers to irrational antagonism towards Islam and/or Muslims also typically based on myth, caricature, and misleading stereotype.[72] Strictly speaking, a 'phobia' is a clinically observable anxiety disorder defined by recurrent and excessive fear of an object or situation. The term has, however, been extended to include individual and collective hostility towards minorities such as homosexuals (homophobia), transexuals (transphobia), foreigners (xenophobia), and Islam/Muslims (Islamophobia).

Although racial and anti-Muslim discrimination can clearly overlap, particularly in England and Wales where, as already observed, over 92 per cent of Muslims are non-white,[73] for several reasons, they are not simply different types of 'racism'. For a start, what constitutes a 'race', or 'religion', and how instances of each differ from one another, is not clear-cut. It is, for example, a mistake to regard 'white'/'non-white' and 'Muslim'/'non-Muslim' as straightforward, mutually exclusive categories. For instance, some of the offspring of a white and non-white parent may look and feel white, while their siblings may look and feel non-white. The only formal test for being a Muslim is to endorse the *shahada*, the affirmation that there is only one true God and Mohammad is his Prophet. Yet, some Muslims, for example Salafis, regard other Muslims, for example Shia, as apostates or heretics, firmly outside the authentic community of the faithful.[74] This, therefore, raises the paradoxical prospect of Muslims being capable of Islamophobic hate crime against other Muslims, including those of the same race. And, in England and Wales, where Muslims constitute just under a third of the non-white population, there is plenty of scope for Islamophobia on the part of non-Muslims irrespective of race.[75]

Each of the prejudices under consideration is also capable of supplanting the other. For example, as already indicated, antagonism towards immigrants in post-Second World War Britain initially manifested, and was debated, in racial rather than religious terms. Yet, the Satanic Verses controversy of the late 1980s, considered more fully below, and the events of 9/11, shifted the focus from colour-based racism against Asians in general (and Pakistanis in

---

71 L. Back and J. Solomos (eds.), *Theories of Race and Racism: A Reader*, 2nd edn. (Routledge, 2009).
72 See, eg, J. Esposito and I. Kalin (eds.), *Islamophobia: The Challenge of Pluralism in the 21st Century* (Oxford University Press, 2011).
73 Muslim Council of Britain, *British Muslims in Numbers*, p. 40.
74 S. Maher, *Salafi-Jihadism: The History of an Idea* (Penguin, 2016), pp. 101–6.
75 According to the census, in 2011, the population of England and Wales was 56.1 million, www.ons.gov.uk/peoplepopulationandcommunity/populationandmigration/populationestimates/bulletins/2011censuspopulationestimatesfortheunitedkingdom/2012-12-17. Of these 14% (8 million) were non-white, www.ons.gov.uk/peoplepopulationandcommunity/culturalidentity/ethnicity/articles/2011censusanalysisethnicityandreligionofthenonukbornpopulationinenglandandwales, 2015-06-18. Of the non-white population, 2,495,446 (31%) were Muslim, Muslim Council of Britain, *British Muslims in Numbers*, p. 40.

particular), to hostility against largely the same minorities on religious, ie anti-Muslim grounds.[76]

Adherents to global proselytizing religions, such as Islam and Christianity, come from many races. Religious prejudice can also occur between people of the same race. Although it is generally impossible to change one's race or apparent race, in principle changing religion is simply a matter of no longer believing in or practising it, and possibly converting to another. However, social and cultural pressures may make this a difficult and costly choice. A name may also continue to imply a religious identity long abandoned. While acts of racial prejudice are often triggered by visual cues, particularly skin colour, religious affiliation is generally less visible without the distinctive clothing or symbols – such as crucifixes, skull caps, or hijabs – which declare it.

Non-Muslim attitudes to Muslims and Islam, in Britain and elsewhere, also span a spectrum. At one end is 'Islamophobia', a visceral and irrational hatred based on myth or negative caricature and misrepresentation. At the other end are those who admire the faith and may even contemplate conversion. Perceiving Muslims to be an oppressed minority, other non-Muslims may identify and express solidarity with them. And there are all kinds of other possibilities, some arguably not even on this continuum at all. For example, some non-Muslims admire the cultural achievements of the great Islamic civilizations of the past, such as their art and architecture, but little else. Yet others may be ignorant of the faith and indifferent both to it and to its adherents. Some may be 'passively critical', aware of the central tenets of Islam but unconvinced by them. Others may be well-informed and 'actively critical' of the faith in general, or certain interpretations of it, from the perspective of an alternative belief system including another religion, atheism, or secularism.

Most, if not all, religions invite reflection and debate, especially about their social, political, and legal implications in ways which race does not. Anti-Muslim prejudice can, therefore, and should be distinguished from evidence-based, and measured criticism of the faith and/or the conduct of those who claim to subscribe to it. The distinction between legitimate critique and prejudice is not, however, always easy to draw. It would, for example, be Islamophobic to declare that all Muslims are wife-beaters, homophobes, and murderously intolerant of apostasy and heresy. But it is not prejudiced to observe that certain interpretations of Islam are difficult, if not impossible, to reconcile with the emancipation of women, the treatment of LGBT+ people, freedom of expression and freedom of thought, conscience, and religion.

There is plenty of evidence of Islamophobia in contemporary Britain, but very little reliable information about its scale and distribution nor, including from jihadis themselves, of a clear causal connection between it and motivation to engage in domestic terrorism. For example, between January and December 2017, Tell MAMA – an independent NGO working with the police and

---

76 S. Warsi, *The Enemy Within: A Tale of Muslim Britain* (Allen Lane, 2017), pp. 21–31.

central government to record, analyze, and tackle incidents of anti-Muslim hatred in England and to support victims – received a total of 1,330 reports, of which 1,201 (0.04 per cent of the Muslim population of the UK) were verified as being anti-Muslim or Islamophobic in nature.[77] Seventy per cent of confirmed incidents occurred 'offline', including on the street, the most serious of which included physical attacks, threatening behaviour, and general abuse. The remainder, originating in the UK, occurred 'online', ie on social media platforms such as Facebook or Twitter, or on other Internet-based platforms. According to Tell MAMA, growing awareness in Muslim communities, among key stakeholders, and partners, that this organization exists, has resulted in greater willingness on the part of victims and witnesses to make complaints. Obstacles to reporting, such as perceived or actual social pressure not to do so, concerns about immigration status, or a sense that it would be pointless in any case, nevertheless, persist.

However, according to a 2018 report by HM Inspectorate of Constabulary and Fire & Rescue Services, 70 per cent of recorded hate crime is racist, 11 per cent concerns sexual orientation, eight per cent is religious (including but not limited to Islam), and seven per cent is related to disability. The number of complaints in all of these categories increased from 2014/15 to 2016/17 by 46 per cent for race, 54 per cent for sexual orientation, 108 per cent for transgender, 115 per cent for disability, and 123 per cent for religion.[78] This may be explained either by an objective rise in the incidence of such activities, or an increased willingness on the part of victims to lodge complaints. It is also clear that recorded anti-Muslim hate crime spikes significantly in the wake of domestic jihadi terrorist attacks.[79]

Grievances and ideology

The grievances and ideology of British domestic jihadis closely mirror the Salafi-Jihadi narrative and ideology discussed in the previous chapter. While this did not fully develop until the late 1990s, precursors, albeit lacking a commitment to domestic jihad, can be found in the post-Rushdie 'Muslim Manifesto – A Strategy for Survival' of the late 1980s. This inspired the establishment of several Muslim organizations considered more fully in the following section. The Manifesto denounces such things as 'the demands of rampant immoral secularism', and states, for example, that 'jihad is a basic requirement of Islam' including for Muslims 'living in Britain or having British nationality', which may involve 'active service in armed struggle abroad and/or the

---

77 MAMA stands for 'Measuring Anti-Muslim Attacks'. https://tellmamauk.org/about-us/.
78 HM Inspectorate of Constabulary and Fire & Rescue Services, *Understanding the Difference: The Initial Police Response to Hate Crime* (HMICFRS, London, 2018), p. 32.
79 A. Travis, 'Hate Crimes against Muslims in Britain Spike after "Jihadi" Attacks, Study Finds', *The Guardian*, 17 June 2015.

provision of material and moral support to those engaged in such struggle anywhere in the world'.[80]

However, the clearest evidence that British domestic jihadi terrorism is a version of Salafi-Jihadism can be found in the belligerent declarations of domestic jihadis themselves. For example, in his pre-recorded martyrdom video testimony, 7/7 bomber Mohammed Siddique Khan said:

> I and thousands like me are forsaking everything for what we believe. Our driving motivation doesn't come from tangible commodities that this world has to offer. Our religion is Islam: obedience to the one true God, Allah, and following the footsteps of the final prophet and messenger, Muhammad ... This is how our ethical stances are dictated. Your democratically elected governments continually perpetrate atrocities against my people all over the world. And your support for them makes you directly responsible, just as I am directly responsible for protecting and avenging my Muslim brothers and sisters. Until we feel security, you will be our targets. And until you stop the bombing, gassing, imprisonment and torture of my people we will not stop this fight. We are at war and I am a soldier. Now you too will taste the reality of this situation.[81]

Similarly, Plymouth-born, white convert to Islam, Nicky 'Mohammed Abdulaziz Rashid Saeed-Alim' Reilly – who injured himself but nobody else while attempting to detonate a nail bomb in an Exeter restaurant on 22 May 2008 – declared in a hand-written note discovered by the police at his mother's home:

> In the name of God, most gracious, most merciful: why I did it. Everywhere Muslims are suffering at the hand of Britain, Israel and America. We are sick of taking all the brutality from you. You have imprisoned over 1,000 Muslims in Britain alone in your war on Islam. You torture and destroy Muslim lives by taking a father or a son or a brother, even you torture Muslim women. In Britain it's OK for a girl to have sex without marriage and if she gets pregnant, she can get an abortion so easily. When you are getting drunk on Friday and Saturday night your behaviour is worse than animals. You have sex in nightclub toilets. You urinate in shop doorways. You shout your foul and disgusting mouth off in the street. It is unacceptable to Allah and the true religion of Islam. Britain and USA and Israel have no real rules. All us Muslims have seen the pictures of Abu Ghraib prison in Iraq, and you all know what you do to our brothers in Guantanamo Bay. Sheikh Usama has told you the solution on how to end this war

---

80 K. Siddiqui, *The Muslim Manifesto – A Strategy for Survival* (The Muslim Institute, London, 1990), pp. 15–16.
81 http://news.bbc.co.uk/2/hi/uk_news/4206800.stm.

between us and many others have as well, but you ignore us. Our words are dead until we give them life with our blood. Leave our lands and stop your support for Israel. I have not been brainwashed or indoctrinated. I am not insane. I am not doing it to escape a life of problems or hardships. I am doing what God wants from his mujahideen. We love death as you love life. Muslims welcome death because we will get *jennah*, inshallah, for defending the weak and oppressed Muslims. You kill one of my people I kill one of yours. I have simply seen for myself the brutality and corruption of America, Britain and Israel and my common sense told me it is unacceptable and wrong. The word is the word of the sword until the wrongs have been righted.[82]

Four common core elements can be identified in these and other statements from British domestic jihadis.[83] First, there is a clear affirmation that Islam, or at least their interpretation of it, is the guiding ideology. Second, the incidents in question are described as acts of war perpetrated in retaliation and revenge for atrocities allegedly committed against Muslims abroad by the democratically elected governments of the UK, the United States, Israel, and others. Khan's reference to 'gassing' is, however, bewildering. The only known use of poison gas as an offensive weapon in the past few decades has been by Saddam Hussein in the Iraq–Iran War 1980–8 and against the Iraqi-Kurdish city of Halabja in 1988, Russia in Chechnya, and allegedly by several of the protagonists in the Syrian civil war including, most credibly, the Assad regime in 2013, 2016, and 2018. Apart from Russia the other two are secular regimes with (at least nominally) Muslim leaders. Third, the citizens of western states are threatened with violent retribution until their defeat is secured. Fourth, there is no indication that any perceived or real disadvantage suffered by Muslims in Britain is a motivating factor.[84]

Three further elements can be found in Saeed-Alim Reilly's statement: it contains 'death cult' and 'blood sacrifice' elements, the west is denounced for its decadence and vulgarity, and Reilly's denial of mental health problems has a sad hollow ring given that he was born into a dysfunctional family in a dysfunctional neighbourhood and that he suffered from Asperger's syndrome and obsessive-compulsive tendencies. Prior to his conversion to Islam, he also self-harmed and experienced suicidal ideations which appear to have led to his death in prison later.[85]

---

82 Pantucci, *Britain's Suburban Terrorists*, pp. 265–6.
83 For example, that of Omar Saeed Sheikh, a British-Pakistani convicted in Pakistan for the murder of *Wall Street Journal* reporter Daniel Pearl, Younis Tsouli, a key UK-based, internet radicalizer with a global reach, said to be Al Qaeda in Iraq's most valuable online administrator, and Richard Reid, the would-be 'shoe bomber'. See Pantucci, *Britain's Suburban Terrorists*, pp. 13, 139, 141, 253, 255, 283.
84 Ibid., p. 13.
85 Ibid., 266–9; S. Morris, 'Death in Prison of Man with Asperger's "Raises Serious Concerns"', *The Guardian*, 7 December 2018.

While anger about UK foreign policy lies at the core of British domestic jihadi grievances, it fails to provide a sufficient explanation for domestic jihadi terrorism. Many non-Muslims are just as angry about it yet have not expressed their rage by murdering fellow citizens in the street. As Pantucci puts it: the events of 7 July 2005 were 'not merely a knee-jerk reaction to British Foreign policy, but rather the product of a confluence of global and local events that in the minds of the perpetrators of the attacks were symmetrical'.[86] Needless to say, it is also a mistake to suppose, that because domestic British jihadis cite 'anti-Muslim British foreign policy' as the primary motive for domestic terrorism, that this is an accurate characterization, or that the policy requires fundamental alteration for this reason alone.

It is, of course, true that the UK has historically been involved, and continues to be involved, in 'Muslim lands'. But the reality is a lot more complex than the simple jihadi misrepresentation maintains. The pre-First World War British empire included significant chunks of the Muslim world, especially northern India and, effectively, Egypt and Sudan. Under the League of Nations mandate regime between the first and second World Wars, the UK also governed the former, and largely Muslim, Ottoman territories of Palestine and what became Iraq. Britain was also instrumental in the establishment of the state of Israel in 1948. But, particularly since the end of the Second World War and the end of the Cold War, the UK has had a complex and multidimensional foreign policy. This currently spans a wide range of interests and relationships – including, for example, with other European states, the Commonwealth, the United States, China, and Japan, not to mention managing Brexit – most of which have little or nothing to do with the Islamic world.

As far as 'Muslim lands' are concerned, there is no evidence that the UK has a 'one-size-fits-all' anti-Muslim foreign policy. For example, for decades the UK has been a staunch ally of the traditional Islamic kingdom of Saudi Arabia and a NATO ally of Turkey, the latter until recently a militantly secular state with a 98 per cent Muslim population. It has also had difficult diplomatic relations with the Islamic Republic of Iran and, in 2016, appointed its first ambassador there since 2011. In the 1990s Britain and its allies were criticized by Muslims and others for being too slow to defend predominantly Muslim Bosnia and Kosovo from armed Serbian aggression. When they eventually did intervene – without UN Security Council approval in the latter – further massacres, mostly of Muslims, were averted. Yet the UK has also been condemned for intervening, with the United States and other nations, in the UN-sanctioned invasion of Afghanistan in 2001, and the invasion and occupation of Iraq in 2003 which lacked clear UN approval. However, the Iraq War, which undeniably inflamed anti-western sentiment amongst Muslims at home

---

86 Pantucci, *Britain's Suburban Terrorists*, p. 3.

and abroad,[87] cannot credibly be said to have been 'anti-Islamic' since it was conducted against a secular tyranny, albeit in an Islamic cultural context. And, in spite of the violence, chaos, and instability which have since resulted, two quite different local Muslim communities – the Kurds and Shias – benefitted from it. The UK also intervened in Libya in 2011, ostensibly to protect the population from crimes against humanity. But in 2013 it decided not to do so in Syria. Furthermore, no one could seriously claim that British foreign policy towards several other Muslim-majority states – including Indonesia and those in central Asia – is Islamophobic.

Mobilization and modus operandi

To begin with, in the 1980s and the 1990s, the 'covenant of security' – which forbids attacks upon a host nation providing it refrains from persecuting the faithful – prevented indigenous Islamist violence against the British homeland. Both mobilization and modus operandi were, therefore, limited to attacks abroad. But this changed as the architects of global jihad increasingly came to regard not only western interests in 'Muslim lands', but western states and their inhabitants, as legitimate targets on account of their perceived shared culpability for the suffering of the global Ummah and their resistance to the establishment of the global Caliphate. While this reached its apotheosis in the events of 9/11 in 2001, other relevant international developments, considered more fully in the previous chapter and earlier in this one, have included the anti-Soviet war in Afghanistan 1979–89,[88] the decades-old struggle between India and Pakistan over Kashmir,[89] the Bosnian, Kosovan, and Chechen conflicts of the 1990s, the US-led invasion of Afghanistan in 2001 followed by the anti-US jihad and subsequent civil wars there from 2001–18, and the US-led invasion of Iraq and subsequent civil wars there from 2003–18. Added to these is the, as yet, unresolved Syrian civil war from 2011 onwards.

It has, however, been argued that mobilization for what ultimately became the cause of domestic jihad in Britain began in 1988 with the 'Satanic Verses' controversy, sparked by the publication of a novel of the same name, by Indian-born British Muslim author Salman Rushdie. The term 'Satanic Verses' refers to an episode in the early history of Islam when, in an attempt to convert the Meccans, the Prophet claimed to have received divine revelation permitting their three most important female deities, Allat, al'Uzza, and Manat, to intercede with the Almighty. Clearly incompatible with the radical 'oneness of God', the foundational precept of Islam, Mohammad is said swiftly to have recanted, attributing the event to Satanic deception. Rushdie's novel, banned

---

87 See Dame Eliza Manningham Buller's evidence to the Chilcot Inquiry into the invasion of Iraq quoted in Pantucci, *Britain's Suburban Terrorists*, p. 158.
88 P. Nesser, *Islamist Terrorism in Europe: A History* (Hurst & Co., 2015), ch. 1.
89 Ibid., ch. 6.

in India as hate speech, yet winner of the 1988 Whitbread Award, and shortlisted for the 1988 Booker Prize, blends then contemporary events and characters with the life of the Prophet in a magic realist format.[90] Its publication provoked mass protests and book burnings in the UK and around the world by Muslims who regarded it as blasphemous and insulting to them and their faith. In February 1989, the Ayatollah Khomeini, Supreme Leader of Iran, issued a religious edict (*fatwa*) condemning to death, Rushdie and anyone associated with the novel's publication. Several attempts were made to assassinate the author who was placed under 24-hour police protection and, in 2007, was knighted by Her Majesty the Queen. A translator, Hitoshi Igarashi, was murdered in Japan.

The Satanic Verses affair galvanized, united, and empowered, in a way hitherto unseen, both the more traditional older generation of British Muslims and their more westernized offspring. It also led to the establishment in Britain of several institutions. These included the Muslim Parliament, Hizb ut-Tahrir and Jam'iat Ihyaa Minhaaj Al-Sunnah (JIMAS), the latter two of which have been accused of being significant staging posts on the road to British domestic jihadi terrorism. Hizb ut-Tahrir, a movement started in Jerusalem in 1953, became particularly active in British universities in the 1990s.[91] Its objectives are to infiltrate public institutions in Muslim countries, especially their armed forces, and to engage in terrorism abroad, ultimately to establish a global Caliphate which would combine modern western institutions, such as democracy, the rule of law, independent courts, and minority rights, with an Islamic way of life. JIMAS – one of the first major Salafi organizations in Britain – did not initially mobilize its members to participate in foreign conflicts. But from 1989 onwards, it sent up to 100 fighters to the battlefields of Afghanistan, Kashmir, Bosnia, Burma, and the Philippines. According to Pantucci, it is difficult not to conclude that, in the 1990s, Hizb ut-Tahrir and JIMAS 'played an important role in the radicalization of British Muslim youth',[92] not least through the influence the former had over university Islamic societies.[93]

However, both Hizb ut-Tahrir and JIMAS have since renounced their support for violent jihad. Respected figures in all three dominant Islamic traditions in the UK, the Deobandis, Barelwis, and Ahl-i Hadith, have also denounced terrorism.[94] The latter has, nevertheless, been associated with the Pakistani terrorist group, Lashkar-e-Taiba, galvanized by the conflict with India over Kashmir.[95] Two of the most prominent Kashmiri jihadi groups, Jaish-e-Mohammed and Harakat-ul-Mujahideen, have also had strong Deobandi connections,[96] and the

---

90 Pantucci, *Britain's Suburban Terrorists*, pp. 80–5.
91 Nesser, *Islamist Terrorism in Europe*, p. 34.
92 Pantucci, *Britain's Suburban Terrorists*, p. 96.
93 Ibid., p. 167; Nesser, *Islamist Terrorism in Europe*, p. 9.
94 Bowen, *Inside British Islam*, p. 33.
95 Pantucci, *Britain's Suburban Terrorists*, pp. 38, 40.
96 Bowen, *Inside British Islam*, p. 31.

Taliban grew out of Deobandi madrassas in Pakistan in the 1990s.[97] Several domestic British jihadis, such as Mohammed Siddique Khan, and others based in Britain, including Abu Qatada and Abdullah el-Faisal, were also associated with the Tablighi Jama'at movement, another austere, fundamentalist, otherworldly, Deobandi offshoot.[98] There are, however, questions about the extent to which the movement itself has been involved in terrorism.[99] Bowen, for example, concludes that Deobandi 'flirtation with jihadi groups in the 1990s can now be seen as an aberration for a network dominated by the apolitical, pietistic strand of Islam'.[100]

Apart from the fact that they are overwhelmingly male, under 30, and Muslim,[101] there is no 'typical' British domestic jihadi and no single route to becoming one either.[102] It is also well recognized, including by government, that there is no straightforward relationship, and certainly no 'conveyor belt', between non-violent and violent 'Islamist extremism'.[103] A wide variety of experiences and backgrounds is represented by the tiny minority of the Muslim population of Britain involved in jihadi terrorism at home or abroad. For example, the British security services regard 23,000 or so (0.7 per cent of the Muslim population of Britain) as 'subjects of interest', 3,000 of whom are suspected of jihadi activity (0.1 per cent) and 500 (0.016 per cent) deemed high priority.[104] Although the total number of British jihadis and those trained in camps abroad greatly exceeds the total for the rest of western Europe put together,[105] resonances can, however, be found between the British experience and those in other European countries. Nesser, for example, distinguishes between 'entrepreneurs' and 'protégés' (each driven by political grievances, ideology, and activism), 'misfits' (motivated by a personal rather than a social or ideological grievance), and 'drifters' (who drift into the movement on account of a social tie to someone already involved).[106] 'Self-radicalization', and the careful targeting and grooming of susceptible young people by jihadi organizations through the internet, also present considerable problems.[107] Some, such as 7/7 bombers

---

97 Fergusson, *Journey through Muslim Britain*, p. 140; Bowen, *Inside British Islam*, pp. 12, 31.
98 Bowen, *Inside British Islam*, p. 82.
99 Pantucci, *Britain's Suburban Terrorists*, p. 39.
100 Bowen, *Inside British Islam*, p. 34.
101 Pantucci, *Britain's Suburban Terrorists*, p. 8.
102 *Ibid.*, pp. 7, 76, 291; S. Khan with T. McMahon, *The Battle for British Islam: Reclaiming Muslim Identity from Extremism* (Saqi Books, 2016), pp. 36–9, 100; Leiken, *Europe's Angry Muslims*, pp. xviii–xix, 216.
103 A. Gilligan, 'Hizb ut Tahrir is not a Gateway to Terrorism, Claims Whitehall Report', *The Telegraph*, 25 July 2010.
104 R. Verkaik, 'Why it's Becoming Impossible to Detect the Terrorists', *The Guardian*, 9 June 2017.
105 Leiken, *Angry Muslims*, pp. 111–12, 184.
106 P. Nesser, *Islamist Terrorism in Europe*, pp. 12–18.
107 Pantucci, *Britain's Suburban Terrorists*, pp. 251–60. See, eg, I. Willgress, 'Teenager Who Spent Student Loan Trying to Join Isil and Used a "Step-by-Step Guide to Terrorism" Is Jailed', *The Telegraph*, 28 July 2016; Staff and agencies, 'Scottish Woman Who Married Isis Fighter "Wants to Become a Martyr"', *The Guardian*, 6 September 2014.

Mohammad Siddique Khan and Shehzad Tanweer, were recruited through prayer circles, Muslim youth groups, radical Islamic bookshops, and open air stalls which facilitate socialization, organize study, and disseminate video and audio recordings and publications of various kinds.[108]

A highly influential role in mobilizing Muslim youth for domestic jihad has been played by UK-based charismatic preachers, such as Abu Hamza al-Masri, Omar Bakri Muhammad, Abdullah el-Faisal, Abu Qatada, Zacaria Moussaoui, and, most recently, Anjem Choudary.[109] According to Leiken, the first four, were in receipt of generous welfare benefits and 'most if not all, were informants for the British domestic security service'.[110] Some like Hamza, veterans of the anti-Soviet Afghan war and the Bosnian conflict, contrast sharply with the often poorly educated, out-of-touch, non-English-speaking, rote-learning-oriented imams, collectively recruited from the Indian subcontinent by first- or second-generation immigrants to provide an orthodox religious education for their children.[111] Most commentators also recognize the role of the prevailing permissive, ineffective British security environment in which a blind eye was turned to radicalization and mobilization with respect to terrorism abroad. In the late 1980s and early 1990s, this prompted the French, among others, to refer to London as 'Londonistan'.[112]

As already indicated, but not yet fully explored here, the available evidence does not establish a simple correlation between British domestic jihadi terrorism, on the one hand, and Muslim material disadvantage, anti-Muslim discrimination, or prejudice, on the other. Although the young urban poor are increasingly prominent among European jihadis, fewer than 20 per cent of British jihadis are said to have come from economically deprived backgrounds.[113] Some have criminal convictions and were radicalized in prison.[114] Others, such as Germaine Lindsay, one of the 7/7 bombers, were born abroad. Some converted from other faiths or none. Many had a very rudimentary understanding of Islam, let alone Salafi-Jihadism, when they were first radicalized.[115] Colour-based racism has affected both those who turned to jihad

---

108 Pantucci, *Britain's Suburban Terrorists*, pp. 69–74, 185–99.
109 Nesser, *Islamist Terrorism in Europe*, pp. 8, 38–47; Leiken, *Angry Muslims*, ch. 10; 'Anjem Choudary Jailed for Five-and-a-Half Years for Urging Support of Isis', *The Guardian*, 6 September 2016.
110 Leiken, *Angry Muslims*, p. 178.
111 See, eg, Pantucci, *Britain's Suburban Terrorists*, pp. 63–6, 78, 115–20, 130–40, 142, 176, 184, 229, 231; V.
112 Pantucci, *Britain's Suburban Terrorists*, p. 17; Nesser, *Islamist Terrorism in Europe*, pp. 37–51; M. Phillips, *Londonistan: How Britain is Creating a Terror State Within* (Encounter Books, 2006).
113 'Omar Was a Normal British Teenager', *The Observer*, 20 January 2008; Leiken, *Angry Muslims*, p. 70.
114 Pantucci, *Britain's Suburban Terrorists*, pp. 142, 206, 210–11, 239–40, 242, 248, 275, 281; R. Mendick 'British Jihadist at Heart of Terrorist Network in Syria and Iraq', *The Telegraph*, 16 August 2014. See ch. 5.
115 Pantucci, *Britain's Suburban Terrorists*, pp. 13, 76–8, 135, 176–83, 221, 223, 242; Khan, *Battle for British Islam*, pp. 42–4, 64–5; V. Ward, 'First White Briton to Join Al Qaeda in Syria is Middle Class Muslim Convert', *The Telegraph*, 19 October 2015; C. Turner, 'Jihadi John "Accomplice" Attended Church in Walthamstow before Becoming a Hardline Islamist', *The Telegraph*, 4 February 2015.

and those who did not.[116] Many recruits have also been personally vulnerable in various ways, including suffering from mental illness, at the time of enlistment.[117]

Some British domestic jihadis have, in fact, come from apparently well-integrated Muslim families and have been privately educated.[118] More than a third have university degrees.[119] Mohammad Siddique Khan, the ring-leader of the 7/7 attacks in London, is a case in point.[120] Born in Leeds to working-class parents of Pakistani origin, he obtained a business degree from Leeds Beckett University where he met his wife and also first became interested in extreme Islamism. Described by those who knew him as well-integrated and able to mix easily with white school friends,[121] he was employed at Hillside Primary School in Leeds as a learning mentor for children from newly arrived immigrant families and was also active in voluntary youth work. Shehzad Tanweer, another of the 7/7 bombers, was born in Bradford to parents of Pakistani origin. His family then moved to Leeds where his father became a respected and prominent businessman, mostly in the catering trade. As an outstanding sportsman at school, excelling at cricket, triple jump, long-distance running, football, and ju-jitsu, it was not surprising that Tanweer specialized in sports science at Leeds Metropolitan University before leaving for Pakistan in 2004 to attend a course in Islamic studies. Andrew (aka Isa) Ibrahim, the privately educated son of a prominent Bristol consultant physician, converted to Islam in his teens. While a student at City of Bristol College in 2008–9, he developed an interest in terrorism. A teacher, noticing his behaviour, the views he expressed, and burn marks on his hands, informed the college authorities. But this information was not passed on to law-enforcement agencies. Not long afterwards, Ibrahim's own mosque tipped off the police. His flat was raided, and he was found ready and equipped to carry out a suicide bombing in a Bristol city centre shopping centre which was narrowly averted.[122]

A particularly potent factor paving the way into domestic jihad for many is the 'crisis', or 'revolt', of 'the second generation'. This can be described as a clash between the generally prosperous, urban, materialistic, hedonistic, secular, individualist, educated, and liberal cultural milieu of the British domestic jihadi's own generation in the country where they were born, and the much more religious, puritanical, conservative, family-and-community-oriented,

---

116 Pantucci, *Britain's Suburban Terrorists*, pp. 51, 51–4.
117 *Ibid.*, pp. 76–7, 94, 201, 263, 268; Khan, *Battle for British Islam*, pp. 37–9, 48–9.
118 Pantucci, *Britain's Suburban Terrorists*, p. 166; Khan, *Battle for British Islam*, pp. 46, 109; CONTEST: *The United Kingdom's Strategy for Countering Terrorism*, Cm.8123, July 2011, para. 5.63.
119 Leiken, *Angry Muslims*, p. 70.
120 For profiles of the four central London bombers, see *ibid.*, ch. 11.
121 Pantucci, *Britain's Suburban Terrorists*, p. 52.
122 S. Morris, 'Bristol Man Guilty of Suicide Bomb Plot on Shopping Centre', *The Guardian*, 17 July 2009; two similar cases are cited in HM Government, *Prevent Strategy*, Cm 8092, June 2011, para. 9.2.

rural, and much less materially prosperous, experience of their parents.[123] They are, as Leiken graphically puts it: 'marginal men ... outsiders in the land of their birth and strangers in the land of their forbears'.[124] Only jihad appears to offer redress for the lack of fulfilment, personal, socio-political, and/or religious injustice (real or imagined), and conflicting identities they feel, and the truth, meaning, belonging, identity, and shared purpose they crave. For others, domestic jihad may offer adventure and a vehicle for the expression of the ultimate form of youthful rebellion.[125]

A particular source of friction in this unstable mix is the expectation, common especially for male second-generation Pakistani immigrants such as Mohammad Siddique Khan, that they should marry their typically illiterate, non-English speaking cousins from the home village. The Salafists offer an enticing escape from this, for some, a distinctly unappealing prospect – return to the pure faith of the founding fathers as expressed in the Qur'an and reject the mediation of clerics, ritual, indulgences, revered holy men, and folk traditions such as cousin-marriage. As Leiken observes, the 'de-territorialized' Salafi faith is 'abstract and learned rather than local and lived',[126] and 'oddly, this fundamentalism is a kind of modernization' depending 'solely on a portable Holy Book rather than immobile local shrines' thereby making it 'more accessible to urban literates'.[127]

Kenny's illuminating ethnographic study of al-Muhajiroun (literally 'a participant in the Hijra', the flight of Mohammad and others from Mecca to Medina in 622 CE or more generally a 'religious migrant') comes to substantially the same conclusions regarding mobilization and modus operandi as those reached by other observers of radical Islam in Britain. In particular, it illustrates how blurred the line between lawful Islamist agitation and terrorism can be.[128] The author concludes, for example, that although instrumental in both diverting activists away from Syria and Iraq and motivating others to go there as foreign fighters,[129] participation in the movement is neither a conveyor belt to, nor a safety valve preventing, terrorism. It may also have been a contributing factor in some cases.[130] Eventually banned following the conviction, in 2016, of its then leader Anjem Choudary, for declaring support for ISIS/DAESH in

---

123 Leiken, *Angry Muslims*, pp. xx, 69–74.
124 *Ibid.*, pp. 102, 265; Pantucci, *Britain's Suburban Terrorists*, pp. 57–66, 74–5.
125 Pantucci, *Britain's Suburban Terrorists*, pp. 8–17; Q. Wiktorowicz, *Radical Islam Rising: Muslim Extremism in the West* (Rowman & Little, 2009); I. Burrell, 'BBC's Newsbeat Reprimanded for Letting Isis Fighter Compare Jihad to Call of Duty', *The Independent*, 10 November 2014.
126 Leiken, *Angry Muslims*, p. 75.
127 *Ibid.*, p. xxi.
128 M. Kenny, *The Islamic State in Britain: Radicalization and Resilience in an Activist Network* (Cambridge University Press, 2018).
129 *Ibid.*, pp. 8–9.
130 *Ibid.*, pp. 28, 205, 208, 220–30.

82 *Domestic terrorism*

Syria and Iraq,[131] in its heyday in the 1990s to the 2000s, the movement had 150–200 dedicated members ('intellectual affiliates') plus several hundred supporters ('contacts'). Its size and strength have, however, been greatly exaggerated both by the movement in order to maximize its profile and by a compliant media eager for sensationalism.[132]

There is no single path as far as recruitment, participation, progression, or leaving are concerned. But social relationships are central at every stage.[133] Kenny found that none of those he interviewed had been raised in Salafi homes.[134] For some, the quest for meaning, identity, belonging, and purpose, including addressing an identity crisis, are dominant.[135] For others it is more a matter of being impressed by activists and succumbing to peer pressure, sometimes preceding endorsement of the movement's ideology which some of those recruited never fully embrace.[136] Some need a father figure and one activist even described involvement as being like a kid with a new toy.[137]

Once recruited, an activist can expect to promote the movement's central purpose, shared with other Islamist groups – calling society to Islam, commanding good and forbidding evil (*Hisbah*, a cornerstone of the movement's activism typically expressed through public protests),[138] establishing a global Caliphate by exploiting western freedoms to undermine them ('jihad of the tongue' rather than 'jihad of the sword'), countering western values, and 'exposing' the west's 'war on Islam'.[139] These are pursued mainly through *Da'wah* ('invitation'), preaching and propagating al-Muhajiroun's distinctive interpretation of the faith, and calling people to Islam, particularly through street stalls, a cornerstone of the movement's activism, and *halaqahs* (local, small Islamic study circles), the basic unit of indoctrination and organization which promotes intense friendship and camaraderie.[140] Other activities include conferences, protests, and media manipulation to gain publicity and present as large a public profile as possible.[141] The internet has also been important.[142]

There is, however, little formal training. Novices learn on the job by imitating established activists.[143] The network may also use threats and other forms of psychological coercion to retain them if they threaten to leave and to

---

131 *Ibid.*, p. 8.
132 *Ibid.*, p. 5.
133 *Ibid.*, pp. 29, 98, 130, 216; P. Nesser, *Islamist Terrorism in Europe*, pp. 1, 7.
134 Kenny, *The Islamic State in Britain*, p. 216.
135 *Ibid.*, pp. 61, 97, 216.
136 *Ibid.*, pp. 28–9, p. 97.
137 *Ibid.*, pp. 48–9.
138 *Ibid.*, p. 262.
139 *Ibid.*, pp. 12, 14, 15, 35, 43.
140 *Ibid.*, pp. 49, 261–2.
141 *Ibid.*, pp. 16, 19, 26, 61.
142 *Ibid.*, p. 219.
143 *Ibid.*, p. 130.

punish them if they do.[144] According to Kenny, resolution of the deep tension between al-Muhajiroun's small-world structure, which facilitated its survival in a hostile environment, and the insularity and dogmatism which threatened it, was achieved by the modification of activities rather than revision of ideology.[145] This included deception when reserving venues and transferring conferences to smaller ones, moving *Da'wah* stalls to new areas and making them less provocative, emphasizing the religious side of preaching, and posting talks online.[146] The outlawing of prominent platforms also prompted new spin-offs and the revival of old ones.[147]

Initially, when police interest was low, al-Muhajiroun had a centralized structure revolving around its founder Omar Bakri Muhammad.[148] But after he left the UK for Lebanon in August 2005, where he was imprisoned for promoting extremist ideologies and inciting violence,[149] it became much more de-centralized. Small networks were linked by multiple nodes, with leadership bridging different clusters.[150] It has always been largely a youth phenomenon and activists often have a poor understanding of the Islamic faith, not least because of the expectation uncritically to endorse the interpretation proffered by its founder and his successors, Anjem Choudary and Mizanur Rahman.[151] Its 'almost cultish' elements, hinging on devotion to these figures, have ensured marginalization and isolation from other Muslims and society at large, a fact acknowledged even by activists themselves.[152] While disagreements can be intense over tactics, this does not include Bakri's vision or al-Muhajiroun's core ideology.[153] The wider environment became increasingly hostile post 7/7,[154] and by the time of Kenny's study, conducted from 2007–14, the movement had dwindled to only a couple of dozen intellectual affiliates and several dozen contacts.[155] Fraternal organizations have also been established in Belgium, Denmark, and Norway.[156]

Life after al-Muhajiroun activism may lie anywhere on a spectrum between total repudiation of its mission, to passive sympathy for jihadi terrorism. However, for most, membership is a passionate, but transient adolescent phase, quietly dropped as a result of maturation and the attractions of leading a normal

---

144 *Ibid.*, p. 205.
145 *Ibid.*, p. 131.
146 *Ibid.*, pp. 30–1, 39–40, 170.
147 *Ibid.*, pp. 34, 170, 210.
148 *Ibid.*, p. 41.
149 *Ibid.*, pp. 42, 51, 59.
150 *Ibid.*, pp. 29, 34, 50.
151 *Ibid.*, pp. 216–8.
152 *Ibid.*, p. 6.
153 *Ibid.*, p. 131.
154 *Ibid.*, pp. 50, 63.
155 *Ibid.*, p. 5.
156 *Ibid.*, p. 8.

life with education, salary, career, family, pastimes, and such.[157] Some activists also burn-out, disillusioned and weary of hearing and relaying the same old message, frustrated about the demands on time, frequent requests for money, conflict with parents and other family members over the cause, a lack of tangible achievements, and the realization that other Muslims have been stigmatized by the movement's activities.[158]

According to Kenny, until it was banned and Choudary was imprisoned following support for ISIS/DAESH, al-Muhajiroun displayed considerable resilience and adaptation to increasingly effective law enforcement.[159] Although leaders and activists were arrested, others forbidden from engaging in public *Da'wah*, protests disrupted, and networks fragmented,[160] the movement was weakened rather than destroyed.[161] As a result of infiltration by informants, activists have also been subject to TPIMs (Terrorism Prevention and Investigation Measures), ASBOs (Anti-Social Behaviour Orders), and MAPPAs (Multi-Agency Public Protection Arrangements).[162] A key operative, Omar Khyam, was also persuaded to testify for the Crown.[163] While the authorities seem to have removed enough nodes to break up the movement, it remains unclear if it is dead or merely dormant.[164] In spite of being involved in de-radicalization programmes, some of those imprisoned have, for example, used their incarceration to deepen their commitment to the cause. *Halaqahs*, also remain active.[165]

Kenny concludes that, from a counterterrorist perspective, disruption of al-Muhajiroun may be considered a success. However, perversely for some activists, it may confirm the conviction that Muslims are being persecuted in Britain. It may also have contributed to the decision on the part of others to become foreign fighters or to abandon the 'covenant of security'.[166] Once radicalized, British jihadis have also typically undergone training in foreign countries, particularly Pakistan, joined the jihad in Syria and Iraq, or simply launched self-initiated attacks on Britain's streets with firearms, knives, other sharp instruments, and/or motor vehicles. The threat posed by those returning from the battlefields of Syria and Iraq is a critical and unique feature of jihadi terrorism, unparalleled with respect to the other two principal domestic types contemporary Britain faces.

---

157 Ibid., pp. 29–31, 201, 204–5.
158 Ibid., p. 204.
159 Ibid., p. 170.
160 Ibid., pp. 31, 38, 63.
161 Ibid., pp. 7, 25–7, 63.
162 Ibid., pp. 210–11.
163 Ibid., p. 25.
164 Ibid., pp. 211–12, 230.
165 Ibid., pp. 209–10, 231.
166 Ibid., pp. 19, 25, 226–9, 230–2; Leiken, *Angry Muslims*, pp. 178–87; Nesser, *Islamist Terrorism in Europe*, pp. 47–51.

Kenny maintains that al-Muhajiroun has been damaged not only by counterterrorism but also by increasing rejection on the part of local Muslim communities.[167] He also argues that formal deradicalization may be less effective than the informal challenging of its mission by friends, family, and former activists. Particularly powerful, in this respect, are exposure to interpretations of Islam which counter that of the movement, coupled with assistance in building new identities outside it – in other words, 'networks in networks out'.[168]

Conclusion

As a result of the peace process and the Belfast/Good Friday Agreement, the scale of Troubles-based terrorism has greatly diminished in Northern Ireland, Britain, and elsewhere. The main residual threat is posed by a tiny minority of armed dissident republicans, wedded to the kind of violent anti-British politics which the vast majority of the republican movement has long since renounced. While there can be no doubt that these die-hards are capable of, and willing to commit murder, as things stand they have nothing like the social, political, and material resources of their predecessors. The bulk of militant far-right activity in Britain takes the form of loose movements dedicated to street and online agitation and mobilization rather than to terrorism as such. However, the evidence indicates that, modelling themselves on their jihadi adversaries, this is beginning to change.

As far as domestic jihadi terrorism is concerned, the answer to the first question posed at the beginning of this chapter is well-known. Invoking a radical, minority, non-mainstream interpretation of Islam, and operating in small cells, or alone with either no links or only loose connections to others at home and abroad, British domestic jihadis seek to commit murder and mayhem through suicide bombings in crowded public places, in public institutions and systems, and/or with any other weapons they can get their hands on, including firearms, meat cleavers, knives, other sharp implements, and motor vehicles.

The answer to the second question is, however, less clear. The conservative Muslim reaction to the decline of, first the Mughal empire in India and then the collapse of the Ottoman empire, has been dominated by opposition to western colonialism, and to the west and modernity in general. Developing across the Muslim world since the 18th century, this has, at most, been passively manifested in Britain's Muslim population, the majority of whom, from Pakistan and Bangladesh, adhere to the Deobandi, Barelwi, and Ahl-i Hadith traditions of Sufi-Sunni Islam. Initially identified as 'the other' by the indigenous population much more by race and country/continent of origin than by religion, there is abundant anecdotal evidence of both cordial and hostile relations. The Rushdie affair of the late 1980s, however, produced a more

---

167 Kenny, *Islamic State in Britain*, pp. 170, 205, 212.
168 *Ibid.*, pp. 233–5.

assertive and self-consciously British Muslim identity, not least among the second generation which, having been born, bred, and educated in Britain, also in principle had better material prospects than its parents. A series of international events from the last two decades of the 20th century compounded these developments by raising the question – how should Muslims around the world, including those in Britain, respond to the violent challenges facing their brothers and sisters abroad? Among a range of answers, only a tiny minority advocated joining jihad abroad, with fewer still opting for indiscriminate murder in the land of their birth.

The threat from British domestic jihadi terrorism is, therefore, essentially a local manifestation of a global problem, from which no country in the world is immune, galvanized and focused by certain specific national social, political, and religious factors. Although a sense of alienation, grievance, and injustice is common to all jihadis, British domestic jihadi terrorism cannot adequately be explained simply in terms of a straightforward reaction by Muslims to material disadvantage, discrimination, and/or anti-Muslim prejudice at the national level, real though these may be for many. At most this has provided the environment for the cultivation of the threat rather than having caused it.

The evidence also indicates that, while some of those attracted to British domestic jihad have come from challenging backgrounds – including broken homes, poverty, and encounters with drugs, crime, prosecution, and imprisonment – others have been well-educated, raised in prosperous, stable, and apparently well-integrated Muslim families with good material prospects. A key factor for some has been the friction, experienced by second and subsequent post-migrant generations between, on the one hand, the dominant British culture characterized by liberalism, secularism, and pluralism, and on the other, the expectations and pressures of their family's 'folk Islam'. However, these variables at most provide only part of the explanation for domestic jihad. After all, other disadvantaged minorities in Britain have not responded to whatever injustice and social exclusion they have, or believe they have, suffered, by resorting to indiscriminate violence on the streets of their own country.

Although perceived by jihadis as anti-Muslim, the UK's current foreign policy is also much too complex and multi-dimensional, even with respect to Muslim-majority states, to be credibly described as such. The UK has undeniably been involved in 'Muslim lands' as an imperial power and as one of several western architects of the post-Ottoman Middle-Eastern settlement. It has also been a particularly influential player in the establishment of the state of Israel, and a key contributor to the western interventions in Bosnia and Kosovo in the 1990s, the invasions of Afghanistan in 2001, in Iraq in 2003, and the battle against ISIS/DAESH from 2015–18. While some, though not all, of these events have undoubtedly exacerbated the problem of domestic jihad, they did not give rise to it either. And it should not be forgotten, of course, that the core of the Muslim world, the Middle East and north Africa, are themselves 'Muslim lands' because of imperial Islamic conquest in the more distant past. Jihadi terrorism, both domestic and global, is, therefore, much less *anti-*imperialist than *alt-*imperialist in the sense that it venerates Islamic imperialism in what were, hitherto, non-Muslim lands, while condemning more recent western imperialism in what has since become the core of the Muslim world.

Amongst the many differences between the British domestic jihadi and Troubles contexts, is that, with the exception of public protest, the protagonists in the former have made no attempt to mobilize politically. This is not least because participation in democratic elections is anathema to jihadi ideology which regards law as deriving from the dictates of Allah in the Qur'an not what human legislators declare in legislation. This has had significant implications for the management of the risk this type of terrorism presents. Even if there ever was an official desire to persuade domestic British jihadis to renounce jihad in favour of peace, there is nobody with whom negotiations could reliably be conducted. And because the current British domestic jihadi threat stems principally from a distinctive mix of background factors, grievances, ideology, and mobilization it cannot be effectively addressed unless these elements are acknowledged and tackled by both state and society acting effectively together. What this has, and should, entail will be the subject of the remainder of this book.

4 *Protect* and *Prepare*

Introduction

As already indicated in Chapters 2 and 3, one of the core characteristics of 21st century British domestic jihadi terrorism is the willingness of its exponents to cause mass casualties and as much other damage as possible. If they acquired weapons of mass destruction this could happen on a horrific scale. This chapter considers the principal, and intertwined, features of *Protect* and *Prepare* – concerned respectively with strengthening protection against terrorist attacks and mitigating their impact if they should, nevertheless, occur.

Protect

The purpose of *Protect* is to improve public safety and to reduce vulnerability to terrorist attack in the UK and against British interests overseas.[1] This includes maintaining the security of borders, aviation, other transport systems, critical national infrastructure, and crowded places, plus controlling access to materials, knowledge, and information that might be used for terrorist purposes. Success is officially defined in terms of awareness of vulnerabilities and their characteristics, attempting to reduce them to an acceptable and proportionate level, sharing priorities and acting wherever possible with the private sector and the international community, and seeking to ensure that the disruptive effects and costs of protective security are proportionate to risk.[2] Depending upon an assessment of the threat level, and guided by considerations of efficacy, cost effectiveness, and proportionality, high-profile individuals deemed at risk may also be provided with official protection.

---

1 HM Government, *CONTEST: The United Kingdom's Strategy for Countering Terrorism*, June 2018, Cm 9608, para. 181. The source for most of the information about the *Protect* strategy in this chapter is derived from pp. 53–62 of this document.
2 Home Office, *Countering International Terrorism*, Cm.8123, July 2011, para. 7.7.

DOI: 10.4324/9781003221104-4

Border and aviation security

As for any state, protecting the borders of the UK involves not just the physical frontier, but also checks and interventions in advance of travel to, and from, abroad. While the physical border is the particular responsibility of the Home Office UK Border Force, all UK law enforcement agencies contribute to its security. Border checks are made, and kept under constant review, against the widest range of domestic and international watchlists, including the international Authority to Carry ('No Fly') scheme. Apart from carriers for scheduled aviation routes to and from the UK within the Common Travel Area (CTA) – which covers the Republic of Ireland, the Channel Islands, and the Isle of Man – advanced passenger and freight data are required before arrival at, or departure from, the UK. All passports are also biometrically checked at points of entry and exit. Sharing information with trusted partners and multilateral bodies, including the Schengen Information System, Europol, and Interpol, also assists in the detection of threats further upstream. The government claims these arrangements will be maintained, and other options explored, now that the UK has left the EU.

Particularly on account of the totemic target it presents to jihadis, global aviation is both intimately connected with border security and raises some specific issues. The UK was instrumental in securing the first relevant UN Security Council resolution, UNSCR 2309, in September 2016, and another, UNSCR 2396, in December 2017. In order to deliver these international commitments, the British government has also worked closely with the International Civil Aviation Organization (ICAO). UK aviation security policy is overseen by the Department of Transport's Aviation Directorate, with the National Aviation Security Programme and Handbook applied at each airport by Risk Advisory Groups (RAG) and Security Executive Groups (SEG).[3] Similar regimes apply to seaports. Domestic law also supplements the substantial body of relevant international law.[4] For example, Part II of the Aviation Security Act 1982 authorizes the Secretary of State for Transport and the Civil Aviation Authority to impose protective measures for aircraft and aerodromes by directive.[5] Part VII of the Policing and Crime Act 2009 also requires the relevant police authority and local chief police officer to negotiate a security-related Police Services Agreement with airports.

---

3 Department for Transport, *Draft Civil Aviation Bill: An Effective Regulatory Framework for UK Aviation*, Cm 8234-I, 2011; Sir John Wheeler, *Report on Airport Security* (Department for Transport, 2002), paras. 1.3, 3.28.
4 P. Wilkinson, 'Enhancing UK Aviation Security Post 9/11' in P. Wilkinson (ed.), *Homeland Security in the UK* (Routledge, 2007).
5 As amended by Civil Aviation Act 2012.

In early 2010 concerns, described by the House of Commons Home Affairs Committee as 'overstated',[6] were expressed about the privacy-related implications of the introduction of body scanners to prevent illegal weapons, explosives, and other dangerous items being taken on board aircraft. In 2016, in order to explore other possible technological and science-based initiatives – such as machine learning algorithms, quantum imaging, and new methods of vapour detection – the Home Office and Department for Transport launched the £25.5 million Future Aviation Security Solutions (FASS) programme. The UK's national Aviation Strategy also outlines how a comprehensive aviation security policy will be conceived and developed in this rapidly changing environment. The 'drone crisis', which grounded 1,000 flights and affected some 140,000 passengers at Gatwick during the Christmas period in 2018, and more briefly at Heathrow early in 2019, prompted both airports to invest in military-style technology. According to press reports, these can crash drones by jamming communications with their operators.[7] In order to intercept any unidentified or unauthorized aircraft compromising UK airspace the RAF is also capable of being airborne in minutes.

Counterterrorist stop and search at ports

Schedule 7 of the Terrorism Act 2000, amended by Schedule 6 to the Antisocial Behaviour, Crime and Policing Act 2014, permits 'examining officers' designated by the Secretary of State (usually the police) to stop and question, search, and detain anyone transiting through ports, airports, international rail stations, or the border area between the Republic of Ireland and Northern Ireland.

Those questioned are required to provide any information or identity documents requested, including passwords to data storage devices they are carrying. Possessions and goods, including data on electronic devices, may also be examined and seized. The purpose is to determine whether those concerned appear to be, or have been, involved in the commission, preparation, or instigation of acts of terrorism. While it is an offence to refuse to cooperate, information obtained during a Schedule 7 examination cannot be used as evidence in a criminal trial except for prosecutions regarding failures to comply with these obligations, perjury, and other offences where the accused makes a statement inconsistent with information they provided at the examination.[8] A legal power is also provided for strip searches to be conducted if the examining

---

6 Department for Transport, *Interim Code of Practice for the Acceptable Use of Advanced Imaging Technology (Body Scanners) in an Aviation Security Environment* (London, 2010); House of Commons Home Affairs Committee, *Counter Terrorism Measures in British Airports* (2009–10 HC 311), para. 30.
7 K. Rawlinson, 'Drone Report Causes Flights to Be Grounded at Heathrow', *The Guardian*, 9 January 2019 and 'Airports to Spend Millions Buying Anti-Drone Defences', *The Guardian*, 4 January 2018.
8 Home Office, *Examining Officers and Review Officers under Schedule 7 to the Terrorism Act 2000 Code of Practice*, August 2020, para. 43.

officer, authorized by a more senior officer not involved in the examination, has a reasonable suspicion that evidence of involvement in terrorist activities is being concealed. But it is extremely rare for this to be exercised. It was used, for example, with respect to a total of only 24 travellers from 2012–19 inclusive.[9] Initial questioning may last for up to an hour. But, subject to formal detention, an officer higher in rank than the examining officer may extend it for a further six hours. Regular reviews, beginning no later than an hour after detention has begun, and then at subsequent intervals of two hours, must be conducted to determine if detention is still necessary. Longer periods, but not for the purpose of examination, require formal arrest.

Exercise of Schedule 7 powers is governed by a code of practice.[10] Amongst other things, this requires examining officers to act respectfully, courteously, fairly, and responsibly in accordance with prescribed procedures, to minimize causing embarrassment or offence, to comply with the Human Rights Act 1998 and the Equality Act 2010, and where necessary to assist with making alternative travel arrangements for those whose travel has been disrupted by an examination. Although exercise of the power to examine is not conditional upon the examining officer having grounds to suspect anyone of being engaged in terrorism, 'the decision to select … must not be arbitrary'.[11] Paragraph 30 provides that it is not appropriate for race, ethnic background, religion and/or other 'protected characteristics' (whether separately or together) to be invoked as a reason for selection except to the extent that they are used in association with considerations that relate to the threat from terrorism. Some examples, such as patterns of travel through specific ports that may be linked to terrorist activity, and referrals by other security, transport, or enforcement bodies, are given.[12] Schedule 3 to the Counter-Terrorism and Border Security Act 2019 effectively extends Schedule 7 powers to include 'hostile activities' – defined as serious crime or threats to national security including those affecting national economic well-being – carried out on behalf of another state. A separate code of practice, similar to that for Schedule 7, has also been provided.[13]

Official statistics reveal several things about the exercise of Schedule 7 powers. First, they are rarely used, and the number of examinations has also been steadily decreasing year-on-year from 61,711 in 2012 to 10,344 in 2019.[14] In the year ending 30 September 2017, over 300 million passengers travelled through UK ports. However, in Britain, to and from which the vast majority enter and leave the UK, only 16,919 (0.006 per cent) were examined

---

9 Home Office, *Operation of Police Powers under the Terrorism Act 2000 and Subsequent Legislation: Arrests, Outcomes, and Stop and Search, Great Britain, Year Ending September 2019*, Statistical Bulletin 30/19, Table S.03.
10 Home Office, *Schedule 7 to the Terrorism Act 2000 Code of Practice*.
11 *Ibid.*, para. 29.
12 *Ibid.*, para. 30.
13 *Ibid.*
14 Home Office, *Operation of Police Powers under the Terrorism Act 2000*, Table S.03.

under these provisions.[15] Between the end of September 2012–19, of a total of 239,241 examinations at ports and airports, conducted under Schedule 7, 224,508 (94 per cent) lasted less than an hour.[16] Of those examined, 83,941 (35 per cent of the total) were white and 135,997 (57 per cent), non-white. The ethnicity of the remaining 19,303 (eight per cent) is not stated. Of the total number of those examined, 10,713 were detained (four per cent), of which 1,224 were white (11 per cent of the total number of detentions), 8,076 (75 per cent of the total number of detentions) were non-white, and the ethnicity of 1,413 (13 per cent) was unstated.

Schedule 7 powers are not expressly targeted against any specific race, religion, or ethnicity. They are not, therefore, discriminatory on these grounds by design. The religious affiliation of those subject to these powers is not recorded. But the overrepresentation of non-whites, particularly among those detained, might suggest racial discrimination in application. It can, however, also be explained in other terms. Since 92 per cent of Muslims in England and Wales are non-white, and all jihadis are Muslim, the vast majority of jihadis in Britain are likely to be non-white. Globally, all jihadis are also Muslim and most are also non-white. On the basis of intelligence assessments, Schedule 7 is likely to be used significantly more in relation to certain flights than others. For obvious reasons, these have not been officially identified.[17] But it is, nevertheless, well-known, as indicated in Chapter 2, that the countries most afflicted by jihadi terrorism are Nigeria, Syria, Iraq, India, Afghanistan, and Pakistan, all of which have almost entirely non-white populations. The majority of those visiting them are also likely to be non-white.

The European Court of Human Rights (ECtHR) condemned the unamended version of Schedule 7 for not being sufficiently circumscribed and for lacking sufficient safeguards against abuse. But it, nevertheless, held that the absence of a reasonable suspicion requirement at the time was not in itself 'contrary to the principle of legality'. It added that there was 'clear evidence' that the unamended Schedule 7 powers 'had been of real value in protecting national security' and were not 'being abused'.[18] However, the UK's Supreme Court has confirmed that the amended legislation is human rights compliant.[19] Between February and April 2019 the government of the UK conducted a consultation exercise about Schedule 7, the results of which had not been announced as this study went to press.[20]

---

15 HM Government, *CONTEST 2018*, p. 56, fn 42.
16 Home Office, *Operation of Police Powers under the Terrorism Act 2000*, Table S.03.
17 HM Government, *CONTEST 2018*, para. 194.
18 *Beghal v United Kingdom*, judgment of 28 February 2019, at paras. 95, 96, 97.
19 *Beghal (Appellant) v Director of Public Prosecutions (Respondent)* [2015] UKSC 49.
20 www.gov.uk/government/publications/circular-0082019-schedule-7-to-the-terrorism-act-2000.

Immigration and asylum

Since 9/11, protecting national security and countering terrorism have had increasing prominence in national immigration and asylum processes the world over. Non-nationals may seek to enter the UK for short or long periods, or to settle permanently. The reasons may include business trips, holidays, study visits, escaping persecution, and in pursuit of, amongst other things, family reunion and greater security, freedom, prosperity, and well-being. In addition to relevant international legal norms, the domestic law and policy are complex, bureaucratic, controversial, and, primarily as a result of Brexit, in a state of flux. Some maintain that, even pre-Brexit, the system was too permissive, and that the departure of the UK from the EU provides a welcome opportunity to tighten controls. Others argue that the regime was, and remains, excessively prohibitive, unjust, and in violation of human rights; characteristics, they maintain, that are likely to be enhanced post-Brexit. Most of the issues in this debate are beyond the scope of this study. However, the preventive element in *Protect* raises the question of when, and under what conditions, refusing certain foreign nationals permission to enter the UK – and the subsequent termination of the right of others to remain – may lawfully and legitimately arise.

In legal, and other, respects a key distinction concerns non-nationals seeking permission to enter the UK to claim asylum, and those presenting for other reasons. This is because, as a signatory to the UN Refugee Convention 1951, the UK is under an international legal obligation to grant asylum to anyone arriving at its borders with a 'well-founded fear' of persecution. However, satisfying this condition does not necessarily mean the claim will be successful. Of particular relevance to this study, Article 1F of the Refugee Convention mandates the refusal of asylum where there are 'serious reasons for considering' that the applicant has been guilty of a crime against peace, a war crime, a crime against humanity (including threatening the integrity of the international refugee regime itself), a serious non-political crime in another country, or has acted contrary to the purposes of the UN.[21] This provision is to be restrictively construed. A considered and reasoned verdict – supported by 'clear and credible' or 'strong' evidence reaching a standard higher than 'reasonable grounds' yet not as high as 'beyond reasonable doubt' – is also required.[22]

The concept of a 'non-political crime' – though interpreted in a manner which 'has not always been consistent'[23] – is also increasingly used by British courts to include those terrorist activities which, though clearly politically motivated, have involved the 'particularly cruel' or indiscriminate use of violence.[24] Section 54 of the Immigration, Asylum and Nationality Act 2006 also

---

21 G. Clayton and G. Firth, *Immigration and Asylum Law*, 8th edn. (Oxford University Press, 2018), pp. 493–511.
22 *Ibid.*, 495.
23 *Ibid.*, 501.
24 *Ibid.*, 500–4.

makes clear that the phrase 'acts contrary to the purpose and principles of the UN', contained in the Refugee Convention, includes committing, preparing, or instigating acts of terrorism and encouraging others to do likewise.[25] Article 33 (2) of the Refugee Convention also entitles states to expel or return refugees, notwithstanding that they otherwise satisfy the conditions for asylum, where there are 'reasonable grounds' for regarding them as 'a danger to the security' of the country of refuge or where, as a result of having been convicted of a 'particularly serious crime', they constitute 'a danger to the community of that country'. Asylum can also be lawfully revoked in accordance with the 1951 Convention if the conditions which gave rise to the well-founded fear of persecution in the country of origin no longer obtain.[26] These exceptions aside, those granted asylum – about 34 per cent of initial cases and 35 per cent of those appealed[27] – are subject to the same counterterrorist regime as British nationals.

Foreign nationals seeking entry to the UK for reasons other than asylum may be refused permission to enter at the discretion of immigration officers, including on the grounds that this would be 'conducive to the public good'.[28] Examples include, amongst other things, the applicant's conduct (including certain convictions), character, and associations.[29] Although the relevant discretion is wide, the courts have held that the decision to exclude on these grounds must be one the immigration officer 'could rationally reach'.[30]

Having lawfully entered the UK, foreign nationals without refugee status can subsequently be expelled (known as 'enforced return') for a variety of reasons including, of particular relevance to this study, if the Secretary of State deems it 'conducive to the public good',[31] a condition most frequently applied with respect to criminal offences. However, even in such circumstances, enforced return is not automatic and depends upon the combined effect of the seriousness of the offence, including the degree of 'public revulsion', the likelihood of reoffending, the deterrent effect it is likely to have upon others, and (rarely as a reason for successfully challenging deportation) the offender's ties with the host and recipient countries, including his/her family life.[32]

Other issues relevant to this criterion include perceived threats to national security and the risk of terrorism. Although such assessments are by nature precautionary and preventive, and inevitably involve future-oriented expectation and prediction as much as, if not more than, reference to past conduct, they must have some evidential basis, the adequacy of which is open to legal

---

25 *Ibid.*, 505–9.
26 *Ibid.*, 425.
27 *Ibid.*, 421.
28 *Ibid.*, 560–71.
29 Immigration Rules, Part 9, para. 320(19), 4 June 2020.
30 *R (on the Application of) Irfan v SSHD* [2013] EWHC 1162 (Admin), para. 87.
31 Immigration Act 1971, s.3(5)(b).
32 Clayton and Firth, *Immigration and Asylum Law*, pp. 560–2.

challenge.³³ A particularly contentious issue concerns evidence connecting the applicant with terrorists, their activities, or their organizations which the applicant either denies or claims was innocent and lawful. Examples include running a bookshop at a mosque frequented by extremists and having allegedly photocopied recipes for poison.³⁴ There has been some judicial debate about the requisite standard such evidence must reach.³⁵ Some judges require the case as a whole to satisfy a 'high civil standard', while others, observing that the core issue is inherently speculative and that relevant proceedings are in the domain of public rather than civil law, have queried whether a formal standard of proof is appropriate at all. While it is also open to the courts to define national security, they have also accepted that the question of what is or is not in the *interests* of national security is a matter for the executive. Immigration cases with national security dimensions are heard by the Special Immigration Appeals Commission where applicants are represented by security-vetted advocates limited in how much information they can disclose to their clients.

An issue raised by the potential forced return of foreign nationals suspected of terrorism or threatening national security, which creates a potential dilemma for the authorities, concerns the principle of *non-refoulment*, the international ban on the compulsory return of foreign nationals to destinations, typically their home state, where they face persecution or a genuine risk of torture, inhuman, or degrading treatment. Where there are grounds for believing that there is such a prospect, but relevant intelligence does not reach the standard required to secure a criminal conviction, two possible options are available: administrative control including house arrest in the UK considered in Chapter 6 or enforced return subject to a Memorandum of Understanding where the recipient state is required to ensure that, following their arrival, the deportee will not be abused or tried upon the evidence of others extracted by mistreatment. The Abu Qatada case provides an example of how Memoranda of Understanding (MoU) operate. On 7 July 2013, after a highly publicized eight-year process, the radical Islamist preacher was returned, subject to an MoU, from the UK to Jordan, where he was subsequently tried and acquitted of terrorist offences. There are, however, two principal problems with the MoU process. Not all recipient states can be trusted to honour relevant commitments and, other than diplomatic pressure, it is difficult to ensure compliance on the part of those which turn out to be less reliable than expected.

In 2019, out of a total of over 60 million non-UK passenger arrivals at UK ports, 17,815 were refused entry and subsequently departed, of whom 514 were failed asylum seekers.³⁶ The four countries leading the top-ten from which

---

33 *Ibid.*, 566–71.
34 *Y v SSHD* [2006] UKSIAC 36/2004 SIAC.
35 Clayton and Firth, *Immigration and Asylum Law*, pp. 566–71.
36 www.gov.uk/government/publications/immigration-statistics-year-ending-december-2019/how-many-people-are-detained-or-returned.

most of these came were Brazil (2,152), Albania (1,356), Romania (1,261), and the United States (827). The remainder had just over 500 or less each. China was in tenth place with 444. Only three of the half dozen or so states with the most serious terrorist problems, Nigeria (503), Pakistan (499), and Iraq (485), appear in the list. Of a total of 7,361 enforced returns (down from 15,828 in 2010), 1,506 were failed asylum applications. While the official figures do not indicate the reasons for refusals to grant entry, or for compulsory returns, counterterrorist concerns do not, however, appear to feature prominently.

Other transport systems

The government works with industry across a range of transport sectors exposed to variable terrorist and other threats. This includes promoting security awareness campaigns, and encouraging data-sharing, risk-sensitive design, and science-based and/or technological solutions, including screening methods and exploring the security potential of behavioural analysis. Because the rail sector also provides a particularly attractive target for terrorists, threats to it have been added to the more familiar assaults, public order, and property offences dealt with by the 2,900 officers of the British Transport Police (BTP).[37] The BTP has also expanded its capabilities, including increasing the number of armed officers patrolling stations and trains. New specialist operations units have been established in Manchester and Birmingham. Working with the rail industry, the Department for Transport and Centre for the Protection of National Infrastructure (CPNI, see below) has also implemented a national awareness campaign – 'See it. Say it. Sorted.' – to encourage public vigilance and the reporting of suspicious activities and/or items on the rail network to the BTP.

Security guidance has also been updated for the bus, coach, and maritime sectors, the latter of which accounted, in 2016, for around 95 per cent of British trade in goods by weight.[38] Since December 2016, with British approval, the French authorities have deployed armed sea marshals on a number of cross-Channel ferries, a programme which, together with a range of other security measures, is likely to form part of a UK–France Maritime Counter-Terrorism Agreement.[39]

---

37 Department for Transport, *Modernizing the British Transport Police* (London, 2001).
38 HM Government, *CONTEST 2018*, para. 207.
39 United Kingdom–France Summit Communique, Royal Military Academy Sandhurst, 18 January 2018, para. 28, https://assets.publishing.service.gov.uk/government/uploads/system/uploads/attachment_data/file/674880/2018_UK-FR_Summit_Communique.pdf.

Critical National Infrastructure

Protective security for the Critical National Infrastructure (CNI) has been the subject of increased attention since 9/11.[40] The CNI includes facilities, systems, sites, property, information, people, networks, and processes which provide essential services, and/or the disruption of which could have a significant impact on national security or the normal functioning of national life. These include those which deal with Chemicals, Civil Nuclear, Communications (comprising Telecommunications, Internet, Broadcast, and Post), Defence, Emergency Services (including Police, Fire, and Rescue Services, Ambulance and HM Coastguard), Energy, Finance, Food, Government, Health, Space, Transport, plus Water and Sewerage.

The Ministry of Defence Police (MDP) – an armed civilian police force with around 3,000 officers created by the Ministry of Defence Police Act 1987 formally confined to around 200 Ministry of Defence establishments[41] – is also well-suited for deployment at gas processing sites. Section 85(1) of the Counter Terrorism Act 2008 allows recovery, from gas transporters, of the costs of 'extra police services' incurred by the MDP or local forces at such installations, where their deployment is considered by the Secretary of State to be: '(a) necessary because of a risk of loss of or disruption to the supply of gas connected with it, and (b) that the loss or disruption would have a serious impact on the United Kingdom or any part of it'. As a result of all these developments, the MDP is, therefore, increasingly assuming the mantle of a CNI police force.

Internet threats, which feature prominently on the CNI agenda, are monitored by the National Crime Agency's National Cyber Crime Unit. The Office of Cyber Security and Information Assurance, a policy unit in the Cabinet Office, also provides strategic direction, while the Government Communications Headquarters (GCHQ) Cyber Security Operations Centre oversees implementation.[42] In November 2016 a five-year National Cyber Security Strategy was launched.

Lead government departments produce annual Sector Security and Resilience Plans for each critical sector, identifying key infrastructures, describing the most significant risks, and explaining protection arrangements. Implementation falls mainly upon the Centre for the Protection of the National Infrastructure (CPNI), established in 2007, operating under the Security Service Act 1989, and formally accountable to the Security Service. The CPNI's key features include special access to intelligence and close working relationships with the private sector and the public. Indeed, the fact that around 75 per cent of the entities subject

---

40 C. Walker, 'The Governance of the Critical National Infrastructure' [2008] *Public Law* 323.
41 *Ibid.*, p. 338.
42 Cabinet Office, *Cyber Security of the United Kingdom*, Cm. 7642 (London, 2009).

to *Protect* are under private ownership[43] makes top-down regulation difficult and presents challenges regarding negotiation and persuasion.[44] Security advice to relevant businesses and organizations is disseminated mainly by specialist police Counter-Terrorism Security Advisers (CTSAs) in each police force. The Serious Organised Crime Agency also has responsibilities in this field and the National Counter Terrorism Security Office (NaCTSO) – established in 2002 under the aegis of ACPO (TAM) (Association of Chief Police Offices – Terrorism and Allied Matters), co-located in the CPNI and overseen by the National Police Chiefs Council (NPCC) – oversees protective security for vulnerable sites.

Although the Pitt Review praised the CPNI's attempts to collaborate with the private sector,[45] the main challenge within its remit concerns the effective constitutional and legal integration of the disparate, highly complex, and typically privately owned enterprises involved. This has been compounded by the fact that neither the establishment of the CPNI, nor its operation have yet been explained in any official consultation paper or debated in Parliament. Given the absence of any comprehensive legislation, market mechanisms, official persuasion, plus assorted legal offences, powers, and regulatory systems, apply instead. These tend to lack a proper legal basis or are governed by inconsistent legal arrangements or by ones which may even conflict.

Materials of concern

In various ways the Home Office seeks to prevent unauthorized use of, and access to, 'materials of concern', such as firearms, explosives, poison, and chemical, biological, radiological, and nuclear resources. This includes legislation to ensure secure storage, legitimate use and sale, and safe disposal schemes. Voluntary codes for businesses also seek to protect supply chains and to detect suspicious transactions. Decisions about whether, and if so how, to intervene are informed by the availability of materials, the likely effectiveness of control measures, the potential impact on personal freedoms, and possible unintended consequences such as displacement to more harmful attacks. Other options include 'designing out' threats through the development of commercially viable safer alternatives for legitimate use, increasing public awareness, and controlling access to, and/or requiring notification of, sales of items that could be used to commit acts of terrorism.

The UK's restrictions on firearms and explosives are amongst the tightest anywhere in the world. The Firearms Acts of 1968 and 1997, for example, have long prohibited private possession of many types of weapon, including handguns. As part of efforts to prevent criminals bringing illegal firearms

---

43 J. Moteff, *Critical Infrastructure: The National Asset Database* (CRS Report for Congress, RL33648, 2007), p. 3.
44 Home Office, *Countering International Terrorism*, para. 7.6.
45 M. Pitt, *Learning Lessons from the 2007 Floods Final Report* (Cabinet Office, 2008), para. 99.

into the UK, automatic detection capability is being strengthened at the border in a double-phase programme which includes private sector initiatives. The 1991 Montreal Convention on the Marking of Plastic Explosives for the Purpose of Detection is implemented by the UK's Marking of Plastic Explosives for Detection Regulations 1996.[46] The control of explosives, primarily a health and safety issue, is governed by the Manufacture and Storage of Explosives Regulations 2005.[47] A licensing regime – which has led to prosecutions and prevented attacks using poison, explosive, and potentially explosive material – applies to members of the public who seek to acquire, possess, or use such items for legitimate purposes. Advice is also officially given to suppliers and buyers of nitrate materials, principally farmers, who are monitored in order to prevent illicit usage.[48] Businesses which sell or supply such items are also required to report suspicious transactions plus significant losses and thefts.

All states have long been concerned with safeguarding chemical, biological, radiological, and nuclear resources which could be used as weapons of mass destruction. The production and storage of radiological and nuclear materials, including the protection and security of civil nuclear sites, is subject to strict international controls and protective security regimes to which the UK subscribes. The 750 armed officers of the Civil Nuclear Constabulary (CNC), as constituted by section 52 of the Energy Act 2004 and funded by the industry, are tasked with policing non-defence nuclear sites and non-designated defence establishments.[49] In addition to the transportation of nuclear materials, this includes 17 civil nuclear facilities and their five-kilometre radius exclusion zones. Parts VII and VIII of the Anti-Terrorism, Crime and Security Act 2001 regulate, respectively, laboratories for security purposes and the security of the nuclear industry. Section 12 of the Terrorism Act 2006 deals with trespass upon nuclear sites. But many of the new criminal offences it creates have yet to result in prosecution. The UK's Radiological and Nuclear (RN) deterrence and detection capability at the border (Cyclamen) is also being strengthened.

Although a terrorist attack using biological materials is officially considered unlikely, the possibility is not being ignored. The UK Biological Security Strategy – published in 2018 and co-sponsored by the Home Office, the Department of Health and Social Care, and the Department for Environment, Food & Rural Affairs – for the first time draws together all relevant activity across Government to protect the UK and its interests from significant biological risks. These include, for example, significant outbreaks of disease occurring naturally or as the result of accidental or deliberate release of hazardous biological material.

---

46 SI 1996/890.
47 SI 2005/1082.
48 National Counter Terrorism Security Office, www.secureyourfertiliser.gov.uk.
49 Department for Trade and Industry, *Managing the Nuclear Legacy*, Cm. 5552 (London, 2002); J. Simpson, 'The UK and the Threat of Nuclear Terrorism' in P. Wilkinson (ed.), *Homeland Security in the UK* (Routledge, 2007).

Crowded places

Following the terrorist attacks in London and Manchester in 2017, a number of changes were made to how crowded places are protected from terrorism. These include the provision of higher quality user-friendly guidance on threats and their mitigation to owners and managers of premises, and the development of new technologies, such as a variety of proportionate and cost-effective high footfall screening measures. However, this has mainly taken the form of practical advice about designs, systems, and processes with an emphasis on local partnerships, involvement of CTSAs, consultation in planning processes, training for business, hotel, and retail staff, and guidelines issued by both the NaCTSO and Home Office.[50]

CTSAs provide bespoke security guidance to the owners and operators of crowded places and deliver annual terrorism-awareness training to hundreds of thousands of staff. Tailored security and awareness advice is also available online. Government-industry partnerships are hosted by the Joint Security and Resilience Centre (JSaRC) and the Security Industry Authority. For example, with police support and assistance, Pool Reinsurance Company (Pool Re) pioneered a scheme offering discounts on insurance premiums for businesses implementing the government's accredited Protective Security Improvement Activity Loss Mitigation Credit.

CTSAs and the CPNI are also interested in contributing at the concept design phase to significant new builds and redevelopments, a collaboration most evident during the Olympic Games in London in 2012.[51] The Olympic and Paralympic Security Directorate within the Home Office took the lead, with operations headed by the National Olympic Security Co-ordinator working alongside the Assistant Commissioner for Specialist Operations in the Metropolitan Police linked to the National Olympic Co-ordination Centre.[52] Highly exceptional, temporary, protective security measures were judicially approved to meet the challenges presented by the occasion. In *Harrow Community Support v Secretary of State for Defence*,[53] for example, the siting of missiles on top of the residential Fred Wigg Tower, Leytonstone, for the defence of the nearby Olympic Park, was held not to be in breach of administrative or human rights law. The court concluded that, apart from bad faith or action outside the limits of permitted discretion, military operational deployments for

---

50 National Counter Terrorism Security Office, *Counter Terrorism Protective Security Advice for Visitor Attractions* (Home Office, 2009).
51 House of Commons Committee of Public Accounts, *The Budget for the London 2012 Olympic and Paralympic Games* (2007–8 HC 85).
52 Home Office, *London 2012 Olympic and Paralympic Safety and Security Strategy* (London, 2011); House of Commons Home Affairs Committee, *Olympics Security* (2012–13 HC 531); A. Richards et al., *Terrorism and the Olympics* (Routledge, London, 2011).
53 [2012] EWHC 1921.

reasons of national security are matters for which the Government is answerable to Parliament and not to the courts.[54]

The MDP also provides assistance at sites attracting public demonstrations, such as the US installation at Menwith Hill, and regularly undertakes patrols, under Metropolitan Police authority, in the Government Security Zone in Whitehall and Westminster.[55] Although Home Office guidelines state that its assistance should not be 'routinely requested',[56] by 2008 this had become semi-permanent, a counterterrorist role officially recognized by sections 85–90 of the Counter Terrorism Act 2008.[57]

Recent terrorist attacks in several states, including the UK, have involved vehicles being driven into crowds. As a result, Hostile Vehicle Mitigation measures, including temporary protective security barriers, have been erected across the country for major events, in big cities, at transport nodes, and on some bridges. The Department for Transport, the Police, the CPNI, and the Home Office are further enhancing protection against relevant risks, including by developing more permanent alternatives, more cost-effective and deployable temporary barriers for one-off events, and working with vehicle hire and haulage industries on measures to improve counterterrorist awareness through training and best practice guidance. New and emerging technologies, such as vehicle immobilization devices, which might further reduce the risk, are also being explored.

Stop and search on the streets

Prior to its amendment in 2012, the Terrorism Act 2000 provided several terrorism-related stop and search powers. The least controversial was, and remains, section 43 which authorizes constables to stop and search anyone reasonably suspected of being a terrorist to discover whether they have anything in their possession which may constitute relevant evidence that this is the case. However, intended to gather intelligence, intercept the transportation of weapons, thwart the planning of terrorist operations, and reassure the public, sections 44 and 45 much more controversially permitted the police, in designated areas and without the need for specific suspicion (reasonable or otherwise), to conduct stops and searches of, respectively, people and vehicles, for articles that could be used in connection with terrorism. Resort to these provisions greatly increased following the 7/7 attacks in London in 2005, rising, for example, from a total of 10,200 in 2001–2 to 256,026 in 2008–9, 72 per cent of the latter conducted by the Metropolitan Police and 23 per cent

---

54 *Ibid.*, para 27.
55 Ministry of Defence Police and Guarding Agency, *Annual Report and Accounts 2007–2008* (2007–8 HC 699), pp. 29, 40.
56 Home Office, *Circular 24/2002: A Protocol between the Ministry of Defence Police and Home Office Police Forces* (Home Office, 2002), para. 11.
57 HC Public Bill Committee on the Counter-Terrorism Bill, 15 May 2008, col. 497.

by the British Transport Police.[58] From 2007–8 until its repeal in 2011, just under 460,000 stop and searches were carried out under the section 44 power, some 3,000 of which (0.7 per cent) led to an arrest.[59] Of the 108,685 people stopped and searched in 2009–10, only 517 were arrested (0.5 per cent), and only two arrests were terrorism-related. Of the significantly fewer (11,787) searches in 2010–11, there were 79 arrests (0.7 per cent), none of which was for a terrorism-related offence. As originally drafted, these powers were widely criticized on the grounds that the lack of adequate legal constraints, especially a 'reasonable suspicion' requirement, had resulted in a massively disproportionate impact upon Muslims and non-whites.[60]

In *R (Gillan) v Commissioner of Police for the Metropolis and Secretary of State for the Home Department*, the House of Lords unanimously held that, provided stops and searches are not based on racial profiling alone, section 44 complied with the European Convention on Human Rights (ECHR).[61] However, on 12 January 2010, the ECtHR ruled that this provision violated the right to respect for private life. The requisite conditions were deemed not to have been defined with sufficient precision to exclude arbitrary interference, particularly because the relevant statutory test for designating an area was 'expediency' rather than 'necessity'. The Court, therefore, concluded that the interference of which the applicant complained was not fully 'in accordance with law' as required by Article 8(2) ECHR. Concern was also expressed about the risk of racial discrimination. While the case did not itself concern non-white applicants, the Court, nevertheless, noted that blacks and Asians were four times more likely than their white counterparts to be stopped and searched. There was also evidence of white people being stopped and searched purely to produce greater racial balance in the statistics. In response to this judgment and concerns raised by others, on 8 July 2010, the Home Secretary, Theresa May, told Parliament that, pending the outcome of a full review of counterterrorism legislation already announced, interim guidelines would be issued to the police banning the use of random stop and search of individuals but not vehicles.

Broadly speaking there are three possibilities regarding police counterterrorist street stop and search powers. At one end of the continuum, it would be possible to subject them all to a 'reasonable suspicion' requirement. But this would rob the police of a potentially vital resource, particularly with respect to large public gatherings where reliable, but not sufficiently specific, intelligence

---

58 D. Povey, K. Smith, K. Hand, and L. Dodd (eds.), *Home Office Statistical Bulletin: Police Powers and Procedures – England and Wales 2007/08*, 07/09, p. 36; Home Office, *Statistical Bulletin – Operation of Police Powers under the Terrorism Act 2000 and Subsequent Legislation: Arrests, Outcomes and Stops & Searches, Great Britain, 2008/09*, 18/09, pp. 43–4.

59 G. Allen and N. Dempsey, *Terrorism in Great Britain: The Statistics*, House of Commons Library Briefing, Number CBP7613, 2018, p. 7.

60 B. Bowling and C. Phillips, 'Disproportionate and Discriminatory: Reviewing the Evidence on Police Stop and Search', *Modern Law Review*, (2007) 70, 936–61.

61 [2006] UKHL 12.

that an attack is imminent has been received with little notice. At the other end, any police officer could be legally empowered to stop and search anyone, or anything, at random at any time and for any reason. But because it would be virtually impossible to control arbitrary abuse and potentially excessive impact upon certain places and populations, this would be very difficult to justify in a democracy committed to human rights and the rule of law.

However, there are various possibilities in between. Stop and search powers can, for example, be limited according to time, place and objective, the solution adopted by the Protection of Freedoms Act 2012 which amends sections 44–47 of the Terrorism Act 2000. Amongst other things this includes replacing the 'suspicion-less' provision with a new section 47A as follows. The power to designate an area for random counterterrorism stops and searches is subject to authorization by a senior police officer and a reasonable suspicion requirement. It also expires after 14 (formerly 28) days and must be confirmed by the Secretary of State within 48 hours. Since this decision must be intelligence-based, the designation of any area for any other purpose such as deterrence, intelligence-gathering, or public reassurance, is no longer permitted. Within a lawfully designated area, uniformed police officers can stop and search people and vehicles as before. But this can now only be 'for the purpose of discovering whether there is anything which may constitute evidence' that the specific vehicle is being used for terrorist purposes, or the person in question is, or has been, concerned in the commission, preparation, or instigation of acts of terrorism, 'whether or not the constable reasonably suspects that there is such evidence'.[62]

Exercise of these powers is now governed by a code of practice which provides, amongst other things, that reasonable suspicion cannot be based on generalizations or stereotypes of certain groups or categories of people deemed more likely to be involved in terrorism than others. And unless the police have a description of a specific suspect, a person's physical appearance cannot be used alone or in combination with any other factor as justification.[63] The code also requires officers to 'take care to avoid any form of racial or religious profiling when selecting people to search under section 47A powers' and to take 'great care' to ensure that this is 'not based solely on ethnic background, perceived religion' or any other characteristic protected by the Equality Act 2010.[64]

Because they are not expressly targeted against any specific race, religion, or ethnicity, neither section 43 nor 47A can be considered discriminatory

---

62 S. 47A(5), Terrorism Act 2000, as amended by section 61(4) and (5) of the Protection of Freedoms Act 2012.
63 Home Office, *Code of Practice (England, Wales and Scotland) for the Exercise of Stop and Search Powers under Sections 43 and 43A of the Terrorism Act 2000 and the Authorization and Exercise of Stop and Search Powers Relating to Section 47A of, and Schedule 6B to, the Terrorism Act 2000*, 2012, para. 4.11.3.
64 *Ibid.*, para. 4.11.4.

on these grounds by design. Section 47A is rarely used[65] and remains largely London-centred.[66] There appear to be no official figures about its racial or religious impact. There are no figures either for the religion of those stopped and searched under section 43, the 'reasonable suspicion' provision. However, in the years ending September 2011–19, there was a steep decline (70 per cent) in the use, by the Metropolitan Police, of the section 43 power from 1,210 in 2011 to 360 in 2014.[67] This was followed by a steady increase over the next three years, including 735 in 2017 and 673 in 2019. Of the 5,842 people stopped and searched whose ethnicity was known (self-defined), 1,931 (33 per cent) were white and 3,146 (54 per cent) were non-white.[68] While only seven per cent of those stopped and searched were arrested,[69] a contribution to deterrence and disruption cannot be ruled out. This is formally excluded as a motive. But it is not legally prohibited as a collateral effect.

The chances of being stopped and searched under the section 43 power is 401 per million for non-whites (3,146/8m) and 40 per million for whites (1,931/48m). In other words, non-whites are ten times more likely than whites to be stopped and searched under this provision. One possible interpretation of these figures is that this is racially discriminatory and that the 'reasonable suspicion' requirement and the Code are being ignored with impunity. But official discrimination is not simply a matter of numbers. It critically depends upon context and justification. The section 47A power is expressly location specific. And while this is not a formal characteristic of section 43, it may also be applied more in certain places than others. Therefore, while it cannot be ruled out that counterterrorist stops and searches on the streets are racially discriminatory, the lack of vital data renders this as yet unproven.

If a serious attempt is to be made to prevent terrorist incidents, an intelligence-based police power to conduct random stops and searches in designated locations, subject to adequate safeguards against unlawful discrimination and other kinds of abuse, must be available. It is difficult to see how section 47A could be further improved to achieve any of the relevant objectives. However, the manner in which stop and search powers are exercised is also critical. If most are of limited duration, applied infrequently to any given individual, and conducted respectfully, there can be little legitimate cause for complaint. However, here again the lack of systematic evidence makes it impossible to draw reliable conclusions about the extent to which this does, or does not, happen in practice.

---

65 J. Hall, *The Terrorism Acts in 2018: Report of the Independent Reviewer of Terrorism Legislation on the Operation of the Terrorism Acts 2000 and 2006*, 2020, para. 4.15.
66 BBC News, 'Police Forces Use New Terror Stop and Search Powers', 7 December 2017.
67 Home Office, *Operation of Police Powers under the Terrorism Act 2000*.
68 Ibid., Table S.02.
69 Ibid., Table S.01.

Prepare

The purpose of the *Prepare* branch of CONTEST is 'to save lives, reduce harm and aid recovery quickly in the event of a terrorist attack',[70] by ensuring there is adequate provision to deliver rapid and coordinated multi-agency responses and to minimize impacts upon local communities and others. Apart from criticism about how specific incidents might have been handled differently – allegedly 'too little too late' in some cases as, for example, with the Manchester Arena attack in May 2017,[71] or 'too much too soon' in others such as the Jean Charles de Menezes tragedy in July 2005[72] – *Prepare* has been the least controversial of the 'four Ps' and has not excited any significant public debate. It shares risk assessment and capacity elements with the other 'three Ps'. But its unique contribution is to manage the immediate and longer term aftermath of an attack ('resilience').[73] A high-profile element of the *Prepare* workstream involves public awareness campaigns which seek to provide practical advice to target audiences – such as young people and UK holiday makers overseas – on what to do in the event of a terrorist attack. However, although the police 'Run, Hide, Tell' campaign has reached at least 25 million people since it was publicly launched in December 2015, the fact that, according to recent research, only 26 per cent of the public are aware of it, suggests that the message is not getting across as well as it might.[74]

Ensuring adequate capacity

The UK approach to preparing for civil emergencies is to build and maintain generic capabilities applicable for use in any eventuality. Additional specialist counterterrorist national expertise, including that required to deal with a chemical, biological, radiological, or nuclear (CBRN) attack, is also provided. Key first responders, especially fire, ambulance, and health services, are supported, mobilized, and integrated by other elements, including the National Risk Assessment (NRA), National Security Risk Assessment (NSRA), the Civil Contingencies Act 2004, the Information Systems Regulations 2018, the Joint Emergency Services Interoperability Principles (JESIPs), Local Resilience Forums (LRFs), and National Counter Terrorist Exercise Programmes. Military aid to the police and other specialized services, including expertise regarding CBRN incidents and bomb disposal, are also available. Broadly speaking, the capacity dimension of *Prepare* reflects this by equipping key agencies and

---

70 HM Government, *CONTEST 2018*, pp. 63–9.
71 T. Chakraborti, 'Manchester Arena Attack: Police Accused of Delaying Fire Fighters', *The Guardian*, 21 August 2018.
72 See Appendix B.
73 HM Government, *CONTEST 2018*, para. 181. The source for most of the information about the *Protect* strategy is derived from pp. 63–9 of this document.
74 *Ibid.*, para. 259.

training their staff. An integral part of the formal contingency plan, Operation TEMPERER, for example, enables the police to call upon a maximum of 10,000 military personnel to be deployed within 12 to 96 hours in support of the civil authorities. One consequence is to enable the redeployment of armed police officers to investigation, as occurred in a more limited manner following the 2017 Manchester and Parsons Green incidents.

The NRA, which informs contingency planning, prioritization, and capability-building at both national and local levels, provides a comprehensive, bi-annual review of the most significant five-year-long civil emergency risk assessments. Although the detailed conclusions are classified, broad brush information is publicly available through the National Risk Register.[75] In 2015, the NSRA – which assesses security risks to the UK and its interests overseas and is used to inform strategic decisions about national defence, resilience, foreign, and security priorities – identified terrorism as a 'tier one' threat, with respect to which the highest impact type (CBRN devices) required contingency planning and capabilities beyond those needed for most other kinds of emergency. In 2021 the Integrated Review of Security, Defence, Development and Foreign Policy identified the reinforcement of the international governance of state access to CBRN weapons, materials, or related technology through relevant treaty bodies as a security and defence priority.[76]

As a result of the devolution of power and authority to the regions and the Human Rights Act in the late 1990s, the Civil Contingencies Act 2004 repealed the Emergency Powers Act 1920 and the Emergency Powers Act (Northern Ireland) 1926 and imposed a number of duties on specified local bodies in England and Wales, Scotland, and Northern Ireland. These include assessing the risk of an emergency and maintaining plans for reacting to it. Certain responders may also be legally required to prevent an emergency or to take other action, including to reduce, control, or mitigate its effects. The Act also confers a legal power on the Crown to make regulations if an emergency has occurred or is about to occur. 'Emergency' is broadly defined to include events and situations which threaten serious damage to human welfare in any part of the UK, any part of the environment of the UK, and war or terrorism which threaten serious damage to the UK's security. More detailed provision is also made concerning specific safeguards designed to prevent abuse of this power, together with what may, and may not, be included in the regulations. The Information Systems Regulations 2018[77] establish a legal framework to ensure that providers of essential and some digital services – particularly those which if disrupted could potentially cause significant damage to the economy, society, and individual welfare – instal adequate measures to improve the security

---

75 www.gov.uk/government/publications/national-risk-register-of-civil-emergencies-2017-edition.
76 HM Government, *Global Britain in a Competitive Age – The Integrated Review of Security, Defence, Development and Foreign Policy*, CP 403, March 2021, p. 85, para. 27.
77 SI 2018, 506.

of relevant networks and information systems, and to report serious incidents promptly to competent authorities.

The JESIPs, initially involving over 12,000 police, fire, and ambulance personnel, were established in 2012 to ensure that the emergency services respond to a major incident effectively and in a coordinated fashion. Since then, the principles have been increasingly adopted by local resilience partners. Several other multi-agency training packages have also been delivered. 'Live play' exercises have been used to test and embed shared approaches, and a new national learning system has been introduced to improve how emergency services learn from incidents and exercises. Although already well-developed, coordination between specialized military and police firearms units is regularly tested in training. And, while the multi-agency response to the attacks in London and Manchester in 2017 demonstrated that JESIPs have become a critical element in the emergency response to a major incident, further work has been promised to refine how they are applied and embedded.

Informed by the NRA, the action plans of LRFs bring together the full range of local partners to plan and prepare for local incidents and largescale emergencies. Central government also liaises with the offices of the mayors of London and Manchester, and with the London CONTEST Board, and participates in the Greater Manchester Resilience Forum. Advice and guidance for the private sector is also available online, including about such things as the handling of bomb threats, providing first aid, and how private security staff should guide the public to safety during an attack. Local businesses are also encouraged to coordinate these with each other and with local public services. LRF action plans, consisting of four key elements, are frequently tested as part of the National Counter-Terrorism Exercise Programme and emergency services assurance programmes which explore whether government departments, the emergency services, military and other public agencies are sufficiently prepared to respond to terrorist attacks both domestically and overseas. Exercises are conducted at all levels, from specialist to local, and also include at least one major annual national live-play event involving the participation of government ministers and COBRA, the high-level crisis response executive committee.

The first three elements of LRFs are considered in this section and the fourth in the one which follows. The Initial Operational Response (IOR) involves first responders from the emergency services tasked with saving lives. Since 2016 more than 150,000 of 190,000 had been trained in relevant IOR procedures. Following the Paris attacks in November 2015, an additional £144m was provided in England and Wales to fund an increase of 1,000 armed police officers plus extra Armed Response Vehicles (ARVs) and Counter Terrorist Specialist Firearms Officers (CTSFOs). The first phase provided around 650 armed officers who responded to all UK incidents in 2017. Although the London Bridge attack was brought to a swift conclusion, there was some criticism, as already indicated, of the reluctance of fire chiefs in Manchester to commit firefighters to the aftermath of the Arena bombing until it was clear that the threat of further acts of terrorism had subsided. The full results of a public inquiry into the atrocity are expected soon. More CTSFOs are also expected to be recruited. Some police forces, including Police Scotland, have also augmented their armed capability outside this programme.

Following an attempted terrorist attack on a train in France in 2015, various measures were also introduced in the UK to improve responses to railway security incidents, including enhancing cooperation between the police and British Transport Police (BTP), improving access for emergency services to the London Underground, and developing targeted public communications campaigns – particularly 'See it. Say it. Sorted.' – to which reference has already been made. A year later, the response to an attack on a train was also tested in a series of national multi-agency trials, including as part of the Tier One (National and Ministerial) Exercise followed in 2018 with a joint Anglo-French Channel Tunnel safety exercise.

A second element of LRFs potentially involves more than 7,000 CBRN specialists in the emergency services, trained and equipped to provide critical lifesaving assistance in the event of such an attack, including urgent medical attention at the scene, decontamination, and support for criminal investigations in a contaminated environment. Responding to, and recovering from, a CBRN incident will also engage a wide range of other government resources and local partners. Informed by the latest scientific and technical knowhow and underpinned by JESIP interoperability principles, the CBRN(e)50 Operational Response Framework, established in 2014, provides the strategic direction for a comprehensive response.

The third element – coordinated scientific and technical support, including early detection of illicit importations of radiological and nuclear materials – is provided by four government agencies: the Defence Science and Technology Laboratory for chemical, biological, radiological, or explosive incidents; the Atomic Weapons Establishment for nuclear events; the Met Office for assessing how weather and climate might impact upon any given attack; and Public Health England (PHE) for more general health issues.

Resilience

The fourth element of LRF action plans – coordinated by the Department for Environment, Food & Rural Affairs in England, supported by the devolved administrations in Northern Ireland, Scotland, and Wales, and tested by the National Counter-Terrorism Exercise Programme – concerns 'resilience', the efficient management of rapid recovery, and the restoration of an affected site to normal use. The Resilience Capabilities Programme ensures that key generic capabilities required for responding to and recovering from emergencies of all kinds, including terrorist attacks, are in place. This includes the rapid restoration of key services, such as power and transport, and managing mass casualties. A more specialized aspect concerns the assistance available from the Government Decontamination Service in the case of a CBRN attack.

Another aspect of resilience concerns the needs of victims and others directly affected by a terrorist incident. In March 2017 a cross-Government Victims of Terrorism Unit (VTU) was established to liaise with local authorities, the police, and regional and national organizations, to ensure that victims, witnesses, and bereaved families receive quick, effective, and coordinated support. This has involved sharing best practice, including from other countries, setting up comprehensive webpages signposting victims to support services, ensuring that payments from charitable funds do not affect state benefits or Council Tax support, and facilitating effective data sharing practices. However, amongst the three schemes of special state compensation to the victims of terrorism, two (one of which has since expired), have concerned mostly property owners/occupiers and airlines rather than individuals.[78] The remaining corporate sector scheme, governed by the Reinsurance (Acts of Terrorism) Act 1993, offers reinsurance against loss of commercial property caused by terrorism. The standard Criminal Injuries Compensation Scheme, administered by the Criminal Injuries Compensation Authority under the Criminal Injuries Compensation Act 1995, is available to individual victims of terrorism. It has, however, been criticized for sluggishness and parsimony and for not applying to British victims of terrorism abroad until 2010.[79]

Conclusion

It is difficult to dispute that, in most particulars, *Protect* and *Prepare* make valid and, indeed, essential contributions to countering terrorism in Britain. Nor could it seriously be denied, that by being vigilant and reporting suspicious behaviour and unattended items to the authorities, the public and the private sector have critical roles to play. There is, however, a very fine line between appropriate and excessive public vigilance. It is also impossible for *Protect* and *Prepare* to strike a balance to everyone's satisfaction in all contexts. However, if the contributions of these CONTEST workstreams are to be as effective and legitimate as they could and should be, the core challenges – including how policy can be coherently conceived and properly resourced, delivered, and managed given the sheer complexity and diversity of relevant sites and contexts – also need to be more thoroughly and consistently addressed.

The underlying problem is that difficulties relating to accountability, transparency, and coherence have arisen in both *Protect* and *Prepare* as a result of a lack of organizational structures comparable to those provided for *Prevent* and *Pursue*. The fact that they have each produced a dense forest of acronyms, and that it is not clear where one programme ends and another begins, is

---

78 C. Walker, 'Political Violence and Commercial Risk', *Current Legal Problems*, (2004) 56, 531.
79 Home Office, *Addressing Lessons from the Emergency Response to the 7 July 2005 London Bombings*, 2006, paras. 30–5; *Pike v Indian Hotels* [2013] EWHC 4096 (QB).

also problematic. Nor is it obvious that the risk of over-securitization is being adequately considered.

There are additional difficulties with *Protect*. It is, for example, unclear how the criteria for success are officially calibrated and who is responsible for auditing them. The absence of a comprehensive, consolidated vision for the various *Protect* personnel, including ports police, the BTP, the MDP, the UK Border Agency, and numerous private security agencies, is also a concern. Relationships between the relevant corporate sector and central government may be relatively well maintained. However, engagement with localities is generally weak. Some agencies have, for example, produced lightweight public documents and, despite their policy importance, there has also been a spate of unpublished reviews. While transparency may have been enhanced by the glossy annual reports produced by many of the specialist police forces, local and national accountability could be improved. Parliament has also been less than robust in maintaining oversight, while the Independent Reviewer of Terrorism Legislation has no jurisdiction over much of the *Protect* agenda. As a result, the setting of priorities about what is protected, and how much public resource is used in a given context, remain obscure.

For two main reasons, the courts have not been particularly involved in the management of either *Protect* or *Prepare*, nor, arguably, should they be. The tension between liberty and security is less acute here than with respect to *Pursue* because, with the exception of stop and search powers, counterterrorist initiatives in these largely technical-bureaucratic domains tend to impact less visibly on individuals than upon corporate bodies. The latter are also likely either to have been consulted by government in advance or, if not, to be largely unconcerned as long as their material interests are not adversely affected. Accountability to shareholders, rather than to customers, unwillingness to share commercially sensitive information, and the comparative ineffectiveness of sectoral regulators, also affect relevant modes of cooperation and transparency.

As far as immigration and asylum are concerned, the core counterterrorist issue is very similar to that considered throughout this study: managing competing risks and legitimate interests. The more permissive the system of controls upon the admission of foreign nationals, the more generous it is to applicants and the more vulnerable to exploitation by foreign terrorists and their sympathizers. But if it is strongly prohibitive, it may reduce the opportunities, not only for foreign terrorists and their fellow travellers to gain admission to the UK, but also those with legitimate and lawful reasons for doing so. An appropriate balance must, therefore, be struck here as elsewhere. The key, as always, lies in the human rights compliant collection, analysis, and use of intelligence which, in this context, requires effective collaboration with other states. Independent, context-sensitive, and effective arrangements for assessing its veracity are also necessary. Broadly the same issues arise with respect to the expulsion of foreign nationals suspected of involvement in terrorism where there is insufficient evidence to sustain a criminal prosecution. In this context the principle of *non-refoulment* and the availability of the kind of administrative controls considered in Chapter 6 provide alternative means of addressing relevant challenges.

The exercise of stop and search powers without reasonable suspicion has provoked controversy. But the view that the relevant provisions were and are inherently Islamophobic is unsustainable because they are neutral with respect to the religious affiliation of those to whom they may be applied. Nor is there any reliable systematic evidence that they have been, and are being, operated in a systematically Islamophobic manner either. However, the same cannot so readily be said about alleged racial bias.

It is, however, difficult to deny that random 'suspicion-less' stop and search powers are necessary and legitimate to tackle terrorism in Britain. But they must be governed by a framework in which credible intelligence assessments are central, and where they are exercised respectfully, within strict limits, and not in a repetitive manner against the same subjects without very good reason. Given the ethnic profile of those likely to be involved in jihadi terrorism, it is also statistically inescapable that such powers will impact more upon non-whites than whites. But, of itself, this does not make them inherently or indirectly racist. In any case, as a result of recent amendments to relevant legislation, it is difficult to see how the balance could be struck more appropriately without unacceptably detrimental consequences to one side of the equation or the other.

5 *Prevent*

Introduction

This chapter is devoted to the most controversial of the 'four Ps'– *Prevent*, which aims to stop people from becoming terrorists or from supporting terrorism in the first place, by countering terrorist ideology and challenging those who promote it ('counter-radicalization'), supporting cooperative individuals who are particularly vulnerable to being drawn into terrorism ('de-radicalization'), and working with sectors and institutions where the risk of radicalization in this sense is considered high.[1] In what follows the strategy and duty will be reviewed. The case against *Prevent* and the official campaign against non-violent extremism will also be considered before some conclusions are drawn. The preventive dimensions of *Protect* and *Pursue* are considered in Chapters 4 and 6, respectively.

The Prevent strategy

The terms 'de-radicalization' and 'counter-radicalization' have been much criticized. But their meaning is, nevertheless, more than adequately clear. Respectively, they mean steering people away from involvement in terrorism, and contesting the ideologies and narratives which underpin it. They also derive from counterparts to *Prevent* pioneered in other parts of the world, particularly the highly successful programmes in Saudi Arabia, Singapore, and Denmark. The core issue is not, in any case, whether the goals in question should be pursued, or how the exercise should be labelled, but how relevant policy should be framed and implemented.

International background

Seeking to convert adversaries, including by pardoning and rehabilitating them, is as old as social conflict itself. More recent programmes include those

---

1 HM Government, *Prevent Strategy*, Cm 8092, June 2011.

DOI: 10.4324/9781003221104-5

developed in the Greek Civil War (1946–9), in British counter-insurgency operations in Malaya and Kenya in the late 1950s, and the Italian 'repentance' or 'pentiti' process of the 1980s. Since the 1990s, a number of Muslim countries, such as Algeria and Egypt, have also used de-radicalization-rehabilitation hybrids to combat Islamist insurgencies. Many states with Muslim majorities (including the Maldives, Yemen, Pakistan, Libya, Tajikistan, Uzbekistan, Indonesia, Malaysia) and others with Muslim minorities of various sizes (such as the Philippines, India, Sri Lanka, Australia, Germany, and Denmark) have also deployed de-radicalization and/or rehabilitation programmes, principally against jihadi terrorism post-9/11.[2]

Since the British *Prevent* programme is modelled on the experience of other countries, it is worth identifying the chief characteristics of other relevant models.[3] One of the most fundamental distinctions is between those schemes which focus solely on diverting those who may be vulnerable to recruitment into terrorism, away from this apparent destination, and those which concentrate instead, or as well, upon seeking to persuade the 'already involved' to disengage, either as an alternative to conviction or consequent upon it. The latter also sometimes requires public renunciation of previous ideological commitments. A second core distinction is between programmes which are largely, or entirely, concerned with breaking the connection between selected individuals and terrorism (call this 'diversion-by-persuasion' or 'de-radicalization'), and those, which, by also including state-sponsored rehabilitation, seek to reduce the risk of relapses by reintegrating subjects back into society (call this 'diversion-by-rehabilitation'). Rehabilitation may include, for example, vocational training, relocation, and the provision of fresh identities supported by 'fake' official documents, which also typically characterize witness protection programmes. Or to put it another way, while rehabilitation presupposes effective de-radicalization, de-radicalization does not necessarily involve formal, state-sponsored rehabilitation.

The most comprehensive and widely celebrated jihadi prisoner rehabilitation, de-radicalization, and counter-radicalization programmes, the Saudi Arabian and Singaporean, rely heavily upon Muslim clerics, and are supported by multi-agency re-education, counselling, and community participation, plus closely monitored aftercare arrangements. Their principal goal is to engage sensitively and patiently with the ideology of jihadi terrorism in order to steer those convicted of such offences, and those deemed vulnerable to recruitment, away from this path. Although there is as yet no clear picture of what works best and why, it has been claimed that there have been 'no known cases of

---

2 C. Baker-Beall, C. Heath-Kelly, and L. Jarvis (eds.), *Counter-Radicalization: Critical Perspectives* (Routledge, 2015), chs. 4, 5 & 13; R. Gunaratna, J. Jerard, and L. Rubin (eds.), *Terrorist Rehabilitation and Counter-Radicalization: New Approaches to Counter-Terrorism* (Routledge, 2011).
3 Baker-Beall et al., *Counter-Radicalization*; Gunaratna et al., *Terrorist Rehabilitation and Counter-Radicalization*.

recidivism' following intervention in Singapore.[4] Saudi officials also report a success rate of 80 per cent for their programme. The other 20 per cent include those who refused to participate.[5]

Domestic background

The UK's *Prevent* strategy reflects these precedents and, although lacking a fully developed formal rehabilitation element, shares many of their core characteristics. It can be traced to 2002 when it was first officially acknowledged that 'a long-term effort would be needed to prevent another generation falling prey to' the 'violent extremism' of jihadi ideology.[6] The challenge became more pressing after the events of 7/7, which, amongst other things, resulted in a more explicit acknowledgment that the current threat is increasingly domestic rather than foreign and that, in addition to traditional security and policing dimensions, requires engagement with, and the active cooperation of, affected communities. As a result, *Prevent* was unveiled to the public in 2006 in the following terms:

> PREVENT ... is concerned with tackling the radicalization of individuals ... by: Tackling disadvantage and supporting reform – addressing structural problems in the UK and overseas that may contribute to radicalization, such as inequalities and discrimination; Deterring those who facilitate terrorism and those who encourage others to become terrorists – changing the environment in which the extremists and those radicalising others can operate; and Engaging in the battle of ideas – challenging the ideologies that extremists believe can justify the use of violence, primarily by helping Muslims who wish to dispute these ideas to do so.[7]

The strategy was implemented in two distinct phases, the first from 2006–11 and the second from 2011 to the present. Little changed in the CONTEST review completed in 2018. Some of the language of *Prevent* and a variant of *Channel* – a linked official multi-agency initiative seeking to identify those vulnerable to being drawn into terrorism and to provide tailor-made support plans based on counselling and engagement in approved activities – have recently made an appearance in Northern Ireland. But, for several reasons

---

4 R. Gunaratna and L. Rubin, 'Introduction' in Gunaratna et al., *Terrorist Rehabilitation and Counter-Radicalization*, p. 6.
5 C. Boucek, 'Extremist Disengagement in Saudi Arabia: Prevention, Rehabilitation and Aftercare' and A. Kruglanski, M. Gelfand, and R. Gunaratna, 'Aspects of Deradicalization' in Gunaratna et al., *Terrorist Rehabilitation and Counter-Radicalization*, p. 88.
6 J. Blackbourn and C. Walker, 'Interdiction and Indoctrination: The Counter-Terrorism and Security Act 2015', *Modern Law Review*, (2016) 79, 840–70, 857–8.
7 HM Government, *Countering International Terrorism: The United Kingdom's Strategy*, Cm 6888, July 2006, para. 6.

the full strategy has never been formally applied there. For one thing, as Chapter 3 demonstrated, the terrorist challenge is very different across the Irish Sea, dealing with it is largely the responsibility of the devolved institutions, and the policy framework was set long before *Prevent* had even been conceived. The ideology of dissident Irish republican terrorism is, in any case, exactly the same as that of the mainstream republican terrorist movement, now an integral part of the peace process. Each is committed to the same underlying goal – the reunification of Ireland in a single, independent, 32-county state. As discussed more fully in Chapter 3, the core issue is, therefore, less about grievance and ideology – key targets for counter- and de-radicalization – and more about mobilization, or more accurately, the failure to demobilize. Given the limited prospects for political/ideological initiatives in Northern Ireland now, there is, therefore, little or no alternative to a security approach. With loyalist terrorist organizations also voluntarily disarmed and fully committed to the 1998 Belfast/Good Friday Agreement, *Prevent* would also, therefore, impact entirely upon nationalist/republican communities with all the negative public relations consequences this implies.

The first phase of *Prevent* in Britain was marked by the absence of significant preceding public debate and a lack of specificity, clear boundaries, and legal foundations.[8] Implementation mechanisms and the allocation of resources were also barely considered and, although some arose on an ad hoc basis later, no processes or standards for evaluation were set either. Attention was focused on several key sectors: local communities; mosques, Muslim schools, and charities; prisons; and non-faith primary, secondary, and tertiary educational institutions.[9] Selected, and willing, local communities – deemed uniquely placed to identify sources of disaffection, to assist those at risk, and to enhance the legitimacy of the strategy – were co-opted as active partners. During 2006, oversight of this dimension was largely transferred from the Home Office to the Department for Communities and Local Government (DCLG). In 2008, active engagement with *Prevent* became a central government expectation for all local authorities.

Muslim charities, together with the UK's 1,800 mosques and 2,000 Islamic religious schools, constituted a second sector. For example, as a result of criticism of the Charity Commission for lack of adequate oversight, new managers were appointed and they provided stronger powers for registered mosques, madrassas, and other associations. But these constitute only a fraction of the total. Regulated and unregulated faith schools have also come under closer scrutiny.

---

8 C. Walker and J. Rehman, '"Prevent" Responses to Jihadi Terrorism' in V. Ramraj, M. Hor, K. Roach, and G. Williams (eds.), *Global Anti-Terrorism Law and Policy*, 2nd edn. (Cambridge University Press, 2012), pp. 730–2.
9 C. Walker, 'Counter-Terrorism and Counter-Extremism: The UK Policy Spirals', [2018] *Public Law*, 725–47, 730–2.

With some of the incarcerated jihadis deemed to present an ongoing threat to security and a serious risk of radicalizing other Muslim inmates, prisons provided a third strand.[10] Official responses in this context have included training for HM Prison Service Imams and the creation, in 2007, of a National Offender Extremism Management Unit. However, the design and funding of a satisfactory rehabilitation/de-radicalization programme has proved more difficult to find. In 2016, an independent report cast doubt on the prospects of successful 'treatment' and recommended greater isolation of those concerned in dedicated specialist units instead.[11]

The fourth sector included non-faith primary, secondary, and tertiary educational institutions where the principal challenge was to balance *Prevent* objectives with the exposure of pupils and students to a range of lawful ideas including the 'radical' and unorthodox. Guidance about how to handle extremist doctrines and speakers in these contexts has also since been issued.[12]

Allied to these initiatives, *Channel* was made available in 12 police force areas. Although operating outside the formal criminal justice sphere, criticisms have, however, been made about net-widening and the implied threat that other legal sanctions, such as child care proceedings, might be applied to those reluctant to cooperate. A lack of transparency beyond bare statistics has also made it difficult to assess the credibility of these concerns effectively.[13]

The Coalition government, which came into office in 2010, was conscious of the flaws in *Prevent*, especially indeterminate boundaries with community cohesion and integration initiatives, the perception by some that the 'Muslim community' as a whole was being spied upon, the employment of 'reformed' extremists, and the lack of impact evaluation reflecting vague performance indicators and diffuse oversight structures. A full official, though not independent, review was therefore instigated. Inaugurating the second phase of the programme from 2011 to the present, the reframed *Prevent Strategy* was intended to:

> (i) Respond to the ideological challenges of terrorism and the threat we face from those who promote it; (ii) prevent people from being drawn into terrorism and ensure that they are given appropriate advice and support; and (iii) work with sectors and institutions where there are risks of radicalization which we need to address.[14]

The 2011 *Prevent Strategy* report sought to remedy some of the initiative's original defects, particularly those concerning agenda-setting and policy-formation.

---

10 See ch. 6.
11 Ministry of Justice, *Summary of Main Findings of the Review of Islamist Extremism in Prisons, Probation and Youth Justice Led by I. Acheson*, August 2016.
12 See below.
13 Walker, 'Counter-Terrorism and Counter-Extremism', 732–3.
14 *Prevent Strategy*, para. 3.21.

But all previous key sites remain of central importance. However, not only do some difficulties with the original iteration remain, others have since arisen. To begin with, it is clear that the transparency deficit has not been remedied. Although broad guidelines have been issued for the increasingly active *Channel* programme, few details about how it works have been made available. Indeed, it was not until 2017 that the Home Office took more control over the publication of quantitative (largely input) data which had hitherto been the responsibility of the police. More information, considered further below, has been provided since 2018 than before.[15]

On the basis of a 'vulnerability assessment' – similar to the framework provided for risk assessment in prison de-radicalization, criticized for its alleged lack of an adequate scientific basis – 'success' is measured in terms of reducing the perceived risk.[16] This may include referrals to other safeguarding processes, such as those for child protection or mental health services. Some accountability has been provided by the National Police Chiefs Council (NPCC) National Co-ordinator of *Prevent* and a *Prevent* Oversight Board.[17] The latter was established in 2011, is currently chaired by the Home Secretary, and has included ministers and officials from relevant departments, Lord Carlile (formerly Independent Reviewer of Terrorism Legislation), and other independent members. But, by contrast with the role of the Independent Reviewer of Terrorism Legislation, neither the NPCC nor the board are genuinely independent.[18] The Home Office maintains that an independent board or regular reviewer is not required for *Prevent* because other aspects of CONTEST, and related policies, do not have specific independent reviewers and that sufficient regular scrutiny is already provided by Parliament. An independent review of *Prevent* was inaugurated in August 2019. However, before its work had even begun its chair, Lord Carlile, was forced to stand down because of his publicly expressed support for the programme. In January 2021, the writer and political commentator, William Shawcross, was appointed to take his place. Accused of being an establishment figure, with centre-right sympathies, in March that year over a dozen NGOs announced their intention to boycott the official review and to set up their own instead. But the independence of this review is also open to question. Since, as discussed further below, most, if not all, of those involved have been campaigning for years for the programme to be scrapped.

The most challenging problem for *Prevent*, therefore, concerns its public image. While the relaunched version focused upon terrorism rather upon than community relations, disentangling it from social integration has not been easy nor have any new coordination processes or resource streams in the Ministry of Housing, Communities and Local Government (formerly the DCLG) been

---

15 Walker, 'Counter-Terrorism and Counter-Extremism', 733.
16 *Ibid.*, p. 734.
17 *Ibid.*
18 *Ibid.*

provided. Furthermore, the official exclusion of ex-extremists as de-radicalizers has been difficult to enforce and has been criticized on the grounds that these are precisely the kinds of people who are most likely to be effective in this role. The attempt to develop counterterrorist narratives by reference to 'British values' has also provoked complaints about the marginalization of arguably no less legitimate non-British equivalents. Some of the more strident critics of *Prevent* also denounce those who cooperate with it as 'government stooges' or 'collaborators'. However, as will be demonstrated more fully below, although the claim that *Prevent* is Islamophobic and in violation of human rights is not supported by the evidence, this perception has, nevertheless, proven very difficult to dispel.

The Counter Terrorism and Security Act 2015

The first attempt to remedy the absence of a legal foundation for *Prevent* was made by the ('CTSA'). The Bill which preceded its enactment was prompted by UN Security Council Resolution 2178 and shared its two central objectives – combatting foreign terrorist fighters and countering violent extremism.[19] The immediate trigger for both was the dramatic appearance and rise of the cruel and uncompromising terrorist and insurgency movement ISIS/DAESH in Iraq and Syria from the summer of 2014 onwards. It was disclosed at the time that over 850 people had gone to Syria or Iraq from the UK to fight or to support those fighting for it.[20] By 2018 more than 20 plots targeting states such as Australia, Belgium, Canada, and France, were also said to have been directed or inspired by extremist groups in Syria.[21] In November 2020 a court hearing an application from Shamima Begum against the removal of her British citizenship for having travelled to live under the so-called ISIS/DAESH 'Caliphate' in 2014 was told that, of 900 Britons estimated to have travelled to Syria to join the jihad, about 20 per cent had been killed and 40 per cent, all deemed a low security risk, had returned. However, in an annex to the Home Office's evidence in these proceedings, MI5 claimed that anyone who had left the UK to join ISIS/DAESH and remained with it until March 2018 was deemed to present an enduring threat to British national security.[22]

---

19 Blackbourn and Walker, 'Counter-Terrorism and Security Act 2015', 840.
20 V. Dodd, 'Isis Commanders "Liaised with Plotters Planning to Attack UK in Past Year"', *The Guardian*, 24 December 2016; Speech by the then-Home Secretary, Theresa May, to the Center for Strategic and International Studies, Washington, DC, 16 February 2016.
21 K. Wilsher, 'Europe Faces New Wave of Terrorism as Jihadis Return, Says Interpol Head', *The Guardian*, 20 December 2018; Blackbourn and Walker, 'Counter-Terrorism and Security Act 2015', 844–5, 849–56; V. Dodd, 'Isis Commanders "Liaised with Plotters Planning to Attack UK in Past Year"', *The Guardian*, 24 December 2016.
22 D. Sabbagh and O. Bowcott, 'Begum Cannot Speak to Her Lawyers from Syrian Camps, Court is Told', *The Guardian*, 25 November 2020.

As the Explanatory Notes put it, the Counter Terrorism and Security Bill had four main objectives: to 'disrupt the ability of people to travel abroad to fight such as in Syria and Iraq', to 'control their return to the UK', 'to enhance operational capabilities to monitor and control the actions of those in the UK who pose a threat', and to 'help combat the underlying ideology that supports terrorism'. The 53 provisions of, and eight schedules to, the legislation cover a range of issues including the seizure of passports, temporary exclusion from the UK, Terrorism Prevention and Investigation Measures (TPIMs), aviation, shipping and rail security, plus other miscellaneous matters, many of which are considered elsewhere in this study.

The Prevent duty

As already indicated, section 26 of the CTSA imposes a statutory duty on specified public authorities to have 'due regard to the need to prevent people from being drawn into terrorism' (the '*Prevent* duty'). Although the central principles are the same, in order to respect relevant differences between Scotland, on the one hand, and England and Wales on the other, the Home Office issues separate generic and sectoral guidance with respect to further and higher education in each of these two contexts. According to the *Prevent Duty Guidance*, revised in April 2019, the term 'due regard' means that specified authorities 'should place an appropriate amount of weight on the need to prevent people being drawn into terrorism when they consider all the other factors relevant to how they carry out their usual functions'.[23] Given the expansion of private enterprise into areas hitherto considered integral to the public sector, questions also arise about the restriction of the *Prevent* duty to certain designated public authorities. Social media have not, for example, been included.

Introduced as amendments to the Bill in the House of Lords, section 31(2) complements the *Prevent* duty in further and higher education with two other statutory obligations already provided by other legislation – to have 'particular regard' to ensuring freedom of speech and for 'the importance of academic freedom'. Under section 43(1) and (2) of the Education (No 2) Act 1986 higher education institutions are required to 'take such steps as are reasonably practicable to ensure that freedom of speech within the law is secured for members, students and employees … and for visiting speakers'. This includes, so far as is reasonably practicable, that the use of their premises is not denied to any individual or group on the basis of his, her, or its beliefs, views, policy, or objectives. Under section 202(2) of the Education Reform Act 1988 university commissioners also have a duty to have regard to the need (a) to ensure that academic staff have freedom within the law to question and test received wisdom, and to put forward new ideas and controversial or unpopular opinions,

---

23 Home Office Statutory Guidance, *Revised Prevent Duty Guidance: For England and Wales*, updated 10 April 2019, para. 4.

without placing themselves in jeopardy of losing their jobs or privileges; (b) to enable qualifying institutions to provide education, promote learning and engage in research efficiently and economically; and (c) to apply the principles of justice and fairness. The Equality Act 2010 also requires higher education providers not to discriminate unlawfully against, to harass, or to victimize[24] students with 'protected characteristics'.[25] This includes on grounds of race, ethnicity, nationality, religion, or belief. In the exercise of their functions, public authorities, including universities, schools, and the NHS, also share the wider Public Sector Equality Duty (PSED) 'to have due regard to the need to … eliminate discrimination, harassment, victimization and any other conduct that is prohibited by or under this Act', to 'advance equality of opportunity', and to 'foster good relations' between persons who share a relevant protected characteristic and those who do not.[26]

The CTSA also provides statutory authority for the Secretary of State to issue both Guidance, to which relevant authorities 'must have regard' when carrying out their *Prevent* duty,[27] and directions enforceable by court order.[28] These are also subject to the 'particular regard' duties referred to above. The *Salman Butt* case, considered further below, confirms that the formal provision of the latter, and repeated emphasis in the guidelines upon the importance of proportionality satisfy the requirements of the right to freedom of expression under Article 10 of the European Convention on Human Rights (ECHR).[29]

Prevent in action

At least 2,500 institutions – including schools, universities, mosques, and other faith groups – have engaged with *Prevent* in over 40 priority areas, relevant training has been completed over a million times, and in 2015–16 alone 142 projects reached over 42,000 participants.[30] Around 300 specialist police officers within 24 forces work on the *Prevent Strategy and Delivery Plan*, launched in 2008 and overseen by the National Coordinator for *Prevent*, appointed by the Association of Chief Police Officers (ACPO).[31] Since it came into effect, the CTSA also requires safeguarding and *Channel* panels to be provided by

---

24 Equality Act 2010, ss. 1, 13, 14, 19–27, 90–4.
25 *Ibid.*, ss. 4–12.
26 *Ibid.*, s. 149(1).
27 CTSA s. 29(2).
28 CTSA s. 33.
29 HM Government, *CONTEST – The United Kingdom's Strategy for Countering Terrorism*, Cmd 8123, July 2011, paras. 1.24, 1.61, 3.11, p. 119; *Prevent Strategy*, paras. 3.26, 3.30, 3.38, 4.2, 6.40, 7.5, 9.5, 9.6, 9.22, 10.44.
30 Counter-terrorism: Written question – 51248; HM Government, *CONTEST – The United Kingdom's Strategy for Countering Terrorism*, Cm 9608 June 2018, p. 31, Fig. 2.3; S. Khan with I. McMahon, *The Battle for British Islam: Reclaiming Muslim Identity from Extremism* (Saqi Books, 2016), p. 90.
31 Home Office, *Prevent Strategy*, Cm.8092, para. 9.16.

local authorities and for appropriate procedures to be established by specified institutions.[32] But because this is intended to be light-touch and risk-based, though 'robust', there is considerable discretion over the details.[33]

The process

There are six main stages to the *Prevent* process, the first two of which largely involve filtering out the majority of those under consideration: initial referral; referral by the police to a *Channel* panel for a decision about the need for official intervention; adoption by *Channel* of those cases deemed to warrant it; exiting *Channel*; official review of those who have departed; and fresh referral to the programme where concerns about radicalization recur.

At the first stage anyone can raise a concern with a specific institution, the police, or local authority about somebody else's perceived vulnerability to recruitment into terrorism. This is no different in principle – and no more an inherent violation of or threat to human rights – than a neighbour complaining to the police about a noisy late-night party, or HMRC being tipped off by a member of the public about suspected non-payment of tax. A referral to *Prevent*, including by a public institution, is also, in principle, no more 'stigmatizing', 'victimizing', 'criminalizing', or 'rights violating' than the opportunity to attend road traffic safety training as an alternative to prosecution for minor road traffic offences.

Those institutions to which the *Prevent* duty applies are required, in the first instance, to filter those arising in their own domains through their own safeguarding processes. Where, for example, university welfare teams have serious concerns about the vulnerability of any student to being drawn into terrorism, they are, in the first instance, likely to seek advice informally from their regular police liaison officer, a practice not unique to the *Prevent* context. Since many of these go no further, they do not, therefore, become formal referrals to *Prevent* and are not recorded in the statistics. All formal referrals to the programme are initially screened by the police to check that the subject is not already under counterterrorist investigation which would exclude them from *Channel* support. There are no legal sanctions under the CTSA or elsewhere, for the failure of any specified authority to act upon information, or to make a formal referral, even when an act of terrorism is subsequently committed which might otherwise have been averted. Nor, in spite of what some might think, does the CTSA impose an individual legal obligation upon the staff of specified institutions to report others, for example students or NHS patients. The formal grounds for a legitimate *Prevent* referral include not just the risk of being drawn into terrorism but also into 'non-violent extremism, which can

---

32 CTSA 36(1).
33 Home Office, *Prevent Duty Guidance: For Higher Education Institutions in England and Wales- Updated 10 April 2019*, paras. 5, 68.

create an atmosphere conducive to terrorism and can popularize views which terrorists then exploit'.[34] This has been the source of some confusion considered by the courts in the *Butt* case discussed further below. Only those forms of 'non-violent extremism' which are conducive to terrorism are included. While the distinction between those which fall into this category and those which do not is intelligible, applying it in practice may not always be easy.

Annual *Prevent* statistics, recorded from the end of March, are generally published the following autumn. The figures for 2020–21 were not available when this book went to press. However, there are grounds for believing that the Covid-19 pandemic, the most serious effects of which lasted in Britain from the spring of 2020 to the spring of the following year, significantly reduced the referral rate and, by implication, the figures for all subsequent elements in the process.[35]

Between 2015–20, a total of 33,067 people were referred to *Prevent*, an annual average of 6,613.[36] Over the four-year period from 2015–19, 13,302 referrals (50 per cent) concerned Islamist extremism, 4,428 (17 per cent) 'right wing extremism', 3,030 (11 per cent) 'other extremism' (including international and far left), and 6,020 (22 per cent) 'mixed, unstable or unclear ideology'. The latter of these categories 'reflects instances where the ideology presented involves a combination of elements from multiple ideologies (mixed), shifts between different ideologies (unstable), or where the individual does not present a coherent ideology yet may still pose a terrorism risk (unclear)'.[37]

While the number of referrals for Islamist concerns has steadily declined, from just under 5,000 in 2015–16 to 1,487 in 2019–20, the number of those referred for all other categories has increased. The figure for concerns about right-wing extremism almost doubled from 759 in 2015–16 to 1,387 in 2019–20, while 'other' plus 'mixed, unstable or unclear ideology' almost tripled from 1,173 in 2015–16 to 3,203 in 2019–20.[38] The percentages of referrals for Islamist and right-wing extremism in 2019–20 were almost identical (24 per cent and 22 per cent respectively), 51 per cent of referrals were for individuals with a mixed, unstable, or unclear ideology, of which, following initial assessment, no concerns persisted for almost half (47 per cent).[39] This constitutes a dramatic increase in those in the 'mixed, unstable or unclear ideology' (48 per cent) from the previous year, coupled with an even more dramatic decrease in those in the 'other extremism' category (−73 per cent). According

---

34 Home Office, *Revised Prevent Duty Guidance*, 2019, para. 8.
35 'Covid-19 Causing Drop in South West Radicalization Referrals', BBC News, 25 November 2020.
36 Author's calculation based on annual Home Office Statistics, *Individuals Referred to and Supported through the Prevent Programme, England and Wales*.
37 Home Office Statistics, *Individuals Referred to and Supported through the Prevent Programme, England and Wales, April 2018 to March 2019*, December 2019, Appendix A, Table D.16.
38 Ibid.; Home Office Official Statistics, *Individuals Referred to and Supported through the Prevent Programme, April 2019 to March 2020 (England and Wales)*, 26 November 2020, Appendix A, Table 6.
39 Ibid.

to the Home Office, each of these effects 'may reflect increased understanding and better recording' following the circulation of relevant guidance to *Prevent* stakeholders.[40]

Where, in any given case, a decision concerning official intervention is deemed to be required, the police refer the matter to a *Channel* panel, the second stage of the *Prevent* process. Of the 26,780 cases originally referred to *Prevent* between 2015–19, only 4,841 (18 per cent) were considered for *Channel* support.[41] This increased to 23 per cent in 2019–20.[42] Acting in accordance with statutory guidance, the local authority panel considers whether the person so referred should be offered support for the purpose of reducing any risk they may present.[43] The legislation and guidelines, the latter of which are regularly updated, recognize that there is no single way of identifying vulnerability to being drawn into terrorism and that, when assessing the risks of an individual being drawn into terrorism, consideration should be given to contextual safeguarding principles, and the full range of relevant indicators, influencing factors and relationships that may have an impact on an individual's susceptibility at any given time. This 'may include direct contact with extremists, community, family influences or the influence of wider networks, such as materials sourced via online or social media platforms'.[44]

At the third stage, from 2015–19, 1,644 referrals were adopted as *Channel* cases, ie deemed eligible for official intervention – six per cent of the total number of *Prevent* referrals and 34 per cent of cases considered at a *Channel* panel.[45] De-radicalization under the *Channel* programme is only one of several options. All *Prevent* referrals are also confidential, do not result in a criminal record, and subjects must consent to whatever support, if any, is recommended.[46] It is not an offence to decline to give consent, and where this occurs, the panel must then consider referral to health or social services.[47] *Channel* cases are also reviewed by *Channel* panels on a monthly basis.

In 2019–20 the proportion of initial referrals adopted as *Channel* cases rose to 11 per cent, and of the total number of referrals adopted by *Channel*, 43 per cent were for individuals referred for concerns related to right-wing radicalization, 30 per cent Islamist radicalization, 18 per cent mixed, unstable, or unclear ideology and eight per cent other radicalization concerns. This represents an

---

40 *Ibid.*, p. 12.
41 Author's calculation based on annual Home Office Statistics, *Individuals Referred to and Supported through the Prevent Programme, England and Wales.*
42 Home Office, *Individuals Referred to and Supported through Prevent Programme*, November 2020, p. 8.
43 HM Government, *Channel Duty Guidance: Protecting People Vulnerable to Being Drawn into Terrorism, Statutory Guidance for Channel Panel Members and Partners of Local Panels*, updated 2 November 2020; CTSA ss. 26(1), 36–8.
44 HM Government, *Channel Duty Guidance*, 2020, paras. 51, 54. See Practice example 1.
45 Home Office, *Individuals Referred to and Supported through Prevent*, December 2019, Appendix A, Table D.15.
46 HM Government, *Channel Duty Guidance*, 2020, paras. 76–81.
47 CTSA, s. 36(6).

increase of 21 per cent (from the previous year) in the number of referrals adopted as *Channel* cases for concerns related to right-wing radicalization. By contrast, the number of referrals adopted as *Channel* cases for concerns related to Islamist radicalization increased by only one per cent.[48] Between 2015–19, of those cases adopted by *Channel*, 1,426 (84 per cent) were aged 30 or under, figures which dropped a little in 2019–20 to 77 per cent. In 2019–20, referrals, panel discussions, and cases concerning right-wing radicalization and mixed, unstable, or unclear ideology were proportionally more likely to involve males (93 per cent, 94 per cent, and 94 per cent; 89 per cent, 94 per cent, and 94 per cent, respectively) than those related to Islamist radicalization (81 per cent, 81 per cent, and 81 per cent, respectively).[49]

At the fourth stage, of those adopted by a *Channel* panel between 2015–19, 79 per cent left the programme without any further official concern about their vulnerability to terrorist recruitment, 20 per cent withdrew, and the remaining one per cent continued to be involved.[50] Of those originally referred to *Prevent*, more than 90 per cent are, therefore, filtered out of the process, or diverted to other services, without being offered any form of support from *Channel*. The fifth stage of the process involves official review of those who have left *Channel*. The sixth, and final, stage concerns fresh referral to the programme where, rarely, concerns about radicalization recur. This happened in only 0.2 per cent of cases between March 2019–20, for example.[51]

As with most statistics these figures are open to a number of interpretations. The fact that very few of those subject to a *Prevent* referral undergo any form of de-radicalization could, for example, be regarded as indicative or either failure or success. It could be interpreted as 'failure' because the trawl has been too wide with too many included who should never have come to the attention of the authorities in the first place. But it could also be considered a 'success' because, although most were deemed not to require deradicalization as such, they were, nevertheless, judged to require some kind of intervention. The same could arguably be said about the fact that over 70 per cent of those receiving *Channel* support exited the process presenting no further terrorism-related concerns or with their vulnerability to terrorism considerably reduced. This could be judged a 'failure' because many of these may not have presented a credible risk in the first place, or a 'success' because, whatever the risk they initially presented, it had been reduced as a result of *Channel* intervention.

But two other less contentious observations can be made. First, these figures drive another nail into the coffin of the claim that the *Prevent* programme is Islamophobic and racist. Not only has there has been a significant decline

---

48 Home Office, *Individuals Referred to and Supported through Prevent Programme*, November 2020, p. 13.
49 Ibid., p. 14.
50 Home Office, *Individuals Referred to and Supported through Prevent*, December 2019, Appendix A, Table C.02.
51 Home Office, *Individuals Referred to and Supported through Prevent Programme*, November 2020, para 2.1.

in referrals relating to concerns about Islamist radicalization, but these now account for only a quarter of the total, the same proportion as those for the far right. Second, the dramatic rise in referrals relating to radicalization which belong to neither of these categories, is both surprising and begs a number of questions, in particular the kinds of activities involved. Is the *Prevent* programme being directed against environmental protesters, for example? The case for greater transparency about this and other issues is difficult to contest.

Prevent in the health sector

The CTSA and the *Prevent* duty apply to the health sector.[52] While much of the public debate about the programme has focused upon education and the NHS, health tends to rank third or fourth in the *Channel* tables. For example, of a total of 1,424 cases discussed at a *Channel* panel in 2019–20, 435 (30 per cent) derived from education, 419 (29 per cent) from the police, 197 (14 per cent) from the health sector, and 170 (12 per cent) from a local authority. And, of a total of 697 cases adopted by *Channel*, 222 (32 per cent) came from the education sector, 197 (28 per cent) from the police, 92 (13 per cent) from health, and 81 (12 per cent) from a local authority.[53]

There is, however, little reliable information about the impact of *Prevent* on the NHS. Among other things, an academic study published in March 2018 claims that the *Prevent* duty risks turning NHS mental health trusts into instruments of surveillance and unfairly stigmatizing mentally ill people as potential terrorist threats.[54] However, in common with other anti-*Prevent* 'empirical studies', these allegations are based on a fatally flawed research method which skews the results and undermines their credibility. Interviews were conducted with only 17 NHS 'experts', two police officers, and safeguarding teams in six NHS trusts and Clinical Commissioning Groups (out of a total of over 300), plus online questionnaires completed by a self-selected, unrepresentative sample of 329 respondents (out of a total of 1.5 million NHS employees).

Prevent in schools

The available evidence suggests that, some initial teething problems aside, the *Prevent* strategy and duty are bedding down well in schools. The requirement to comply with the duty tends to be regarded, not as a security matter, but as an additional strand in existing risk-based welfare, safeguarding, and pastoral

---

52 CTSA, Schedule 6; HM Government, *Prevent Duty Guidance*, 2019, paras. 77–98.
53 Home Office, *Individuals Referred to and Supported through Prevent*, November 2020, Appendix A, Table 1.
54 C. Heath-Kelly and E. Strausz, *Counter-Terrorism in the NHS: Evaluating Prevent Duty Safeguarding in the NHS* (Warwick, 2018).

support systems for vulnerable students, such as those suffering from mental illness or lack of motivation, at risk of suicide, or of becoming victims or perpetrators of non-terrorist crime.[55] If welfare staff think any concerns require it, they may make a formal referral to a Chief Police Officer who may then refer the person concerned to a local authority *Prevent* panel, but 'only if there are reasonable grounds to believe the individual is vulnerable to being drawn into terrorism'.[56] Schools and colleges have been at pains to emphasize that they are not interested in 'spying' on students, as the more strident critics of *Prevent* claim, nor do they have the authority to refer anyone directly to a deradicalization programme themselves. Any subsequent sharing of information between educational institutions and other bodies is governed by existing data protection laws which also make spying difficult.[57]

The results of a study, published in July 2017, shed light on how the *Prevent* duty is being managed in schools and colleges in England.[58] In-depth interviews were conducted with 70 educational professionals connected with 14 schools and colleges in West Yorkshire and London, and eight local authority level *Prevent* practitioners supporting schools and colleges. A national online survey of 225 school/college staff, plus a series of feedback and discussion sessions with Muslim civil society organizations, school/college staff, educational trade unions, government departments, and local authorities, was also conducted. Although the project suffered from significantly fewer methodological defects than is common in *Prevent*-related research, the authors are nevertheless disarmingly honest about the limitations of their methods. They state, for example, that although the in-depth interviews constitute a good sample size, respondents were distributed across only two geographical areas with high urban density, ethnic and religious diversity, and considerable *Prevent*-related investment. Respondents with a left-wing political persuasion, women, and Muslims are also significantly overrepresented in the sample in the following proportions respectively: 80 per cent, 61 per cent, and ten per cent (five per cent in the population at large). Although the survey enables some hypotheses suggested by interview data to be tested, the authors admit that the sample is not 'representative ... of educationalists in England'.[59]

The study found some criticism of the *Prevent* duty and scepticism about its efficacy. But very few respondents directly questioned its legitimacy, expressed wholesale opposition to it, or regarded it as counter productive. It was also widely understood that *Prevent* is fundamentally about safeguarding, that this is a valid objective given current circumstances, and that in principle, the duty

---

55 HM Government, *Prevent Duty Guidance*, 2019, paras. 51, 52.
56 CTSA s. 36(3).
57 HM Government, *Prevent Duty Guidance*, 2019, paras. 21, 22; HM Government, *Channel Duty Guidance*, 2020, para. 46, Annex A, 'Sharing Information with Partners'.
58 J. Busher, T. Choudhury, P. Thomas, and G. Harris, *What the Prevent Duty Means for Schools and Colleges in England: An Analysis of Educationalists' Experiences* (Aziz Foundation, July 2017).
59 Ibid., p. 22.

applies to all forms of extremism. Some reservations were, however, expressed about whether this is genuinely the case in practice. There was relatively little support for concerns that the *Prevent* duty has had a 'chilling effect' upon discussion in schools and colleges in the classroom and beyond. On the contrary, there was some evidence that it had, in fact, *promoted* debate about *Prevent*-related issues. The authors also found, however, that there was less certainty about, and some resistance to, building resilience against extremism around British values. Widespread, and 'in some cases very acute concerns', were also expressed about increased stigmatization of Muslim students in the context of the *Prevent* duty.[60] But it is unclear how this was manifested. It also sits uneasily with other findings, particularly recognition that *Prevent* is fundamentally about safeguarding. In any case, most of those who expressed this view acknowledged that schools and colleges are actively seeking to ensure that these risks are avoided. The study also found that attempts to respond to the *Prevent* duty, both in the curriculum and beyond, had incurred hidden financial costs and had significantly increased workloads, particularly for senior staff.

Prevent in higher education

While there is no straightforward link between participation in terrorism and previous exposure to non-violent extremism, whether encountered in education or elsewhere, concerns about the risk of 'being drawn into terrorism' are particularly acute in the tertiary sector for several reasons. Higher education provides social spaces characterized by close inter-personal connections and often maelstroms of ideas. Thinking young people are often attracted by radical proposals for solving the world's problems, yet are also uncertain about who and what to believe. As a result, some will be vulnerable to manipulation. Extreme right-wing activism has also recently been reported in higher education.[61] There is also evidence that student 'no-platforming' and 'safe space' campaigns impact more restrictively upon free expression than the *Prevent* duty.[62] And, because this is likely to ensure that few if any secular far-right activists get anywhere near addressing university audiences, radical Islam may appear to be disproportionately targeted by *Prevent*.[63]

Over the past few years an increasingly clear picture has begun to emerge about the impact of *Prevent* on university campuses. For example, summarizing the report of its inquiry into freedom of speech in universities conducted in 2017–18, the Joint Parliamentary Committee on Human Rights stated that it 'endorsed the need for *Prevent* as a strategy for preventing the development of

---

60 Ibid., pp. 54, 65.
61 J. Bateman, 'The Far Right Holds a Grip on European Campuses', *The Nation*, 12 October 2020.
62 I. Cram and H. Fenwick, 'Protecting Free Speech and Academic Freedom in Universities', *Modern Law Review*, (2018) 81, 825–73, 847.
63 Ibid., pp. 837, 872.

terrorism' in this context but had concerns about the definition of extremism and the clarity of the guidance. It also repeated its earlier recommendation for an independent review of the *Prevent* duty.[64]

A survey of student opinion about a wide range of issues relating to Islam and Muslims in UK universities also provides some surprising, and a few problematic, insights.[65] The authors found, for example, that 59 per cent of respondents had never heard of *Prevent* but that 40 per cent of these were, nevertheless, willing to express an opinion about it.[66] Of those who said they had heard of it,[67] a total of 75 per cent agreed that it is either 'essential to protecting the security of our universities and combatting terrorism' (30.1 per cent), or that it 'can be helpful in tackling these issues but can be damaging to universities if not implemented sensitively' (44.9 per cent). Less than ten per cent of all those surveyed – and less than 15 per cent of Muslim respondents, who the study also found are more likely to have heard about *Prevent* than their non-Muslim peers – unequivocally condemned the programme. Sixteen per cent of all respondents were 'don't knows'.

Although more professionally conducted than is common in social scientific research about *Prevent*, the study, nevertheless, suffers from a number of serious flaws. These fall into three principal categories. First, the executive summary includes several speculative claims about the allegedly negative effects of *Prevent* which are either unsupported by any data in the report at all, or by none that is statistically significant. Two other underlying and interconnected core issues in this respect are the failure to distinguish more sharply, on the one hand, between cause and effect, and, on the other, between *perceptions* about how *Prevent* works and hard evidence about how it *in fact* operates. The report also shares a flaw common to all research hostile to *Prevent*: 'negative effects' are uncritically blamed on the programme rather than on other factors, including the mythology which surrounds it. This is particularly true of the claim, which the authors repeat several times, that anxieties about the Prevent strategy have had a chilling effect on campus life, especially among Muslim students, some of whom claim to have consciously modified their engagement with higher education in order to avoid being labelled an extremist and subjected to unfair discrimination.[68] There is no evidence either to sustain the hypothesis that *Prevent* 'appears' to be 'discouraging free speech' and compromising academic freedom.[69] The authors also fail to explain how, given that very few students

---

64 Joint Parliamentary Committee on Human Rights, *Freedom of Speech in Universities: Responses*, 13 July 2018.
65 M. Guest, A. Scott-Baumann, S. Cheruvallil-Contractor, S. Naguib, A. Phoenix, Y. Lee, and T. Al Baghal, *Islam and Muslims on UK University Campuses: Perceptions and Challenges*, (SOAS, Coventry/Durham/Lancaster Universities, 2020).
66 Ibid., pp. 43, 47.
67 Ibid., pp. 43, 45.
68 Ibid., pp. 55, 61.
69 Ibid., pp. 6, 42, 54.

have heard about it and the majority of those who have support it, the programme has acquired the negative effects alleged.

While the report recognizes that a correlation between support for *Prevent* on campus and negative attitudes about Muslims does not establish a causal link either way, this insight is not universally adhered to throughout. No evidence is presented, for example, that government policies addressing radicalization have 'reinforced' racial and religious discrimination in the UK.[70] Nor is there any evidence for the claim that *Prevent* has undermined the mechanisms universities have for subjecting negative stereotypes to critical scrutiny.[71] Other hypotheses, unsupported by any evidence, include the following: *Prevent* has 'arguably helped to embed a form of institutionalized and state-sponsored Islamophobia' in UK tertiary education, and 'the strategy is vulnerable to hasty, ill-informed or prejudiced accusations, leading to wasted police time and the stigmatization of misunderstood minorities'.[72]

A second difficulty is that the authors claim there is a 'lack of evidence' concerning the 'presumed risk' of recruitment into terrorism on campus,[73] when there is, in fact, abundant evidence. For example, agitation to join jihad abroad has been rife in the tertiary sector since the 1990s,[74] at least 20 prominent jihadis were educated at British universities,[75] and 'around 30 per cent of those who have been convicted of jihadi terrorist-related offences have been through universities'.[76] The risk may, however, have declined since the mid-2000s precisely because of *Prevent* and other interventions, a possibility *Islam and Muslims on UK University Campuses* simply ignores.

However, thirdly, the most fundamental problem of all is that, by disregarding many of the key facts about *Prevent*, uncritically endorsing the myths, and ignoring or misunderstanding the legal and regulatory environment, the authors fail to realize that their most contentious conclusions are simply unsustainable and that their most convincing proposals are already being fully implemented. They refrain from calling for the abolition of the strategy, generally or in higher education specifically, but recommend instead that it be 'discontinued in its current form'[77] and applied critically and with sensitivity to local circumstances. Students and staff should be consulted about how it is being implemented at their own institutions, clear expert guidance should be available to protect freedom of expression, and free and frank debate about

---

70 *Ibid.*, pp. 4, 61–2.
71 *Ibid.*, p. 6.
72 *Ibid.*, pp. 40, 42.
73 *Ibid.*, p. 61.
74 R. Pantucci, '*We Love Death as You Love Life*': *Britain's Suburban Terrorists* (Hurst, 2015), pp. 93, 98, 100, 116, 173.
75 *Ibid.*, pp. 77, 94–5, 97, 136, 152, 160, 162, 176, 183, 226, 234–5, 244, 252, 253, 257, 273, 278, 283, 284.
76 House of Commons Home Affairs Committee, *Roots of Violent Radicalization*, Nineteenth Report of Session of 2010–12, HC 1446, 6 February 2012, Q 420, Ev 80.
77 Guest et al., *Islam and Muslims on Campus*, p. 62.

all ideologies should be encouraged in an atmosphere of critical thinking and mutual respect.[78] This has, however, been happening across the sector for years. UK universities consistently and repeatedly express a strong commitment to both freedom of speech and academic freedom and recognize that higher education provides a unique opportunity for radical thinking and for a wide range of ideas to be expressed, explored, and contested. Relevant institution-specific codes of practice, subject to regular review, including consultation with student unions, have been widely established. Nor is it clear if the recommendation in the report that *Prevent* should operate 'openly' means the current confidential nature of referrals should be abandoned.

Crucially, although stating the *Prevent* duty correctly, the report also ignores the fact that, in the tertiary sector, it is balanced by two competing and more weighty legal obligations to which reference has already been made – to have 'particular regard' for the importance of academic freedom and for ensuring freedom of expression.[79] Nor do the authors seem to be aware that implementation is routinely monitored by the Office for Students (OfS). There is, for example, no mention of this fact, nor even of the office itself, anywhere in the study. In its *Prevent*-related report for the academic year 2017–18 the OfS states, for instance, that 'the first three years of monitoring showed a high compliance rate across the sector: there was strong evidence that providers had successfully embedded *Prevent* within their wider welfare policies and procedures'.[80]

In 2017–18 of 307 universities and other higher education providers only one failed to demonstrate due regard for the *Prevent* duty, while further action was required from another.[81] Seeking to allay concerns that the duty is being used to spy upon students, the report also points out that Accountability and Data Returns (ADRs) do not include information which would enable any student to be identified.[82] Excluding self-referrals by students and staff, and those where the provider took no action, of the 307 higher education providers complying with the *Prevent* duty in the year in question, 202 (66 per cent) referred a total of 83,419 cases for specialist welfare advice and support, including but not confined to *Prevent* issues. Of these, 174 (0.21 per cent) were escalated to the point where the *Prevent* lead became involved. Over 70 per cent (122) were referred to local *Prevent* panels for external advice. Only 15 (12 per cent of those referred for advice from *Prevent* panels, 0.017 per cent of the total number of welfare cases) were subsequently referred by *Prevent* panels to the *Channel* process.[83] In the financial year 2017–18, the wider education

---

78   Ibid., p. 6.
79   Ibid., p. 40.
80   Office for Students, *Prevent Monitoring Accountability and Data Returns 2017–18: Evaluation Report*, 21 June 2019, para. 8.
81   Ibid., Table 1, p. 8, para. 54 g.
82   Ibid., para. 28.
83   Ibid., Table 2, p. 9.

sector made 2,426 referrals which were allocated to the *Channel* programme, only 0.6 per cent of which came from higher education.[84]

The OfS also reports that in 2019 no providers had failed to demonstrate due regard for the *Prevent* duty.[85] Procedures were in place to manage security-sensitive research at universities, *Prevent*-related acceptable IT usage protocols were clear, and providers continued to engage and consult with students on how safeguarding from radicalization was and is being conducted.[86] Of greatest significance, however, is the fact that, based on its system-wide monitoring, the OfS authoritatively expresses its confidence that providers are balancing their *Prevent* duty with other statutory obligations which, as already indicated, include having 'particular regard' for the importance of academic freedom and for ensuring freedom of speech.[87]

A distinct issue arising from the discharge of the *Prevent* duty in the tertiary sector, but much less so in other branches of education, concerns external speakers at, and activities on, higher education premises, where the gender segregation of meetings and the hosting of openly misogynist, homophobic, and anti-Semitic Muslim speakers has been a well-documented trend in recent years.[88] The *Prevent Guidelines* require universities to carry out institutional assessments to determine the risk of students being drawn into terrorism, including 'not just violent extremism but also non-violent extremism, which can create an atmosphere conducive to terrorism and popularize views which terrorists exploit'.[89] Where concerns arise that an event may create such risks, invitations to outside speakers may be revoked, and events either cancelled or allowed to proceed only upon condition, for example, that the views likely to be expressed are publicly challenged.[90] Such decisions are also subject to an appropriate balance being struck between the 'due regard' and 'particular regard' duties.

The OfS's *Prevent Review Meetings – Findings from the 2019 Programme* found, amongst other things, that providers have appropriate systems in place for assessing *Prevent*-related risks posed by external speakers and events, plus appropriate and proportionate mitigations. There is 'clear evidence that providers continue to make nuanced decisions and to balance their legal responsibilities with the requirements of the Prevent duty' in addition to ensuring

---

84 *Ibid.*, para. 40.
85 Office for Students, *Prevent Review Meetings – Findings from the 2019 Programme*, 6 February 2020, para. 4.
86 *Ibid.*, para. 5.
87 *Ibid.*, para. 6.
88 Cram and Fenwick, *Free Speech and Academic Freedom in Universities*, 831–3; Khan, *Battle for British Islam*, pp. 61, 68–70, 73–4, 119–50.
89 HM Government, *Prevent Duty Guidance*, 2019, para. 64; HM Government, *Prevent Duty Guidance for Higher Education*, 2020, para. 19.
90 HM Government, *Prevent Duty Guidance for Higher Education*, 2020, paras. 7–15.

'proportionate and consistent implementation'.[91] No 'cause for concern' was found 'that free speech was being undermined by Prevent in external speakers policies and in their implementation'.[92]

Concerns about the implications of the *Prevent* duty for guest speakers on university campuses were also authoritatively addressed on 26 July 2017 when the high court rejected a claim brought in judicial review proceedings. Dr Salman Butt maintained that the inclusion of his name in an official press release about tackling extremism in universities and colleges was unlawful and in breach of his human rights.[93] Relying on information provided by the Home Office Extremism Analysis Unit (EAU), which had opposed the publication of any names, the press release referred to 70 events on university premises in 2014 featuring 'hate speakers'. However, as the result of an 'oversight', six people including Dr Butt, were also identified as 'expressing views contrary to British values' on campus.

The claimant, a practising Muslim with a PhD in biochemistry, is editor-in-chief of *Islam21C*, a publicly available website which describes itself as 'articulating Islam in the 21 Century [sic]'. He was also an occasional speaker, chair, and panel participant at university student, particularly Islamic, society events. Dr Butt maintains that he rejects terrorism and denies he is an 'extremist'. He also claims to hold lawful 'orthodox conservative religious views', shared by many others, and to support the core British values of 'democracy, the rule of law, liberty and respect and tolerance of other faiths and beliefs'. However, the judgment cites information, compiled by the EAU, that Dr Butt has, amongst other things, 'equated homosexuality with paedophilia ... defended gender segregation', claimed 'criticism of segregation and FGM is an attack on Islam ... celebrated the kidnapping of Israeli soldiers and referred to Israelis as "pigs"'.[94] The court expressed no opinion about whether these views are 'extremist' or not. Dr Butt also alleged that the press release implied he was a 'hate speaker' and that it had resulted, not only in a decrease in invitations to address tertiary sector audiences, but also in his own decision to decline other invitations in order not to embarrass his prospective hosts. A claim for damages – for defamation, for breach of the right to respect for private life under Article 8 ECHR, and for breach of the Data Protection Act 1998 – was held to be beyond the scope of judicial review but may be pursued in separate proceedings.

Mr Justice Ouseley's thorough, robust, and at times strongly worded 68-page judgment, uncompromisingly rejects each of the arguments relied upon by the claimant. It was held that, properly construed, the *Prevent Duty Guidance* and *Higher Education Prevent Duty Guidance* ('the guidance') is not

---

91 Office for Students, *Findings from the 2019 Programme*, para. 77.
92 Ibid., para. 5.
93 *Salman Butt v Secretary of State for the Home Department* [2017] EWHC 1930 (Admin).
94 Ibid., para. 197.

beyond the scope of the *Prevent* duty, as Dr Butt alleged. Rather than equating 'non-violent extremism' with 'terrorism', they merely recognize that the former could potentially, though not invariably, be an element in the process of 'being drawn into' the latter. Mr Justice Ouseley acknowledged that this distinction is not easy to draw, and there may be forms of non-violent extremism which do not risk drawing others into terrorism. But he stated that this does not mean non-violent extremism is beyond the scope of the *Prevent* duty. Nor does the guidance fail to comply with the section 31 CTSA duty which requires, when the *Prevent* duty is exercised, that 'particular regard' (a stronger obligation than 'due regard') be paid to freedom of expression and to academic freedom. According to the judge, rather than directing conduct, the guidance merely seeks to guide it, and the legal duty under section 29(2) CTSA is to have 'regard' to it, a weaker obligation than having 'due regard' as in section 26, or 'particular regard', as in section 31.

The court also rejected the claim that the guidance violated Dr Butt's right to freedom of expression under Article 10 ECHR on the grounds that he was not a victim of the alleged breach as the Convention requires. He had no legal right to express his views on university campuses and there was no evidence that any event at a university involving him, or anyone else, had been cancelled in exercise of the *Prevent* duty. At most, therefore, Dr Butt's complaint concerned possible future, rather than actual, violations. Moreover, the *Prevent* duty could not be said to have had a 'chilling effect' upon his freedom of expression because he remained free to express his views in numerous other ways.

However, Mr Justice Ouseley also held that, even if Dr Butt had been a victim of an interference with his Article 10 rights, the guidance fulfilled the ECHR 'legality test'. Although it permitted discretion in how certain identifiable factors were taken into consideration and did not mandate any particular result, it was sufficiently accessible and its effects were reasonably foreseeable. Since it also pursued the legitimate aim of preventing people from being drawn into terrorism, and was proportionate, it also complied with the ECHR 'democratic necessity test'. However, the judge expressly recognized that different circumstances might give rise to an Article 10 violation.

It was also held that, because the information collected by the EAU concerned views Dr Butt had expressed in public, and which he wished publicly to promote, there was no interference with his right to respect for his private life under Article 8 ECHR. In any case, the legality and democratic necessity tests had also been fulfilled with respect to this provision for substantially the same reasons as for Article 10. Finally, Mr Justice Ouseley also found, largely for the reasons supporting his rejection of the claimant's other arguments, that the activities of the EAU did not amount to surveillance under the Regulation of Investigatory Powers Act 2000.

On 8 March 2019, the Court of Appeal upheld the High Court decision in the *Butt* case on the grounds that the official collection of information which led to the applicant being designated an extremist did not breach his right to respect for his private life.[95] It also concluded that there was no surveillance, but even if there had been it could have been justified, and that, in any case, there is no reasonable expectation of privacy with respect to statements made in public. A single paragraph in the relevant *Prevent* duty guidance was, however, ruled unlawful because it failed to express with sufficient clarity, the need for a balance to be struck between the statutory obligation upon universities to consider denying particular 'extremist' speakers a platform (because of the risk that others might be drawn into terrorism), against other statutory duties including having 'particular regard' for the importance of freedom of expression and academic freedom. Minor redrafting is all that is required to rectify this anomaly.

The *Butt* case did not raise or ventilate all the controversial issues raised by the *Prevent* duty in higher education. Both sides accepted, for example, that there is no evidence that the guidance has led to unlawful indirect discrimination against Muslims. The first instance judgment, nevertheless, authoritatively addresses the central concerns about the *Prevent* duty and guest speakers on campus. It also confirms that although 'non-violent extremism' may be taken into account when the duty is exercised, this is only lawful and legitimate where it is deemed to contribute to averting the risk of being drawn into terrorism. Some forms of 'non-violent extremism' will, in other words, be implicated but others will not. While this distinction is not easy to draw, it is not for this or other reasons untenable.

The politics of Prevent

As already intimated, *Prevent* is controversial and has inspired a vigorous debate amongst campaigners, academics, and other commentators. However, polling evidence indicates that this has had very little impact upon the public at large, most of whom have never heard of it. As with many issues, opinion in the debate spans a spectrum ranging from those who support *Prevent*, including some who favour reform within the existing framework, to those who reject it in its entirety and call for a boycott until it is scrapped.

Amongst other things, the reformers have expressed concerns about the efficacy of the programme and the need for greater transparency about operating criteria, performance indicators, and outcomes, enhanced legal clarity and accountability for both *Prevent* and *Channel*, more information about how each programme operates in practice, and regular independent review of all aspects.[96] Addressing these issues would not only be desirable for their own sake; if satisfactorily achieved, the strategy would be strengthened.

However, by contrast, there is also a highly vocal and visible anti-*Prevent* movement. In addition to a significant stream in the social science literature, this includes at least 45 separate organizations, such as Stop the War Coalition,

---

95 *R (Salman Butt) v The Secretary of State for the Home Department* [2019] EWCA Civ 256.
96 Cram and Fenwick, 'Free Speech and Academic Freedom in Universities', pp. 871–3.

Students Not Suspects, Educators Not Informants, the National Union of Students (NUS), and the University and College Union (UCU), the trade union for academic and other staff at universities and colleges.[97] According to this perspective, the *Prevent* programme should be abolished on the following grounds. It is a toxic brand, deeply unpopular with the 'Muslim community', and driven by official racism and Islamophobia. It subjects harmless, law-abiding Muslims to intelligence-gathering and spying, systematically criminalizes, victimizes, and stigmatizes them, turns them into a 'securitized community' and blames them for the jihadi threat. This, it is said, jeopardizes community cohesion and undermines the efficacy of counterterrorism. Even before the *Prevent* duty came into effect in 2015, those subscribing to this view predicted that it would not only compound these defects but would also legitimize Islamophobia in society at large, chill public debate, seriously threaten academic freedom, stifle campus activism, require staff at educational institutions to engage in racial profiling, and undermine safe and supportive learning environments.[98]

The explanation of how the programme operates in practice provided above has already addressed the bulk of these complaints. It is, however, unclear to what extent, if at all, those who advocate its abolition have modified their position to take account of these developments. But whether they have or not, the following issues nevertheless require further consideration: *Prevent* is a toxic, anti-Muslim brand driven by official racism and Islamophobia; it violates or threatens human rights; it has chilled public debate; it should be boycotted until scrapped.

Is Prevent toxic and anti-Muslim?

There is a fatal problem with the claim that *Prevent* is toxic, anti-Muslim, deeply unpopular with the 'Muslim community', and driven by official racism and Islamophobia: there is no reliable systematic evidence that it is true. The allegation manifests in several ways.

For example, sweeping generalizations to this effect are often made without any supporting evidence whatever. Alam and Husband, for instance, claim that 'the logics of surveillance' have 'resulted in a breakdown of trust between large sections of the British Muslim population and the agents of the state'.[99] Yet they fail to provide any evidence at all. As already indicated, this is at variance with polling data, particularly the study by Clements et al., cited above.

The claim also relies heavily upon widely circulated anecdotes which typically suffer from several core problems. The veracity of most are difficult to

---

97 S. Greer and L. Bell, 'Counter-Terrorist Law in British Universities: A Review of the "Prevent" Debate', *Public Law*, (2018), 83–104, 85.
98 *Ibid.*, p. 98.
99 Y. Alam and C. Husband, 'Islamophobia, Community Cohesion and Counter-Terrorism Policies in Britain', *Patterns of Prejudice*, (2013) 43, 235–52.

confirm. Those that are true, though indicating regrettable and unjustified conduct, are not for that reason alone indicative of systemic problems with either the *Prevent* programme or the duty. It is not known, for example, how many school students, Muslim or otherwise, have been taken aside by teachers in exercise of the *Prevent* duty without this giving rise to any complaints by their parents or others. Some of the most prominent and widely circulated rumours have also been discredited by subsequent revelations. Take, for example, the case of the Muslim schoolboy, interviewed by teachers apparently in exercise of the *Prevent* duty and visited by the police, allegedly because, in an essay, he referred to living in a 'terrorist' rather than a 'terraced' house. When the storm of protest about this episode had abated, it turned out that the teachers had become concerned, and the police became involved, not because of Islamophobia triggered by adjectival confusion, but because, in his essay, the boy had also claimed that he was being beaten by his uncle.[100] In another case a Muslim schoolboy was allegedly traumatized as a result of being questioned by his teachers for having referred to eco-terrorism in a French class discussion.[101] Yet, in the High Court Mr Justice Blake dismissed, as 'totally without merit', a judicial review application lodged by his mother, Ifhat Smith, an activist in the anti-*Prevent* group *Prevent Watch* who claimed that the strategy 'is unlawful because it is more likely that concern may be directed to children of the Muslim faith'. She was ordered to pay £1,000 for wasting court time.[102]

There are also significant problems with what the anti-*Prevent* movement takes to be reliable evidence in support of its cause. For a start, deficient research methods in the 'empirical' studies undermine the credibility of their conclusions.[103] Typically, limited to a few dozen respondents, constituting tiny, unrepresentative fractions of both the general and Muslim populations, and usually self, rather than randomly selected, data collection tends to be distorted and partial at best. Nor has any study yet made an attempt systematically to collect, and separately to record and analyze, empirical data from officialdom, or from those who have been referred to *Prevent* and *Channel*. As a result, the take-away messages rest upon inferences about how these programmes operate, drawn from typically negative attitudes of respondents whose experience of being directly involved is at best unknown.

---

100 The original story was also later modified by the BBC. See also Khan, *Battle for British Islam*, pp. 94–5.

101 V. Dodd, 'School questioned Muslim pupil about Isis after discussion on eco-activism', *The Guardian*, 22 September 2015.

102 *Salahudeen Smith v Secretary of State for Home Department and Headteacher and Governors of Central Foundation Boys' School*, CO/4064/2015.

103 See, eg, Heath-Kelly and Strausz, *Counter-Terrorism in the NHS*; K. Spiller, I. Awan, and A. Whiting, 'What Does Terrorism Look Like?': University Lecturers' Interpretations of Their Prevent Duties and Tackling Extremism in UK Universities', *Critical Studies on Terrorism*, (2018) 11(1), 130–50; K. Sian, 'Born Radicals? Prevent, Positivism, and Racial Thinking', *Palgrave Communications*, (2017) 6, 1–15; A. Singh, *Eroding Trust: The UK's Prevent Counter-Extremism Strategy in Health and Education* (Open Society Justice Initiative: New York, 2016).

When we turn to the analytical and interpretive dimensions, we find that the case against *Prevent* is characterized by non sequiturs and speculation rather than objective fact. These include, for example, the assumptions that: if x per cent of Muslims in a given survey *think* the *Prevent* duty is Islamophobic it *is* Islamophobic; because some Muslims *feel* they and/or all Muslims are under unjustified systematic official suspicion, Muslims as a whole *are* under unjustified systematic official suspicion;[104] because counterterrorist law impacts negatively upon some Muslims, *all* Muslims have become systematically officially suspect simply because they are Muslim;[105] because Muslims perceive some aspects of counterterrorist law and policy to be racist, unfair, unjust, and discriminatory, such laws and policies *are* racist, unfair, unjust, and discriminatory; because some students and staff at British universities may be avoiding research or teaching related to topics which they fear may get them into trouble with *Prevent*, the programme is to blame, when this effect may result as much as, if not more, from the mythology surrounding it.[106]

There are also grave problems with the concept of 'the securitized Muslim community in Britain' which underpins the case against *Prevent*. As Chapter 3 demonstrates, while there are certainly Muslim *communities* in the UK, the term 'the Muslim community in Britain' is misleading because Islam in Britain is so diverse in national, ethnic, racial, doctrinal, social class, and other terms. Furthermore, *Prevent* does not criminalize or securitize anyone because it operates entirely outside the criminal justice and security systems and is oriented towards safeguarding not criminalization, stigmatization, or victimization. Exponents of the securitization thesis accuse the state of negatively stereotyping Muslims. But they themselves not only stereotype the state as monolithically anti-Muslim, but also stereotype 'the Muslim community' as uniformly vulnerable, passive, powerless, harmless, blameless, criminalized, stigmatized, and victimized.[107] Each of these is, at best, a distortion of a much more complex reality.

In fact, the underlying rationale of *Prevent necessarily* assumes a complex *mix of trust and suspicion* on the part of all relevant parties. Inevitably, official agencies will be suspicious of those intent on radicalization and possibly some of

---

104 C. Pantazis and S. Pemberton, 'Resisting the Advance of the Security State: The Impact of Frameworks of Resistance on the UK's Securitization Agenda', *International Journal of Law, Crime and Justice*, (2013) 41, 1–17; A. Lynch and N. McGarrity, 'Counter-Terrorism Laws: How Neutral Laws Create Fear and Anxiety in Australia's Muslim Communities', *Alternative Law Journal*, (2008) 33, 225–8; A. Blick, T. Choudhury, and S. Weir, *The Rules of the Game: Terrorism, Community and Human Rights: A Report by Democratic Audit, Human Rights Centre, University of Essex for the Joseph Rowntree Trust* (Joseph Rowntree Trust, 2007).
105 C. Pantazis and S. Pemberton, 'From the "Old" to the "New" Suspect Community: Examining the Impacts of Recent UK Counter-Terrorist Legislation', *British Journal of Criminology*, (2009) 49, 646–61.
106 Guest et al., *Islam and Muslims on Campus*.
107 Alam and Husband, 'Islamophobia, Community Cohesion and Counter-Terrorism', p. 250; S. Croft, *Securitizing Islam* (Cambridge University Press, 2012), pp. 183–99.

those vulnerable to it. Yet, the recruitment of a particular Muslim organization to work with *Prevent* also indicates official trust in its capacity and commitment to assist with de-radicalization. Muslims who participate in *Prevent* on a bona fide basis must also necessarily trust the state to act responsibly in countering radicalization – an interest they themselves must also, by definition, share. Since there is no credible evidence that Muslims *as a whole* have been systematically 'securitized' in the UK, or any credible evidence that being a Muslim is systematically sufficient to raise official suspicion, the securitization thesis remains a misleading and potentially dangerous myth.

A welcome exception to the complaints about the toxicity of *Prevent* is provided by *Listening to British Muslims: policing, extremism and Prevent*, published in March 2020.[108] Although, as the title suggests, *Prevent* features prominently, the study has a wider focus. Funded by a charitable trust, conducted by a non-partisan consultancy, and based on methodologically strong qualitative and quantitative methods[109] – including structured focus groups plus representative samples of both Muslims and the general population of Britain – the authors draw the following *Prevent*-related conclusions. First, the 'popular narrative' that *Prevent* is a 'toxic brand'[110] is difficult to reconcile with the discovery that most British Muslims (56 per cent) have not even heard of it, although the 44 per cent of those who have is greater than the comparable figure of 32 per cent for the general population.[111] Nevertheless, 'when offered a neutral explanation', 80 per cent of Muslim respondents expressed either unqualified (47 per cent) or qualified (33 per cent) support, only slightly lower than the 85 per cent support for *Prevent* amongst the general public.[112] White Muslims and those with higher education were the most likely of Muslim respondents to support *Prevent*.[113] The study also found that Muslims in Britain appreciate the threat of Islamist extremism and accept that the police, in whom trust is high, should have a prominent role in combating it. Seventy-four per cent of those surveyed also understand the need for the strategy to be targeted upon Muslims, especially those communities and localities where the risk of recruitment into terrorism is greatest.

Arguably even more surprising is that Muslims in Britain are also more likely (66 per cent) than the population at large (63 per cent) to refer to *Prevent* someone they suspect of being vulnerable to being drawn into terrorism. This figure is highest for white Muslims, and for both white and non-white Muslims who have been through higher education.[114] However, slightly more

---

108 J. Clements, M. Roberts, and D. Foreman, *Listening to British Muslims: Policing, Extremism and Prevent* (Crest Advisory, 2020).
109 Ibid., p. 8.
110 Ibid., p. 90.
111 Ibid., p. 11.
112 Ibid.
113 Ibid., p. 89.
114 Ibid., p. 89.

than half of those supporting *Prevent* also expressed concerns about *Prevent*, the most common being the perception that it subjects all Muslims to suspicion and that it is 'unfair on innocent Muslims'.[115] Twenty-one per cent of adult Muslim respondents were strongly of the view that the police 'unfairly target British Muslims as they believe they are a terrorism risk', compared with five per cent of the general population.[116] However, as with other studies to which reference has already been made, this falls far short of establishing that *Prevent* has *in fact* turned Muslims into a 'securitized community', one under pervasive official suspicion, or that it is *in fact* unfair to innocent Muslims. Abjuring the term 'Muslim community' on the grounds that it has 'limited or no utility',[117] the authors also conclude that 'there is no single Muslim voice' on the issues surveyed, and that the range of opinion held by Muslims about *Prevent* broadly corresponds to that in British society at large.

The authors conclude that their research 'undermines the argument that *Prevent* should be scrapped due to lack of trust' but 'it does suggest that there is ample scope to improve confidence in the programme'.[118] As they and many others maintain, there could and should be better communication and consultation between the state and Muslims over *Prevent* and other issues.[119]

Does Prevent threaten and/or violate human rights?

Various individuals and organizations, particularly those involved in the combined NGO review of the programme, have warned that *Prevent* threatens and/or violates human rights.[120] But this is by no means universally accepted by human rights specialists and activists.[121] The allegation suffers from the same absence of reliable, systematic evidence discussed above. It also tends to lack close engagement with both how *Prevent* operates in practice, as opposed to the mythology which surrounds it, and with the fact that the human rights paradigm permits the kind of exceptions to relevant norms critics so readily condemn as violations.[122] Indeed the framework employed by the anti-*Prevent* movement to judge the appropriateness or acceptability of the strategy and the duty tends to be referenced to implicit, shadowy, vague, and poorly thought-through conceptions of core 'progressive values' such as human rights, equality,

---

115 *Ibid.*, pp. 11, 45.
116 *Ibid.*, p. 87.
117 *Ibid.*, p. 9.
118 *Ibid.*, p. 91.
119 *Ibid.*, pp. 35, 43.
120 See, eg, Human Rights Watch UK, and Liberty.
121 See, eg, Equality and Human Rights Commission, *Delivering the Prevent Duty in a Proportionate and Fair Way*, 9 February 2017, pp. 3, 5.
122 See, eg, Alam and Husband, 'Islamophobia, Community Cohesion and Counter-Terrorism'; Pantazis and Pemberton, 'Resisting the Advance of the Security State', p. 8; J. Cesari, 'Securitization of Islam in Europe', pp. 21, 23.

integration, and recognition of social diversity.[123] Typically, however, there is no engagement with the detailed implications of any of these, nor any recognition that they may often be difficult to reconcile with each other, and when they do, it is rarely if ever obvious which should prevail.

In order to take this claim seriously the human rights allegedly threatened or violated by *Prevent* need to be identified. How the programme threatens or violates them needs to be explained in much more detail. Prima facie, three human rights are implicated – to privacy (or more strictly to respect for private and family life, home, and correspondence), to freedom of thought, conscience, and religion, and to freedom of expression. The claim that *Prevent* violates, or even threatens, any of these is not self-evident. Nor is it strong because the programme is less concerned with what anyone believes, thinks, or says, or how they behave, than with how what they believe, think, say, or do that may threaten their own safety or that of others. And even if *Prevent* referrals may be said to interfere with any of these rights such intrusions are, nevertheless, capable of being formally justified as lawful, necessary, and proportionate in the interests of, amongst other things, the rights of others found in the second paragraphs of relevant ECHR provisions.

There is no credible basis either for believing that *Prevent* is discriminatory on racial or religious grounds by intention or design. This is not least because, as already indicated, it is modelled on similar initiatives used against Islamist terrorism by predominantly non-white, Muslim majority states. For another, *Prevent* is formally neutral about the kind of terrorism to which it can be applied and, as also already indicated, it is increasingly being used against right-wing and other forms of extremism in spite of the fact that each of these currently presents a much less deadly threat than the jihadi counterpart. The fact that *Prevent* was introduced to tackle, and has been mostly used against, domestic jihadi terrorism, simply reflects the fact that, for the past decade and a half, this has been by far the most serious domestic terrorist challenge.

The claim that *Prevent* is being applied in a systematically racially or religiously discriminatory manner is also difficult to reconcile with the statistics cited above. As already indicated, these demonstrate that both the purpose and effect of the strategy are to safeguard those referred to it rather than to spy upon anyone, turn any social group into a 'securitized community', violate human rights, or damage any other legitimate interest. There is no trace of Islamophobia, racism, or anti-Muslim prejudice in the CTSA or in any of the supporting documents. Indeed, on the contrary, relevant guidelines repeatedly stress the need for proportionality, that *Prevent* must not be used as a means for

---

123 A. Kundnani, *The Muslims Are Coming! Islamophobia, Extremism and the Domestic War on Terror* (Verso, 2014), 11–15, 285–9; C. Husband and Y. Alam, *Social Cohesion and Counterterrorism: A Policy Contradiction?* (Policy Press, 2011); M. Hickman, L. Thomas, S. Silvertri, and N. Nickels, *'Suspect Communities'? Counter-Terrorism Policy, the Press, and the Impact on Irish and Muslim Communities in Britain, A Report for Policy Makers and the General Public – July 2011* (London Metropolitan University, 2011), pp. 6, 24, 27.

covert spying,[124] that in the jihadi context, the target is not Muslims as a whole but only a tiny dangerous minority, and that perspectives on the extreme right of the political spectrum are also included.[125] The fact that the bulk of those referred to *Prevent* and *Channel* are young, non-white, Muslim, men is also simply a reflection of the demography of those involved in the principal threat Britain faces. The possibility that *Prevent* may have been applied in a racist or religiously discriminatory manner on isolated occasions cannot be ruled out. But rumour and anecdote aside, there is no credible evidence that this has happened often or even at all.

An example of many of the difficulties with the case that *Prevent* violates or threatens human rights can be found in a report for the Open Society, one of the more sustained attempts to consider the human rights implications. The author recommends that the duty should be scrapped in the education and health sectors because the programme 'suffers from multiple, mutually reinforcing structural flaws, the foreseeable consequence of which is a serious risk of human rights violations'.[126] This, he also predicts, could have a potentially counter-productive effect upon counterterrorism. In common with most other anti-*Prevent* 'empirical' research, this analysis is, however, itself deeply flawed at the methodological, empirical, analytical, and policy levels. To begin with, the 17 case studies, and the survey data upon which the report is based, fall below the threshold for minimal scientific reliability. Interviews are said to have been conducted with 87 people, including parents, academics, and university and government officials amongst others. But no information is provided about how they were recruited or what questions they were asked. Numerically, they constitute only a tiny sliver of the relevant populations and the only information about how they were selected is that this was the result of 'outreach' in 'multiple public outlets'.[127]

The report also fails properly to consider, or even to mention, the following: the impossibility of exempting universities and other institutions from the universal democratic public obligation to contribute to counterterrorism; the constitutional and wider legal context and the immediate background to and justifications for the CTSA; that the CTSA does not impose a statutory duty to report individuals at risk of being drawn into terrorism but rather an institutional duty to have 'due regard' to the need to prevent people from being drawn into terrorism balanced against the 'particular regard' duties (which it notes but discounts);[128] that the *Prevent* duty is managed by universities' welfare and not their security services; that participation in de-radicalization programmes is

---

124 *Prevent Duty Guidance*, para. 21; *Prevent Strategy*, paras. 1.15, 3.15, 6.34–6.43, 7.1, 11.30.
125 *Prevent Duty Guidance*, para. 11; *CONTEST*, paras. 2.39–2.40; *Prevent Strategy*, Preface, paras. 5.10–5.11, 5.36–5.37, 5.42–5.46, 6.9–6.12, 7.8, 8.70, 9.23; *Counter-Extremism Strategy*, paras. 6, 10, 11, 56, 57, 62, 123.
126 Singh, *UK's Prevent Counter-Extremism Strategy*, p. 16.
127 *Ibid.*, p. 11.
128 *Ibid.*, pp. 31, 60.

voluntary, that failures to comply with the duty have no legal consequences, and that referral does not in itself raise a human rights issue let alone disclose a violation; the distinction between restrictions upon and violations of human rights (which the report also notes but fails to appreciate);[129] the crucial distinction between counterterrorism and counterextremism, a confusion which leads the author wrongly to assume that the CTSA permits referrals for the mere expression of unorthodox views where there is no risk of being drawn into terrorism; that while confidential interactions between clients and professionals, including between students and staff at British universities, are legally protected, this does not cover those where a risk of harm is disclosed;[130] that information revealed in other public or semi-public university activities and contexts, including seminars, classes, and lectures, is not legally protected by duties of confidentiality and not obviously by the right to privacy either; and merely because Muslims may once have been more likely to be at the receiving end of the *Prevent* duty does not in itself constitute a violation of the right not to be discriminated against, since being a Muslim is a necessary, though not a sufficient, condition for participation in jihadi terrorism, the primary terrorist threat the UK faces.

Generally ignoring the significance of the principle of proportionality, the report also lists some international human rights norms and domestic human rights laws but fails to explain precisely how the CTSA poses a serious risk of their violation.[131] Nor does the author present any credible evidence that the legislation is 'eroding trust' in the institutions concerned as the title of the report suggests, or that it is likely to do so. In fact, the evidence of widespread compliance throughout the sector, cited above, strongly suggests otherwise.

Rather than advocating boycott, abolition, or revision of the *Prevent* duty, the UK's Equality and Human Rights Commission (EHRC) instead recommends responsible and properly managed positive engagement by universities. It notes that concerns have been raised that the Prevent duty is sometimes being implemented in ways which could: undermine the fundamental rights and freedoms of staff and students, stifle free speech and academic freedom, lead to discrimination and other conduct prohibited by the Equality Act 2010, and stigmatize or alienate segments of staff and student populations.[132] But, rather than condemning the duty as a violation of, or even a threat to, human rights, it reminds universities of their Public Sector Equality Duty, commends them for their strong commitment to it already, notes their positive engagement with *Prevent*, and encourages responsible, reflective, evidence-and-impact based, proportionate, fair, properly recorded, and properly monitored management of all relevant obligations. It also recommends the framing of

---

129 Ibid., pp. 53, 56, 90.
130 The confidentiality issue is only discussed in the health sector, ibid., pp. 47–50.
131 Ibid., pp. 51–63.
132 Equality and Human Rights Commission, *Delivering the Prevent duty*, pp. 3, 5.

action plans following adequate consultation with all relevant parties, which should be capable of responding promptly and appropriately to complaints, including modifying existing arrangements where necessary, and delivered by fully trained staff sensitive to all relevant issues.

Does Prevent chill public debate in society at large?

As noted in a previous section, the claim that *Prevent* is 'chilling' public debate in education, and in universities in particular, is at variance with the evidence. Given that the programme is not well-known more widely, including amongst Muslims, it is unlikely that this is any truer in society at large. This complaint is also difficult to reconcile with the fact that the stridency and intolerance with which the strategy has sometimes been condemned – often coupled with denunciation as stooges, collaborators, racists, and Islamophobes of those Muslims and others with a more cooperative perspective – tends to drown out more moderate and nuanced opinion.[133] This may itself have a 'chilling' effect upon the public debate, potentially producing precisely one of the effects of which the programme itself stands accused.

Policy implications of scrapping Prevent

While most of the assumptions underpinning the demand for *Prevent* to be scrapped have already been called into question in the discussion above, others remain. For example, since no evidence has yet been provided to substantiate it, the allegation that the *Prevent* programme and the duty are counterproductive remains speculative. In fact, the opposite is suggested by the studies by Busher, Clements, Guest, and their respective co-authors cited above, and by the fact that nearly 400 mosques and other Islamic organizations participate willingly and actively in it.[134] As the Manchester and London attacks in May and June 2017 also demonstrate, many Muslims are also ready and willing to report suspicious activity on the part of other Muslims to the authorities.[135]

Those who demand the abolition of *Prevent* have so far failed to identify the kind of counterterrorist law and policy against domestic jihadi terrorism which would escape condemnation for being Islamophobic and for turning Muslims into a securitized community. Nor is it clear if the abolitionists object to participation in a de-radicalization programme as a condition of release on licence from prison. If they do, they should indicate how they think such reoffending is to be avoided. And if they do not, they should say why we should wait until an offence has been committed before such intervention can occur.

---

133 Khan, *Battle for British Islam*, p. 135.
134 *Ibid.*, p. 113.
135 *Ibid.*, pp. 15–24. See, eg, J. Grierson, 'Khuram Butt – Attacker Was Involved in "Violent Scuffle"', *The Guardian*, 7 June 2017.

The inescapable fact is that seeking to prevent any kind of terrorism in Britain, be it jihadi or far right, will *inevitably* require focusing security attention upon, respectively, those predominantly non-white Muslim, and those non-Muslim white communities from which, according to reliable intelligence, each originates. But, providing an appropriate regulatory framework is complied with, and in particular that counterterrorist measures are proportionate to risk, this is not open to reasonable objection.

There are further policy-related problems with the various *Prevent* boycotts. They fail to offer a viable alternative to the challenge presented by the actual and potential recruitment of young people in particular to far right or jihadi terrorist causes. Nor is it clear what any given boycott requires or what would count as successful participation. It is, for example, difficult to resist the conclusion that a deliberate refusal on the part of a member of staff at a given university who, for anti-*Prevent* reasons, refused to report concerns about a right-wing student who later killed dozens by mowing them down in a motor vehicle, would be a success for the boycott. But it would be a catastrophic failure in every other respect.

There are further difficulties with the UCU's campaign. It was, for example, approved at the May 2015 Congress without members having been consulted in advance, in a closed session with the media excluded, and apparently on a vote so tight that a recount was required.[136] Following legal advice that a boycott would be unlawful, the campaign was then devolved to branches with the UCU itself acknowledging that local non-compliance would also constitute unlawful continuous industrial action without ballots approving it.[137] It is not clear if any branches have followed through on this commitment. Some, such as the University of Bristol's, both sit on the University's Prevent Compliance Group while simultaneously canvassing support for non-compliance, without organizing a ballot, and also having neglected to inform members that participation in a boycott could expose them to legal action for breach of their employment contracts.[138]

Countering non-violent extremism

Terrorism undeniably involves 'violent extremism'. But many, including the government, are convinced that 'extremism' more generally increases the risk of terrorism and also undermines social cohesion. The study by Clements et al. referred to above, found, for example, that a significant majority of Muslim and non-Muslim respondents were worried about extremism of the Islamist

---

136 UCU, *The Prevent Duty: A Guide for Branches and Members*, para. 21; Khan, *Battle for British Islam*, p. 111.
137 UCU *Prevent Duty*, para. 22.
138 Bristol UCU, *The Prevent Duty@Bristol: The Duty in Context, Bristol UCU Response and Next Steps*, 9 March 2016.

variety (63 per cent and 67 per cent respectively) and of the far right (71 per cent and 62 per cent respectively).[139] Particular challenges arise from the profile of ideas and behaviour hostile to humane values, tolerance, and mutual respect, on the internet and in social media. As Chapters 2 and 3 sought to show, it is also clear that whatever other factors may be in play, ideology lies at the foundations of the two main types of domestic terrorism Britain currently faces. But it is less clear what precisely the connection between terrorist ideology and 'non-violent extremism' is and how, if at all, the state and society should be mobilized to address the latter. At the heart of the counterextremism debate, therefore, lie three core, and as yet not fully answered, questions: what precisely is 'extremism'? What kind of threats and risks does it pose? And what, if anything, should state and society do about it?

Background

The counterextremism debate stepped up a gear with the establishment of a Tackling Radicalization and Extremism Taskforce in the Cabinet Office following the murder of Lee Rigby in 2013. In the absence of prior public consultation and little detail, the seven-page report, *Tackling Extremism in the UK*, stated that 'Islamist extremism':

> is an ideology which is based on a distorted interpretation of Islam, which betrays Islam's peaceful principles, and draws on the teachings of the likes of Sayyid Qutb. Islamist extremists deem Western intervention in Muslim-majority countries as a 'war on Islam', creating a narrative of 'them' and 'us'. They seek to impose a global Islamic state governed by their interpretation of Shari'ah as state law, rejecting liberal values such as democracy, the rule of law and equality. Their ideology also includes the uncompromising belief that people cannot be Muslim and British, and insists that those who do not agree with them are not true Muslims.[140]

The proposed counterextremism agenda included providing civil law powers to ban extremist groups and to curtail the behaviour of individual extremists, legislation to strengthen the role of the Charity Commission, countering extremist narratives by reinforcing the capabilities of communities and civil society organizations, working with internet providers, encouraging public reporting of extremist content online, sharpening legal obligations with respect to *Prevent* and *Channel*, strengthening social integration, and supporting vulnerable institutions including schools, universities, and prisons. Two years later

---

139 Clements et al., *Listening to British Muslims*, p. 79.
140 HM Government, *Tackling Extremism in the UK: Report from the Prime Minister's Task Force on Tackling Radicalization and Extremism*, December 2013, para. 1.4.

an Extremism Analysis Unit was established in the Home Office to develop relevant policy.

The Queen's Speech on 27 May 2015 announced a Counter-Extremism Bill. In October that year, a 40-page *Counter-Extremism Strategy* paper defined extremism as calling for the death of members of 'our armed forces' and/or 'the vocal or active opposition to our fundamental values, including democracy, the rule of law, individual liberty and the mutual respect and tolerance of different faiths and beliefs'.[141] Although the term 'British values' is also widely used, the document, nevertheless, states that 'our' includes allies and friendly nations. On the express assumption that there is no single model, the Extremism Analysis Unit was tasked with building a better understanding of what constitutes 'extremism'. Reviews of Sharia law, and of extremists in public services, were promised. It was also suggested that criminal sanctions should make participation in the *Channel* programme mandatory for those 'further down the path to radicalization', and that the public should be encouraged to denounce extremists through an 'Extremism Community Trigger'.[142]

A year late, the Queen's Speech on 18 May 2016 promised a Counter-Extremism and Safeguarding Bill with, according to press reports, the equivalent of anti-social behaviour orders for extremists, Ofcom regulation for internet-streamed TV, and intervention in unregulated religious schools. However, publication was delayed, not only by the difficulty of finding more legally robust definitions than those found in the strategy document, but also by a raft of other more urgent priorities to which the Brexit vote of June 2016 gave rise. Also in 2016, a libel action was brought by the chief Imam at Lewisham Islamic Centre, criticized by the BBC for his allegedly extremist views. The judge sought to define 'extremism' by reference to 'moderation'. But since this also proved inconclusive ten examples of the former – including 'Manichean', ie binary black and white world views, advocating civil disobedience, and/or espousing the views of other 'extremists' – were offered instead.[143] The Conservative and Unionist Party Manifesto for the 2017 general election contained a commitment to defeating extremism and proposed new criminal offences in pursuit of this objective. But the Queen's Speech on 21 June 2017 merely promised the establishment of a Commission for Countering Extremism and reiterated the government's commitment to the counterterrorist strategy review announced in November 2016.

In December 2016 the Casey review recommended enhancing the profile of British values in law and in school history syllabuses and enshrining them, plus a commitment to the rule of law, in an oath for holders of public office.[144]

---

141 HM Government, *Counter-Extremism Strategy*, Cmd. 9148, October 2015, p. 9.
142 Ibid., paras. 89, 117.
143 [2016] EWHC 2688 (QB).
144 Dame Louise Casey, *The Casey Review: A Review into Opportunity and Integration* (Ministry of Housing, Communities and Local Government, 5 December 2016), pp. 168, 169.

Briefly reviewed, the *Prevent* policy was also described as 'impressive and heartening', and the government was encouraged to defend it more robustly against criticism which the report dismisses as distorted and exaggerated.[145] While admitting that 'extremism is a subjective concept', the report also maintains that social integration would reduce it.[146]

In January 2018 the new Commission for Countering Extremism was given a wide-ranging mandate, including paying particular attention to women's rights, supporting communities and the public sector, promoting British values, training schools and colleges in how to confront extremism, and advising the government on relevant policy, laws, and other actions that may be required to tackle it. Sara Khan, a Muslim, former pharmacist and prominent human rights activist, was appointed Lead Commissioner. While the core questions of what constitutes extremism and the risks and threats it poses remain largely unanswered, greater progress has been made on what ought to be done about it, arguably putting the cart before the horse. However, rather than presenting a flagship bill to Parliament, the Home Office currently prefers a civil society approach in which grants from the Building a Stronger Britain Fund are provided to groups tackling racism, segregation, FGM, Islamophobia, and anti-semitism. Although reminiscent of some pre-2011 *Prevent* activity, applicants eligible under these new arrangements are from the third sector rather than from local authorities.

Legal and human rights environment

Much of the counterextremism agenda is, in fact, already governed by legislation, including the criminalization of indirect incitement to commit terrorism[147] and harmful cultural practices such as genital mutilation and forced marriage.[148] Advocating violence and/or hatred is already legally banned both by counterterrorist and ordinary criminal law. Disruptive measures are also available under the Anti-social Behaviour, Crime and Policing Act 2014 and have already been applied in relevant contexts. For example, in 2014 five-year orders – including a ban on associating with named radicals such as Anjem Choudary, entering educational establishments, the use of loudhailers, the distribution of unsolicited materials, and defacing public advertisements – were imposed upon three members of London's Tower Hamlets 'Muslim patrols'. In 2016 injunctions were also issued against the right-wing group *Britain First*.[149]

In the absence of any specific law on the matter, the human rights ideal provides the most appropriate set of standards enabling, amongst other things,

---

145 *Ibid.*, paras. 10.24, 10.32, 10.37.
146 *Ibid.*, paras. 9.16, 9.27.
147 Terrorism Act 2006, ss.1 and 2.
148 Female Genital Mutilation Act 2003 and Anti-social Behaviour, Crime and Policing Act 2014, Pt X.
149 *Chief Constable of Bedfordshire v Golding* [2015] EWHC 1875 (QB).

a distinction, albeit a less than sharp one, to be drawn between those forms of expression which should be tolerated in a free society from those which should not. The right to freedom of expression, found in every credible list of civil and political rights, rests on the bedrock principle that the expression of any idea or belief should be permitted unless a good reason – including threats to public safety or national security – can be found to restrict or ban it. Or, to put it another way, freedom of expression is a non-absolute human right. The European Court of Human Rights (ECtHR) has also affirmed that this right, provided by Article 10 of the ECHR, is vital for the kind of ideas, views, opinions, and outlooks – including those which 'offend, shock and disturb' – upon which a pluralistic, tolerant, broadminded, progressive, and democratic society depends. However, the appropriate standard of proof required for legitimate interference with free expression in the name of countering extremism remains unclear. While there is obviously some overlap with *Prevent*, how a distinct policy agenda will be set for 'counter Extremism', and how it might be implemented and its performance evaluated, are difficult to predict.

The counterextremist agenda, therefore, raises three core human rights questions, the last two of which cannot be clearly demarcated from each other: what counts as 'expression', what kinds of expression are protected, and what kinds of restriction may legitimately be imposed under what circumstances?[150] 'Expression', for the purpose of Article 10 ECHR, includes the spoken and written word, drama, art, graphics, dress, nudity, symbols and symbolic acts, which convey opinions and ideas of a political, social, cultural, artistic, or commercial kind. This may be through, amongst other means, publications, meetings, broadcasting, theatre, cinema, the internet, and advertising. The rights to freedom of assembly and association would also be largely redundant unless they too were supported by a right to free expression.

However, as a matter of principle, certain forms of expression are not protected by Article 10. These include views inherently hostile to core Convention values, those which seek to deny, belittle, or defend the Holocaust (and possibly other clearly established crimes against humanity), and those which incite violence or hatred.[151] According to Article 10(2), the exercise of the right to freedom of expression also 'carries with it duties and responsibilities' which may be 'subject to such formalities, conditions, restrictions or penalties', provided these are prescribed by law and are necessary in a democratic society in pursuit of specific 'legitimate aims'. These are listed as follows: national security, territorial integrity, public safety, the prevention of disorder or crime, the protection of health or morals, the protection of the reputation or rights of others, preventing the disclosure of information received in confidence, and maintaining the authority and impartiality of the judiciary. However, any

---

150 S. Greer, J. Gerards, and R. Slowe, *Human Rights in the Council of Europe and the European Union: Achievements, Trends and Challenges* (Cambridge University Press, 2018), pp. 172–9.
151 *Ibid.*, pp. 174–9.

limits imposed upon expression for any of these reasons must be proportionate. Providing they act in good faith, the ECtHR also permits some latitude to states in determining where relevant lines should be drawn. And, in cases where an official interference is admitted but a justification pleaded, the severity of the penalty will often be the deciding factor in determining whether or not freedom of expression has been violated.

The ECtHR also requires bans and/or restrictions on the right to freedom of expression to be regulated by laws which are clear, provide adequate safeguards against arbitrary abuse, and enable adverse official responses to be reasonably foreseen. In most circumstances, content, form, tone, context, and consequences – including the applicant's status, the addressees, the likely public impact, the extent of any restriction, and the possibility of alternative outlets for the views in question – will often be critical in determining whether any particular expression is compatible with Article 10 or not. For example, on account of its importance for the proper functioning of democracy, the Court permits greater scope for social and political debate, particularly by politicians and journalists, than for artistic and commercial expression. It also recognizes that audio-visual media have greater immediacy and impact than print. In considering whether, in any given circumstances, the right to freedom of expression should prevail over any legitimate exception, or vice versa, the Court is not only concerned with the particular dispute before it, but also with the possible 'chilling effect' upon freedom of expression generally if the restriction were to be upheld.

The legitimate grounds for curtailing freedom of expression are not always easy to distinguish from each other and the ECtHR does not always indicate clearly which may have justified the particular limitation in question. In cases involving terrorism, for example, criminalizing the expression of certain views may be permitted in the interests of national security, public safety, and/or the prevention of disorder or crime. But the Court is generally unsympathetic to blanket bans and is typically most concerned about the proportionality of restrictions and sanctions, and with the provision of adequate procedural safeguards against abuse. As already intimated, incitement to religious hatred is not protected by Article 10. But the legitimate limits upon the right to express critical, satirical, or 'obscene' views about a given faith have proven difficult to specify with precision. As a result, gratuitous insult and/or abusive attack may or may not be tolerated according to the circumstances.

Conclusion

Seeking to prevent jihadi and far-right terrorism in Britain will inevitably involve both the 'securitization' of the population as a whole, and also focusing additional security attention upon, respectively, those predominantly non-white Muslim, and non-Muslim white networks, associations, and communities, from which, according to reliable intelligence, each of these types of terrorism derive. But, providing this complies with an appropriate regulatory framework, and in particular is proportionate to risk, it will fall far short of systematically securitizing, criminalizing, officially stigmatizing, or victimizing the 'national communities' concerned.

The *Prevent* programme has a crucial role to play in tackling terrorism, not least because it underscores that this is a responsibility shared by state and society. And yet, with the possible exception of stop and search, it has been the subject of more vitriolic criticism than any other element of CONTEST. Nevertheless, the more it has developed and bedded down, and the more independent, methodologically robust, and evidence-based research has been conducted about it, the less credible the case for it to be scrapped has become. Anti-*Prevent* scholarship suffers from several fatal flaws. It is characterized by the failure to apply basic social science methods, particularly random-sample surveying. It has also failed to explain how domestic jihadi and far-right terrorism could and should be prevented in a manner which would avoid the charge that relevant 'communities' have been unfairly 'securitized'. It is not clear if the anti-*Prevent* movement objects to the de-radicalization and rehabilitation of convicted terrorist offenders, an issue explored more fully in the following chapter. If it does, we need to be told how they are to be discouraged from returning to the terrorist cause upon release from prison. And, if there is no such objection, why should official intervention occur only after a terrorist offence has been committed and not before?

A *Prevent* referral has nothing like the sinister undertones its more strident critics allege. Its core objective is fundamentally about protecting those referred from the risks they pose to themselves as it is to protect others. Because the entire programme operates outside the criminal justice process it cannot 'criminalize' anybody. And since any given subject's involvement is confidential, it is difficult to see how it can 'stigmatize' or 'victimize' anyone either, let alone entire national 'communities'. Most referrals go no further and only a tiny minority result in de-radicalization. Participation in whatever intervention is offered is voluntary and there are no formal sanctions for refusing to cooperate. A *Prevent* referral is, therefore, no more objectionable than a complaint to the police by a neighbour about a noisy late-night party and less objectionable to being officially invited to attend road traffic safety training as an alternative to receiving three points on a driving licence. The use of *Prevent* to spy and gather intelligence is formally prohibited. This is also constrained by data protection laws which limit information-sharing. The claim by some critics of *Prevent* that these are, nevertheless, features of the programme has yet to be supported by any evidence.

Since *Prevent* is formally neutral about the kinds of extremism to which it can be applied, and based upon models developed to tackle the threat of Islamist terrorism in non-white majority Muslim states, it is difficult to see how it could be racist and/or Islamophobic in intent or design. Nor is there any evidence that it has been systematically used in a racist or Islamophobic manner either. Indeed, it is impossible to square this complaint with the fact that it is now being deployed more against white, non-Muslim, right-wing, and other forms of extremism, than against their Islamist counterpart. Legitimate concerns have, however, recently arisen about the increase in referrals related neither to Islamism nor the far right. Much greater disclosure about the kinds of activities involved would be welcome.

The claims that *Prevent* jeopardizes community cohesion, undermines the efficacy of counterterrorism, and legitimizes Islamophobia in society at large, rest upon unproven speculation, particularly regarding cause and effect. They are not only difficult to reconcile with official figures, but also inconsistent with reliable evidence from independent polling. This has found that very few people, including Muslims, have even heard of the programme, and that when they find out about what it entails, substantial majorities, including of Muslims, support it.

All of this casts considerable doubt upon allegations that *Prevent* chills public debate, seriously threatens academic freedom, stifles campus activism, requires staff at educational institutions to engage in racial profiling, and undermines safe and supportive learning environments. In fact, since reliable polling evidence also indicates that very few students have heard about the strategy either, these alleged cause and effects, remain at best unproven. And even if some of these problems have genuinely arisen, an at least equally plausible hypothesis is that this has been produced by the mythology surrounding *Prevent* rather than by the programme itself.

It is, nevertheless, clear that the debate about *Prevent* would benefit from much more disclosure about how it operates in practice, ideally provided by independent and scientifically credible studies, including from those who have been through it. Several modifications such as, for example, greater transparency about operating criteria, performance indicators, and outcomes, plus enhanced legal clarity and accountability, would be welcome. But, in order to forestall the possible development of effective resistance to de-radicalization, there is a legitimate security interest in not disclosing too much. Appointing a regular independent reviewer, or expanding the mandate of the current Independent Reviewer of Terrorism Legislation, and developing a much more fully resourced rehabilitation programme, are also worth considering.

It is also undeniably appropriate for a liberal democracy to outlaw those religious and secular ideologies which promote violence and hatred. But the same is not so obviously true of official attempts to counter, and to encourage others to counter, non-violent extremism. Allied to the problem of defining what 'non-violent extremism' means, the right to freedom of expression includes the right to express non-violent opinions even if they offend, shock, and disturb. The more the *Prevent* programme is formally structured and clarified, the less scope there may be for an official campaign against non-violent extremism. And by the same token, the greater the official commitment to countering non-violent extremism, the more this may limit the reach of *Prevent*. Much, therefore, needs to be done to clarify the relationship between these two programmes, worthy though the objectives of each are.

Finally, no matter what the conclusions of the official and unofficial reviews, there is next to no prospect of *Prevent* being scrapped or replaced by anything significantly different in the foreseeable future. No UK-wide party likely to form or participate in government is committed to such an objective. It is particularly unlikely that the Conservatives – having convincingly won the 2019 general election and seemingly set to remain in office for many years – will renounce the programme. Some on the Labour left are sympathetic to the campaign against *Prevent*. But the party's manifesto for the 2019 general election merely called for an official review which has since been granted. Any genuinely independent examination of the programme is likely to recommend improvements in accountability, transparency, and legal clarity rather than abolition. Finally, in his first speech as party leader to the party's Covid-restricted virtual conference in September 2020, former Director of Public Prosecutions Sir Keir Starmer signalled a major challenge to the perception that Labour is soft on threats to national security, an adjustment difficult to reconcile with all but a modest reform of the *Prevent* strategy.

6 *Pursue*

Introduction

The purpose of the *Pursue* element in CONTEST is to respond to the challenge presented by terrorism in Britain, or to British interests overseas (the latter beyond the purview of this study), by detecting, prosecuting, punishing, controlling, and/or disrupting those who engage in it.[1] These objectives, some of which also pertain to *Prevent* and *Protect*, have long featured in counterterrorism across the globe, including throughout the liberal democratic world. Indeed, it would be difficult to imagine how terrorism could be tackled effectively anywhere without them. The only questions for serious debate, albeit significant and multi-faceted ones, therefore, concern how they should be achieved.

Pursue, is complex, dense, sophisticated, technical, and highly bureaucratic. It includes such issues as the criminalization of terrorism-related conduct, collecting and analyzing information/intelligence about it, investigating those suspected of being involved, and deciding whether, and if so how, to proceed against them by prosecution, trial, and punishment, or through non-judicial executive measures. It is impossible for relevant law and policy to be comprehensively described, explained, and assessed here. But an attempt will, nevertheless, be made to consider the following key questions, common also to non-terrorist contexts: how well-conceived is it, particularly regarding checks, balances, and respect for human rights? Who is authorized to exercise the powers in question and according to what standards? And to what institutional controls are they subject?

As already indicated elsewhere in this study, it has been claimed that *Prevent* is racist and/or Islamophobic and has turned Muslims in Britain into a 'securitized community'. But these allegations have not been made to the same extent with respect to *Pursue*. This raises two equally problematic possibilities. Either *Pursue* is free from these defects – but if so why? – or it also suffers from

---

1 HM Government, *CONTEST: The United Kingdom's Strategy for Countering Terrorism*, June 2018, Cm 9608, pp. 43–52.

them – in which case why has there been less vocal concern about it and where is the evidence? Relevant official figures clearly show variations in impact with respect to gender, age, race, religion, and nationality. But, for several reasons, these do not, of themselves, support the conclusion that *Pursue*-related laws and policies are inherently sexist, ageist, racist, Islamophobic, or xenophobic, or that they systematically operate in such a manner either. Over the past few years, the majority of those arrested, charged, prosecuted, convicted, and sentenced in Britain for terrorism-related offences, have been young, male, non-white Muslims. This is also true of those subject to executive controls regarding such activities. Given the chief characteristics of the dominant terrorist threat, it would be very surprising if it were otherwise.

Criminalization

It can be argued that the risks posed by terrorism could, and should, be tackled by the ordinary criminal law without the need for any specific terrorist offences or special criminal justice processes at all. But few serious commentators take this view not least because precision engineering is an increasingly widespread characteristic of law, including criminal law, the world over. Law enforcement and security agencies, together with UK governments and legislatures of all political complexions, have also long been persuaded that such laws and policies are no less required in the counterterrorism sphere. The key questions are instead: how is, and should, this be achieved? What kinds of conduct are and should be included? Is the line between activities which ought, and which ought not, to be criminal, drawn with sufficient clarity and, in particular, are there appropriate defences to relevant charges?

The approach taken in the UK to the criminalization of terrorism has the following broad characteristics.[2] First, there is no bright line separating every 'terrorist' from every 'non-terrorist' offence. As in most jurisdictions, the core acts of terrorism – for example, murder, other offences against the person, offences involving firearms or explosives, and criminal damage[3] – are proscribed by the standard criminal law. However, some offences only assume a distinctively 'terrorist' characteristic according to context and the motives of those who commit them. In the UK offences which may be committed by terrorist or non-terrorist offenders can be charged as having 'a terrorist connection' if appropriate.[4] The Terrorism Act 2000 consolidated counterterrorist legislation, including offences, arising from the conflict in Northern Ireland. This has since been both revised and extended for the UK as a whole by fur-

---

2 C. Walker, *Blackstone's Guide to the Anti-Terrorism Legislation*, 3rd edn. (Oxford University Press, 2014), chs. 2 and 3; pp. 7–19, 211–37, 279–86.
3 Those involved in the 'Airline Liquid Bomb plot' in 2006 were, for example, convicted of the common law offence of conspiracy to murder, *R v. Ali (Ahmed)* [2011] EWCA Crim 1260.
4 Schedule 2 of the Counter-Terrorism Act 2008 contains a list of such offences.

ther post-9/11 enactments. As a result, even statutory terrorist offences are not contained in a single source but are scattered across the legislative landscape.

There is no offence of 'terrorism' as such in the UK either. However, since many substantive offences refer to 'terrorism' without themselves defining it, it has proven necessary to provide a general statutory definition. As indicated in Chapter 1, this is now contained in section 1 of the Terrorism Act 2000, which defines 'terrorism' as action or threats, in pursuit of a political, religious, racial, or ideological cause, designed to influence the government, or an international governmental organization, or to intimidate all and/or part of the public through serious life-threatening violence, serious damage to property, the creation of a serious risk to public health or safety, and/or by interfering seriously with or disrupting an electronic system. As also already indicated, this may be regarded as over-inclusive. But it has, nevertheless, been adopted by other jurisdictions, is broadly compliant with international law, and has not often be litigated in the UK.[5]

Terrorist offences are also 'generic' in the sense that they apply, in principle, to any and every kind of terrorism. There are, therefore, no offences specifically concerning 'jihadi terrorism' with separate ones dealing with 'dissident Irish' or 'right-wing terrorism'. The complaint that counterterrorist offences inherently, and by nature, 'criminalize' a particular minority is, therefore, unsustainable. While, in principle, this still leaves open the question of how they are applied, there is no evidence of systemic racism or Islamophobia on this dimension either.

In addition to regular criminal offences such as killing, causing injury, and damaging property, examples of specific statutory terrorist offences include involvement in the preparation of acts of terrorism or assisting others in doing so; membership of, or support for, a proscribed organization including by wearing clothing or displaying symbols to this effect; providing financial services and money laundering in relation to terrorism; training for terrorist purposes; directing a terrorist organization; possession of an article for terrorist purposes; encouragement of terrorism (often mistakenly referred to as the offence of 'glorifying terrorism' when 'glorification' is merely an example of how the offence could be committed); dissemination of terrorist publications; providing or receiving instruction or training for terrorism.

Technical challenges arise with respect to terrorist as with any offences, particularly their scope and defences, and what counts as evidence of the prohibited behaviour ('actus reus') and the mental element including knowledge, belief, and intent ('mens rea'). However, comparatively few of these have excited much interest beyond the largely self-referential community of judges, lawyers, and jurists.[6] The dominant criticisms tend to be that the offences in question potentially criminalize what should be lawful, or that they risk convicting the

---

5 Walker, *Anti-Terrorism Legislation*, p. 18.
6 *Ibid.*, ch. 6.

innocent by not drawing a sharp enough distinction between what constitutes the crime and what does not. Determining how innocent, though ill-advised, conduct should be distinguished from that genuinely connected with terrorism is particularly problematic with respect to some ancillary offences. The offence of supporting a proscribed organization can, for example, be committed in various ways, including by providing material or ideological support, though without belonging to it as such.[7]

The offence of withholding information about terrorism has also gone in and out of official fashion as the pendulum has swung between the view that it could contribute positively to counterterrorist law enforcement and the alternative opinion that those who have not chosen to receive such information should not be compelled to turn informer with all the potential risks this might present. Having been a crime in Northern Ireland at the peak of the Troubles, it was dropped from the catalogue of terrorist offences in the mid-1990s, only to be revived in the post-9/11 context.[8] Carrying a sentence of up to five years imprisonment, the offence is committed where, without reasonable excuse, a person fails, as soon as reasonably practicable, to disclose information they know or believe might be of material assistance in preventing someone else from committing an act of terrorism, or in securing, in the UK, the apprehension, prosecution, or conviction of another person for an offence involving the commission, preparation, or instigation of such an act.[9] It may also be committed by mere inactivity (for example, by not answering police questions or not volunteering information), through the partial suppression of information, or by relating an account known to be false. While an act of terrorism is required, the mens rea – 'knows or believes' – means that an offence will technically have been committed where this test is satisfied, even if the information in question was neither material nor accurate. However, in such cases the appropriateness of prosecution would be open to question. A reasonable excuse for not making the disclosure – such as fear of reprisal, though not the desire merely to remain uninvolved – provides a defence.[10] However, some uncertainty persists about whether, and if so the extent to which, professional privilege – for example between doctor and patient, lawyer and client, priest and supplicant, journalist and source – and the privilege against self-incrimination are included.[11]

It is also an offence under section 57 (1) of the Terrorism Act 2000 to possess an article – even lawful and commonplace items such as wire, batteries, rubber gloves, scales, electronic timers, overalls, balaclavas, agricultural fertilizer, and gas cylinders – in circumstances which give rise to a reasonable suspicion that this is for a purpose connected with terrorism. If knowledge of, and control

---

7 Terrorism Act 2000, s. 12.
8 Walker, *Anti-Terrorism Legislation*, p. 146.
9 Terrorism Act 2000, s. 38B.
10 Ibid.
11 Walker, *Anti-Terrorism Legislation*, pp. 149–51.

over, the item(s) are established, the prosecution must then prove beyond reasonable doubt that the relevant circumstances give rise to a reasonable suspicion that the defendant possessed them for a terrorist purpose.[12] It is a defence, which the prosecution can then seek to undermine, for the defendant to show that, although they possessed the article, this was not for a purpose connected with the commission, preparation, or instigation of an act of terrorism.

It is also an offence under section 58 of the Terrorism Act 2000, punishable by a maximum sentence of ten years' imprisonment, to collect, record, or possess information in a document or record likely to be useful for terrorism, even if there is nothing unlawful about the information itself. However, the prosecution must prove beyond reasonable doubt that the defendant knew about, and had control over, the document or record in question, and was aware that it was likely to provide practical assistance to a person committing or preparing to commit an act of terrorism, even though they themselves did not have such a purpose.[13] For example, the so-called 'Lyrical Terrorist', who wrote poems including 'How to Behead', was convicted under this provision, not for her literary output, but for possession of documents about military techniques and other propaganda. She, nevertheless, had her conviction quashed on appeal on the grounds that, in his summing up to the jury, the judge failed to distinguish those documents which satisfied the test of practical utility to terrorism from those which did not.[14] It is a defence to a charge for this offence that the defendant had a 'reasonable excuse', which the prosecution can then seek to discredit beyond reasonable doubt. In principle this should protect those who have legitimate reasons for possessing relevant material, for example journalists and those involved in the armed defence of beleaguered communities abroad.[15] It is not, however, a 'reasonable excuse' under section 58 to collect information for a private criminal purpose, for example breaking into the Home Secretary's home to steal rather than to carry out an act of terrorism.[16] By contrast, it would be a defence to a charge under section 57(1) for the defendant to show that the actual purpose in having an explosive was to blow open a bank vault. But this would leave them open to prosecution under the Explosive Substances Act 1883. The offence of preparation for terrorism, provided by section 5 of the Terrorism Act 2006, has to some extent reduced the need for reliance upon sections 57 and 58.

The Counter-Terrorism and Border Security Act 2019 seeks to update and to close gaps in relevant legislation, primarily in order to tackle digital challenges and to respond to developing patterns of radicalization. It seeks to do so by, amongst other things, increasing sentences for serious terrorist offences,

---

12 *R v G* [2009] UKHL13.
13 *Ibid.*, para. 46.
14 *R v Samina Malik* [2008] EWCA Crim 1450.
15 *R. v Rowe; R v AY* [2010] EWCA Crim 762.
16 *R v G* [2008] EWCA Crim 922.

158 Pursue

improving post-release police management of those who have served relevant custodial terms, and strengthening the country's border defences against the activities of hostile states. Key provisions relevant to criminalization extend the existing offence of inviting support for a proscribed organization to cover recklessness as to whether others will be so encouraged; making clear that the existing offence of displaying, in a public place, an image which arouses reasonable suspicion that the person in question is a member or supporter of a proscribed organization, includes online images such as photographs taken in a private place; updates the offence of obtaining information likely to be useful to a terrorist to incorporate terrorist material that is merely viewed or streamed over the internet rather than downloaded; and provides a new offence of entering or remaining in an area outside the UK designated in regulations by the Secretary of State to protect the public from the risk of terrorism.

While improvements in definition and defences may be desirable in some respects, there are no compelling grounds for any terrorist offence in UK law to be scrapped. The concept of 'reasonableness', though an inherently vague and discretionary one, plays a vital though not a uniform role in setting thresholds for both actionable official suspicion and legitimate defences. Since all relevant statutory offences are post-Human Rights Act, they prima facie pass the democracy, constitutionalism, rule of law, and human rights tests. And where challenged in court for the failure to comply with human rights, judges have either rejected such claims or been instrumental in requiring parliament to correct the defect.

Information and intelligence

As already indicated in Chapter 1, there can be no doubt that the key to the effective management of the risk posed by terrorism in Britain, as elsewhere, lies in the collection, analysis, and use of information which enables violent incidents to be prevented, suspects to be caught and tried, or the threat they present to be otherwise neutralized by, for example, the kind of administrative measures considered further below. Although the distinction is not clear cut, broadly speaking 'information' refers to unprocessed data which may or may not be relevant for these purposes, while 'intelligence' refers to that which is. 'Evidence' is intelligence which reaches a sufficiently probative standard to justify prosecutions.

A distinction can be drawn between several different types of intelligence: human sources, including prisoners, detainees, contacts, informants, agents, and anybody else; signals intelligence collected from communications and electronic sources; image intelligence derived from radar, photographic, infrared, and electro-optic imagery; technical intelligence concerning technological capacity, performance and operational capability of terrorist organizations; and measurement plus signature intelligence, the collection of technically derived data describing distinctive characteristics of specific incidents. However, in the final analysis, all information which becomes intelligence and evidence ultimately derives from a single source – people: how they behave, how and what they communicate and record, the things they own, possess, and touch, and the locations where they are, have been, and/or may go.

While some information about terrorist activity comes from open sources, such as newspapers and the internet, and can, therefore, be gathered without any special legal powers, as a general rule the more intrusive the intelligence-gathering, the tighter the legal regulation. Broadly speaking surveillance can include direct physical means (such as tailing and photographing subjects of interest, training binoculars on windows, installing CCTV at certain locations, penetrating terrorist organizations by informants/agents), the interception of communications (both with and without physical interference), searches of people, vehicles, and property, and the seizure of objects (including documents, notebooks, and electronic data storage equipment). Notwithstanding the resilience of many terrorist suspects, counterterrorist powers of arrest and detention, considered below, may also make a significant contribution to intelligence-gathering, not least because they provide an opportunity for intense, prolonged, and controlled interaction with potentially valuable sources.

In the UK lawful counterterrorist surveillance derives from general statutory powers of surveillance directed against any, and every, form of criminality. Concerns about compliance with human rights (particularly privacy), constitutionalism, and the rule of law have become increasingly accepted by legislators over the past few decades. As a result these powers have acquired the following general characteristics: a legislative and institutional framework which seeks to constrain their arbitrary abuse; requiring their instigation to be authorized by a senior officer in the agency concerned with judicial warrant in some cases; the keeping of comprehensive records; oversight of the relevant system, but not specific decisions, by a Parliamentary committee; and an independent commission and/or tribunal to which complaints about allegedly unlawful use may be brought. In the course of the past two decades the legal/regulatory framework has undergone significant transformation, particularly as a result of the Regulation of Investigatory Powers Act 2000 and the Investigatory Powers Act 2016 (as amended) considered further below.

Official surveillance and intelligence-gathering have long been subjects of lively debate, particularly about how the relationship between individual liberty and collective security can, and should be, managed. However, by far the most contentious is the claim that post-9/11 counterterrorist intelligence-gathering has turned Muslims in Britain into a 'securitized community' or a community under pervasive systematic official suspicion and that surveillance amounts to Islamophobic and/or racist discrimination and a violation of human rights. Other dimensions of this accusation are contested throughout this study and the various threads drawn together in the concluding chapter. However, apart from sparse anecdotes and angry complaints, there is no reliable systematic evidence that counterterrorist surveillance and intelligence-gathering in Britain suffer from these defects. There is, for example, no reliable evidence that being a Muslim is sufficient to arouse the interest of the police or security services, or that official security-related databases are being kept on Muslims, purely because of their religious affiliation, but not on anyone else. It is highly unlikely that the courts would tolerate such conduct if it were happening and was legally contested.

The Regulation of Investigatory Powers Act

Over the past two decades or so it has also become increasingly evident that the internet is a significant communication, propaganda, recruitment, and training resource for terrorists and their sympathizers. However, as a result of western democratic reservations about legal restrictions on freedom of expression, the UN has made little progress in encouraging relevant national legislation and the most concrete initiative taken by the EU, requires states to criminalize online recruitment and training for, and incitement of, terrorism.[17] In many respects the UK has been ahead of the international game.[18]

The passing of the Regulation of Investigatory Powers Act 2000 ('RIPA') was prompted by technological developments, including the internet, and the sophisticated encryption of electronic correspondence. It seeks to empower public bodies to carry out surveillance and investigation including the interception of communications – for the purpose of counterterrorism, and the policing of other types of crime – and to regulate how this is conducted. Certain public authorities are also permitted to carry out mass surveillance of communications in transit, to monitor internet activities, and to demand from internet service providers secret access to a customer's communications and cooperation in conducting surveillance. The Act also authorizes the withholding of information about the existence of interception warrants, and any data thereby obtained, from disclosure in court. Secondary legislation by ministerial order is required for some parts of the Act to come into force.

The legislation also created the offices of the Interception of Communications Commissioner, Intelligence Services Commissioner, and Investigatory Powers Commissioner for Northern Ireland.[19] An independent judicial body, the Investigatory Powers Tribunal, presided over by a senior judge and including judges and senior QCs, was also established.[20] Replacing the Interception of Communications Tribunal, the Security Service Tribunal, and the Intelligence Services Tribunal, this hears complaints about any conduct or alleged infringement of human rights by, or on behalf of, MI5, MI5, and GCHQ. It also seeks to provide opportunities for redress to anyone concerned that they may have

---

[17] Council Framework Decision 2008/919/JHA of 28 November 2008, amending Framework Decision 2002/475/JHA on combating terrorism.
[18] C. Walker and M. Conway, 'Online Terrorism and Online Laws', *Dynamics of Asymmetric Conflict*, (2015) 8, 156–75.
[19] Regulation of Investigatory Powers Act, ss. 57–64.
[20] Ibid., ss. 65–70.

been the victim of an unlawful use of covert investigative techniques by a public authority.

RIPA has been heavily criticized, though not especially for alleged abuse in the context of counterterrorism. The primary complaints have instead concerned its failure to cover the full range of surveillance techniques including bulk data, the exposure of journalists to being compelled to disclose their sources, and the investigation by local authorities of possible breaches of planning regulations, whether families in fact live in the catchment area for popular schools, and other relatively trivial anti-social activities such as dog-fouling, under-age smoking, and fly-tipping. While journalists' sources are generally privileged under European data protection laws, with which the UK complies, RIPA enables an investigating officer to seek authorization for compulsory disclosure from a senior officer rather than from a court.

While Parliament was considering these criticisms, section 3 of the Terrorism Act 2006 empowered the police to issue a notice to service providers requiring public access to material believed to be 'unlawfully terrorism related' to be barred or for it to be modified. Failure to comply is an offence. However, these provisions have yet to be formally invoked. Instead, informal requests are preferred. The public is also encouraged, via a government website linked to the Counter-Terrorism Internet Referral Unit launched by the police in 2010, to alert the authorities about online extremism and terrorism. BT, Virgin, Sky, and TalkTalk have also sought to facilitate the identification of terrorist material by installing public reporting buttons on their services. Facebook, Google, Yahoo, and Twitter have also agreed to mentor smaller internet companies regarding the monitoring of content.

Parliament eventually responded to the controversy which RIPA inspired by passing the Investigatory Powers Act 2016 which, in addition to providing extra safeguards, creates new powers, and consolidates existing ones. Amongst other things, these enable UK intelligence and law enforcement agencies to conduct targeted interception of communications, bulk collection of communications data, and bulk interception of communications. A legal power, similar to that provided by the Anti-terrorism, Crime and Security Act 2001 and the Data Retention and Investigatory Powers Act 2014, was also provided to require Internet Connection Records to be retained. However, on 21 December 2016, the European Court of Justice (ECJ) declared the generalized retention of certain types of personal data unlawful.[21]

The Act also enables the police, intelligence officers, and managers of certain government departments to view internet connection records without judicial warrant as part of a targeted and filtered investigation. The police and intelligence agencies are permitted to access data by hacking into computers and other devices. Local authorities are provided with some investigatory powers, for example with respect to suspected fraudulent benefits claims, but

---

21 Joined Cases C-203/15 and C-698/15 Tele2 and Watson (Grand Chamber).

not to access internet connection records. Communication Service Providers (CSPs) are also required to retain, for a year, the internet connection records of UK internet users, including which websites were visited, but not the particular pages or the full browsing history, to assist with targeted interception of data, and communications, and to interfere with equipment in pursuit of an investigation. The Act obliges telecommunications operators to maintain the capability to remove encryption or provide data in an intelligible form when, where necessary and proportionate, they are served with a warrant, notice, or authorization by both the Secretary of State and a Judicial Commissioner. It is also now an offence for a CSP, or one of its employees, to reveal that data has been so requested. Foreign companies are not required to engage in bulk collection of data or communications or to remove encryption.

In order to oversee the use of all investigatory powers, the Act replaces the Interception of Communications Commissioner, the Intelligence Services Commissioner, and the Chief Surveillance Commissioner with an Investigatory Powers Commissioner, supported by an office – the Investigatory Powers Commissioner's Office (IPCO) – staffed by 15 serving and former senior judges plus a scientific advisory panel and 50 officials. Warrants to access the content of communications must be reviewed by a judge serving on the IPCO, and any interference with equipment requires the authorization of the Secretary of State in advance. A new criminal offence of unlawfully accessing internet data has been created, with safeguards also provided for sensitive professions such as journalists, lawyers, and doctors.

The Investigatory Powers Act 2016 also strengthens the provisions governing the Investigatory Powers Tribunal by providing a new right of appeal where a point of law raises an important issue of principle or practice, or where there is some other compelling reason for appealing. On 27 April 2018 the UK High Court ruled that the Investigatory Powers Act violates EU law.[22] In response, the Data Retention and Acquisition Regulations 2018 came into force on 31 October that year. These limit access to communications data to that concerning serious crime – defined as offences which attract sentences of imprisonment for a term of 12 months or more – and require the authorities to consult the independent IPCO before requesting data. However, the regulations also enable rapid access without independent approval subject to a three-day expiry and with subsequent review. Although the Act provides a particularly rigorous and comprehensive surveillance regulatory regime, its human rights compliance remains contentious.[23]

---

[22] *The National Council for Civil Liberties (Liberty), R (On the Application Of) v Secretary of State for the Home Department & Anor* [2018] EWHC 975.

[23] *Privacy International v UK* 46259/16, 4 September 2020; *Privacy International v Investigatory Powers Tribunal* [2021] EWHC 27 (Admin).

Investigation

The primary purpose of counterterrorist criminal investigations is to convert information derived from intelligence and other sources into evidence capable of sustaining convictions in the criminal courts. It has many elements, the most important of which include police searches of premises, the seizure of objects and documents, and the arrest and questioning of suspects which may lead to detention. Most of the details were settled in the Terrorism Act 2000, the implications of which have since been thoroughly considered in the case law and legal literature.[24]

However, before considering these, a perennial theme in this study merits some attention. There is no evidence that counterterrorist investigations in Britain are systematically motivated by racist or Islamophobic considerations. While it cannot be ruled out that such defects have contaminated specific investigations, there is as yet no credible evidence that this has happened either.

A simple thought experiment exposes the muddled thinking which tends to underpin such accusations. Imagine that several mosques in an English town are vandalized in broad daylight by someone yelling Islamophobic abuse. Every witness to these events tells the police that the culprit was a tall man in his 20s or 30s with ginger hair and an Irish accent. Though open to the possibility that the accent may be fake, the police initially concentrate their inquiries upon Irish men with ginger hair in this age-range in that town. No one could seriously claim this is 'racist' or 'Hibernophobic', or that it turns the 'Irish community', 'the ginger-haired community', or 'the ginger-haired Irish community' there into an 'officially suspect' or 'securitized community'. For one thing, it is open to question whether people of Irish extraction in any English town constitute a 'community' in any intelligible or useful sense. It cannot even be known with certainty that they would regard themselves as such. For another, even if they did, more than half this 'community', namely the women, children, and older men, would not be of any interest to the police for the purpose of this particular investigation. Furthermore, membership of the 'Irish community', like most national/ethnic 'communities', is indeterminate and, in this case, is much more a matter of subjective choice on the part of anyone with Irish antecedents than objective fact. It is not clear, for example, if children born in England to at least one Irish parent belong to it. It may, therefore, be said that, in this imagined scenario, all ginger-haired Irish men in their 20s and 30s in the town in question would, in a formal and loose sense, be 'subjects potentially of interest to the police'. This is unobjectionable because it is simply an unavoidable consequence of the reported characteristics of the offender.

Now, let us depart from the imaginary and focus upon the real. As already observed elsewhere in this study, over 90 per cent of the fatalities in terrorist incidents in Britain since 9/11, and just short of 100 per cent of the non-fatal

---

24 Walker, *Anti-Terrorism Legislation*, chs. 4 and 5.

casualties, were caused by young, male Muslims who justified their conduct in terms of defending their co-religionists overseas and contributing to the establishment of a global Islamic Caliphate governed by a particularly brutal, ultra-traditional interpretation of the Muslim faith. In some of these incidents the culprits were killed, either in suicide bombings or while resisting arrest. Although it is possible that the apparently solitary offender in the imaginary Islamophobic scenario in the previous paragraph may have had far-right connections, prima facie, the incidents were time-limited and local. By contrast, the perpetrators of domestic jihadi terrorism in Britain have come from places apart from those in which the attacks themselves took place. The evidence also suggests that wider networks linked by the same ideology were involved.

As already indicated elsewhere in this study, young men are overwhelmingly more likely to engage in terrorism of all kinds than women of any age and older men, and that only eight per cent of Muslims in England and Wales are white. It follows, therefore, that the relevant criminal investigations into incidents of domestic jihadi terrorism must inescapably focus predominantly upon young Muslim men in, and/or from, Britain as a whole, most of whom are likely to be non-white. While, as in the imaginary scenario, it may be said that all young, non-white Muslim men in Britain are, in a formal and loose sense, 'subjects potentially of interest to the police', this is also unobjectionable because here too it is an inescapable consequence of the objective rather than the assumed or attributed characteristics of the offenders. As long as the investigation does not take an unwarranted turn, such as the arrest and detention of all young Muslim men in the cities in which the incidents occurred, it cannot credibly be regarded as discriminatory because it would clearly be proportionate to a legitimate purpose.

In fact, two problems would arise if, in either the imagined or real scenarios, seeking to avoid accusations of 'racism' and/or in the latter Islamophobia, the criminal investigations were to be extended to include suspects who do not share the relevant racial/ethnic and/or religious characteristics of the offenders. First, scarce resources would be wasted by considering those who could not possibly have been responsible for the crimes in question. Second, drawing into the investigation those who do not share the identities of the culprits potentially threatens their human rights more than it does those who do.

Search and seize

Street and port stop and search powers, which could just as readily be considered part of the *Pursue* agenda, were considered in relation to *Protect* in Chapter 4. Half a dozen or so special counterterrorist search powers are also available to enter and search premises and to search anyone found therein, and to seize documents and other items. The relevant law is complex and technical, with different circumstances giving rise to different requirements and safeguards.[25] Key distinctions concern whether searches are conducted in residential or non-residential premises, a specific address or all premises in a cordoned area, whether they are urgent and exercisable by the police on their own authority with or without the sanction of a senior officer, or less urgent and require judicial warrant, and whether the purpose of seizing property is to prevent it from being concealed, lost, damaged, altered, destroyed, or to examine it more closely for evidence. In all cases, except great urgency, reasonable cause, framed slightly differently for the police and for the judiciary, is required. Special rules, also subject to various kinds of reasonableness requirement, govern confidential journalistic material and the compulsory production of, or access to, 'excluded' and 'special procedure material', ie personal records deriving from trade, profession, etc., human tissue or tissue fluid held in confidence for medical purposes. The Policing and Crime Act 2017 also provides the police with a power to enter premises to seize passports cancelled under the Royal Prerogative in relation to national security, as considered further below.

Terrorist funds

Triggered by the UN Security Council Resolution 1373, CONTEST singles out terrorist funds for particular *Pursue*-related attention.[26] A Joint Money Laundering Intelligence Taskforce (JMLIT), set up in 2015, facilitates the exchange and analysis of information and intelligence between the financial sector, Government, and law enforcement in order better to detect the movement of terrorist funds. Within this network the Terrorist Finance Experts Group was established to support the exchange and analysis of financial information which may be linked to terrorism.

In order to enhance the sharing of information when such suspicions arise, the Criminal Finances Act 2017 (CFA) established the office of Counter-Terrorism Financial Investigator and also gave law enforcement agencies and partners new powers to investigate and disrupt terrorist financing, money laundering, and criminal finance. Amongst other things, this extends certain financial investigative powers, previously reserved for the police, to civilian financial investigators. The Sanctions and Anti-Money Laundering Act 2018 provides a framework for sanctions, including but not confined to counterterrorism, hitherto implemented through the EU, to take effect in the UK. Replacing powers contained in the Terrorist Asset Freezing etc. Act 2010 and the Anti-Terrorism, Crime and Security Act 2000, it permits the UK to exercise sanctioning powers autonomously. However, UN guidance remains very influential.

---

25 *Ibid.*, ch. 3.
26 HM Government, *CONTEST 2018*, para. 140.

Arrest, charge, and detention

Section 41 of the Terrorism Act 2000, arguably the most important single provision in the entire statute, simply provides: 'a constable may arrest without a warrant a person whom he reasonably suspects to be a terrorist'.[27] Several features differentiate this from powers of arrest in the non-terrorist sphere. First, although the European Court of Human Rights (ECtHR) has accepted that, in this context, the term 'terrorism' is equivalent to 'criminal offences relating to terrorism',[28] the grounds are broader because the arrest is on reasonable suspicion for 'being a terrorist' rather than for a specific offence. What is required, in other words, is a reasonable suspicion that the person being arrested is, or has been, involved in the commission, preparation, or instigation of acts of terrorism.

However, the courts accept that while 'reasonable suspicion' need not amount to proof beyond reasonable doubt,[29] it must be established as both a genuine suspicion in the mind of the person making the arrest, and be justified on objective grounds even though this may derive from secondary sources such as the evidence of informants or police briefings rather than from events or information received first-hand by the arresting officers themselves.[30] The result is that the suspicion justifying a section 41 arrest need not be as specific as for non-terrorist offences. Second, it follows that fewer details about the grounds need be disclosed to the suspect upon arrest. The courts have held, for example, that, as more details are likely to emerge from briefing documents preceding subsequent police interviews, it is sufficient at the time of arrest to inform those being arrested that they are suspected of being a terrorist and that they are being arrested under section 41 of the Terrorism Act 2000.[31]

The principal purpose of a special arrest power of this kind, coupled with longer-than-normal periods of detention considered further below, is to interrogate suspects in pursuit of several objectives. First, terrorist offences may give rise to urgent public safety concerns, for example the need to ensure that any undetected bombs are located and defused, or imminent plots detected and disrupted. Second, searches may need to be conducted in order to collect forensic evidence. Third, police interviews facilitate the gathering of intelligence. A fourth reason concerns the international dimension of the current (particularly jihadi) terrorist threat. It may be necessary for terrorist suspects to be held longer than their non-terrorist counterparts, not only because they are

---

27 Walker, *Anti-Terrorism Legislation*, pp. 158–70.
28 *Brogan v United Kingdom*, App. nos. 11209, 11234, 11266/84, 11386/85, Ser. A. 145-B (1988), para. 50.
29 *O'Hara v United Kingdom*, App. no.37555/97, 2001-X.
30 *McKee v Chief Constable for Northern Ireland* [1984] 1 W.L.R. 1358.
31 *Forbes v HMA* 1990 SC (JC) 215; *Brady v Chief Constable for the RUC* [1991] 2 NIJB 22; *Oscar v Chief Constable of the RUC* [1992] NI 290. In *Sher v Chief Constable of Greater Manchester Police* [2010] EWHC 1859 (Admin).

more likely to be highly dedicated and dangerous, but because the police may face considerable difficulties establishing identity, translating foreign languages, and liaising with foreign security agencies. Another goal is to discover evidence likely to be admissible in court. In the 1970s and 1980s, counterterrorist prosecutions relied heavily on confessions, particularly in Northern Ireland. However, improvements in forensic testing and much tighter limits on the pressure which can be exerted upon suspects in interviews have since reduced the significance of confessions for the purpose of prosecution and trial.

In order to enhance police investigations, periods of post-arrest detention permitted under section 41 are much more substantial than those available in non-terrorist contexts.[32] Suspects arrested and detained with respect to terrorist offences can be held for up to a total of 14 days. Decisions about the length of detention are taken in three principal phases. First, the police can detain such suspects at their discretion for 48 hours from either the time of arrest or examination at a port. But, provided an application to this effect has been approved by 'a judicial authority', this is extendable, in the second phase, for a further five days (seven days in total).[33] A fresh application, the third phase, must be made for any subsequent extension up to a maximum of seven further days, making a possible total of 14 days from arrest. Draft legislation, providing for extensions of up to 28 days in exceptional circumstances, has been prepared but will not be enacted unless judged necessary.

In the mid-2000s, there was a vigorous public debate about proposals that the duration of pre-charge detention should last up to 42, or even, 90 days.[34] But this ultimately failed to persuade Parliament for the following, amongst other reasons. Except for civil law jurisdictions where a magistrate directs the investigation, this would be significantly out of line with the law and practice of most other democratic states, it might be incompatible with the European Convention on Human Rights (ECHR), and any statement obtained during a detention beyond, say, four days, might be deemed inadmissible as evidence at trial due to unfairness.[35] In the event, the Criminal Justice Act 2003 limited extensions to a total of 14 days while the Terrorism Act 2006 permitted a total of 28 days. The 2006 Act also authorized extensions after 48 hours to be made by prosecutors in addition to the police and required a High Court judge to approve those for longer than 14 days.[36] However, following the election of the Coalition government in 2010, the provision permitting a 28-day

---

32 Walker, *Anti-Terrorism Legislation*, pp. 161–70.
33 Part III of Schedule 8, Terrorism Act 2000; *Sher v Chief Constable of Greater Manchester Police* [2010] EWHC 1859 (Admin).
34 Walker, *Anti-Terrorism Legislation*, p. 162.
35 See, eg, Joint Committee on Human Rights, *Counter-Terrorism Policy and Human Rights: Terrorism Bill and Related Matters* (2005-6 HL 75, HC 561), paras. 87 and 92; House of Commons Home Affairs Committee, *The Government's Counter-Terrorism Proposals* (2007–08 HC 43); Lord Carlile, *Report on Proposed Measures for Inclusion in a Counter Terrorism Bill*, Cm 7262, 2007.
36 Terrorism Act 2006, ss. 23–5.

detention period was repealed and the former 14-day limit was reinstated as from 25 January 2011.

Anyone arrested under section 41 must be taken, as soon as reasonably practicable, to a place of detention designated by the Secretary of State. Other safeguards, provided by codes to the Terrorism Act 2000, include strict record-keeping, monitoring by closed circuit television, and regular medical checks. The police also have powers to take steps, where reasonably necessary, to identify the suspect by, for example, photographing, measuring, and conducting voice recognition tests. Fingerprinting and the taking of non-intimate samples may be authorized by a superintendent. But an intimate sample may only be taken with consent. Interviews are audio and video recorded.

Suspects in terrorism cases also have rights to have someone informed of the detention and to seek legal advice. Delays may be authorized by a superintendent for up to 48 hours, by contrast with the 36 hours for non-terrorist contexts. The grounds are the same as those in non-terrorist cases except for the following additional risks: interference with the gathering of information about the commission, preparation or instigation of acts of terrorism, and alerting someone, thereby making it more difficult to prevent an act of terrorism or making it more difficult to apprehend, prosecute, or convict in connection with the commission, preparation, or instigation of an act of terrorism.

If authorized by an officer of at least the rank of Commander or Assistant Chief Constable, the right of access to a lawyer may only be exercised within sight and hearing of a 'qualified officer' (ie a police inspector), where there are reasonable grounds for believing that any of the consequences specified for delaying access might otherwise arise. While the government expects deferment to be limited to 'exceptional cases',[37] there are doubts that access under these circumstances meets the standards of fairness required by Article 6 of the ECHR.[38]

Police 'review officers' must conduct formal reviews of counterterrorist detentions to ensure they remain lawful.[39] The first must be carried out as soon as reasonably practicable after arrest and then at intervals of not more than 12 hours, ending after detention has been extended by warrant. The grounds for police authorizations include checking fingerprints; conducting forensic tests; checking detainees' replies to questions against intelligence; opening new lines of enquiry; identifying accomplices; correlating information obtained from one or more persons detained with respect to the same case; awaiting a decision by the Director of Public Prosecutions; finding and consulting other witnesses; arranging an identification parade; checking an alibi; translating

---

37 HC Debs. vol. 346, col. 375, 15 March 2000, Charles Clarke.
38 *Brennan v United Kingdom* App. no. 39846/98, 2001-X; *(John) Murray v United Kingdom*, App. no. 18731/91, Reports 1996-I, para. 66; *Averill v United Kingdom* App. no. 36408/97, 2000-VI; *Magee v United Kingdom* App. no. 28135/95, 2000-VI.
39 Walker, *Anti-Terrorism Legislation*, pp. 167–8.

documents; employing an interpreter and interviewing the detainee with their assistance; communicating with foreign police forces; evaluating translated documents and pursuing further lines of inquiry these might suggest.[40]

Detainees have an opportunity to make oral or written representations to the judicial authority considering whether or not their detention should be extended, and to be legally represented at the hearing. While the judicial authority may withhold information about particularly sensitive aspects of the investigation, such as the specific issues the police wish to explore, failure to take adequate account of the detainee's representations might result in the quashing, by judicial review, of decisions to extend detention.[41] After having been given an opportunity for representations to be made by, or on behalf of, the applicant and the person to whom the application relates, a judicial authority may direct that the detainee and/or any legal representative be excluded from the subsequent hearing provided effective means of communication are, nevertheless, established.[42] The judicial authority must be satisfied that there are reasonable grounds for believing that further detention is necessary to obtain evidence relevant to the suspicion that the detainee is a 'terrorist', and that the investigation is being conducted diligently and expeditiously.

Providing they are satisfied that it is necessary in the interests of justice, and by contrast with the practice in the non-terrorist context, section 22 of Part II of the Counter-Terrorism Act 2008 authorizes a Crown Court judge to permit questioning up to a total of 48 hours after a defendant has been charged with a terrorist offence. This is subject to certain conditions, such as appropriate transfer from prison to a police station, that the investigation is being conducted diligently and expeditiously, and that it will not interfere unduly with the preparation of the defendant's defence to the specific, or to any other, criminal charge. Questioning by the police after the trial commences is not expressly prohibited but would generally be difficult to reconcile with the interests of justice. Adverse inferences can be drawn from the failure of defendants to mention facts when questioned or charged they later rely upon in their defence at trial and/or to decline to give evidence at the trial itself.[43]

Various other options under discussion for continuing police questioning post-remand include extending to all counterterrorist investigations the procedure specified by section 6 of the Explosive Substances Act 1883 which provides that a judicial examination can be conducted on the order of the Attorney General when it is reasonably suspected that an offence under the Act has been committed; more extensive use of preparatory offences; permitting intercept evidence to be admitted at trial; and fuller use of the threshold test

---

40 Terrorism Act 2000, Sch. 8, para. 23. See the Colville Report, *Review of the Operation of the Prevention of Terrorism (Temporary Provisions) Act 1984*, Cm. 264, 1987, para. 5.16.
41 *Re Quigley's Application* [1997] NI 202.
42 Criminal Justice and Police Act 2001, s. 75.
43 Terrorism Act 2008, ss. 29(9), 36, 37.

for charging which requires reasonable suspicion where there is a reasonable expectation of further evidence becoming available in a complex investigation. Since the police do not have the physical facilities to detain people in humane conditions for prolonged periods, suspects held for longer than 14 days could be transferred to prison with the proviso that, unless the defendant does not object, any statement obtained beyond 14 days should be deemed inadmissible at trial on the grounds of unfairness.

Statistics for 2019–20 have been distorted by the effects of the Covid-19 pandemic considered in Chapter 1. However, between the years ending September 2001–19, a total of 4,598 people were arrested for terrorism-related activities, 2,045 (44 per cent) of whom were held under section 41 of the Terrorism Act 2000 and the remainder, 2,553 (56 per cent), under other legislation including that directed at terrorist and non-terrorist crime.[44] Of the total, 1,890 were charged with an offence, the majority (1,247) terrorism-related,[45] and 2,281 were released without charge.[46] The remainder (427) were bailed, were pending, or were dealt with in other ways, including by cautioning or transfer to immigration authorities. The number of section 41 arrests has declined as a proportion of all terrorism-related arrests from a high point of 97 per cent in 2004–5, to 12 per cent in 2019–20.[47] Of the 2,045 arrested under section 41, 1,790 were held for up to seven days, and 2,034 for up to 14 days. Since 2007 inclusive, no detention has lasted for longer than 13 days.[48]

The majority of those arrested, charged, and prosecuted in Britain for terrorism-related offences over the past few years have been young, male, non-white, British Muslims. For example, in the years ending September 2001–19, according to ethnic appearance as recorded by the police at the time of arrest, 1,425 (31 per cent) of the 4,598 suspects arrested in connection with terrorism-related activity were white and 3,139 (68 per cent) non-white.[49] The majority of those arrested, 2,373 (52 per cent) were under the age of 30 as were those charged (56 per cent).[50] The vast majority of those arrested, and the majority of those charged with a terrorist-related offence, 91 per cent in both cases, were male.[51]

---

44 Home Office, *Operation of Police Powers under the Terrorism Act 2000 and Subsequent Legislation: Arrests, Outcomes, and Stop and Search, Great Britain, Year Ending September 2019*, Statistical Bulletin 30, 19, Table A.01.
45 Ibid., Table A.04.
46 Ibid., Table A.03.
47 Ibid., Table A.01.
48 Ibid., Table A.03.
49 Ibid., Table A.11.
50 Ibid., Table A.10.
51 Ibid., Table A.09.

Prosecution and trial

In the UK, counterterrorist criminal proceedings are those involving the commission, preparation, instigation of, and/or support for, acts of terrorism, acts which appear to have been carried out for the purpose of terrorism, and/or those concerning the resources of a proscribed organization. Subject to qualms about the breadth of the definition of terrorism in the Terrorism Act 2000 considered in Chapter 1, it is, nevertheless, accepted on all sides of the serious debate, that the optimal way of dealing with terrorist offences already committed is prosecution in a fair trial on the basis of fairly obtained and reliable evidence, and conviction by a properly constituted independent and impartial court on the basis of proof of guilt beyond reasonable doubt. This is not only the most effective way of seeking to distinguish the guilty from the not-guilty and to ensure that only the former are punished; it also offers the best prospects of securing the legitimacy of counterterrorist law enforcement and of maintaining public confidence in it.

However, for two main reasons there is less consensus (than is desirable) about what constitutes fairness in this field. The most authoritative standards, found in international human rights law and the ECHR in particular, are abstract and require interpretation. National courts and the ECtHR have also recognized that countering terrorism may justify restricting them in ways some may regard as violations by, for example, relaxing rules on the exclusion of certain forms of potentially incriminating evidence and tightening bail conditions. It is also not uncommon in liberal democracies for distinctive trial processes, and in some cases special courts, to be instituted for terrorist offences.[52] These may include proceedings held wholly or partly in secret, modifications to the constitution of the tribunal itself such as the substitution of judge(s) alone for juries, changes to the rules regarding burden and standard of proof and the admissibility of evidence, reduced disclosure of the prosecution case to the defence, limiting the role of defence lawyers, and providing a role for special advocates. There are also arguments for and against removing the prohibition against treating information obtained by the interception of communications as evidence, as provided by section 17 of the Regulation of Investigatory Powers Act 2000, and permitting such information to be admitted at trial at the discretion of the prosecuting authorities.

As already indicated in Chapter 1, in order to facilitate the phasing out of internment in Northern Ireland, from 1973 onwards terrorist offences, ie those 'scheduled' in the Northern Ireland Emergency Provisions Act, were tried in Belfast's single-judge, non-jury, Diplock courts. This had several principal consequences with no counterpart elsewhere in the UK then or since. One was the campaign against the phasing out of 'special category status' for those

---

52 See, eg, F. Ni Aoláin and O. Gross (eds.), *Guantanamo and Beyond: Exceptional Courts and Military Commissions in Comparative and Policy Perspective* (Cambridge University Press, 2013).

convicted by the Diplock courts which eventually led to the deaths of ten republican prisoners on hunger strike. Second, heavy reliance upon confessions led to the abuse of some suspects in police custody. When this was exposed and stopped, a series of mass trials on the testimony of 'supergrasses', elicited by the offer of inducements such as immunity from prosecution or reduced sentences, ensued. However, the only lasting contribution the supergrass process made to the Diplock conviction-rate was to provide an alternative means of obtaining confessions.[53]

As a result of the peace process, the Justice and Security (Northern Ireland) Act 2007 both provides special arrangements to protect jurors in all trials, by ensuring greater anonymity and fuller checks in jury selection, while reserving non-jury trial for highly exceptional circumstances. Subject to a presumption that trial will be by jury, it is the responsibility of the DPP for Northern Ireland to opt for trial without a jury if, in any given circumstances, there is a risk that the administration of justice may be impaired by jury trial and one of at least four conditions is satisfied – the defendant is linked to a proscribed organization, an offence has allegedly been committed by a proscribed organization, a proscribed organization attempts to interfere with the investigation or prosecution, or the offence occurred as a result of or in connection with sectarianism. The fact that the decision to opt for a trial without a jury lies with a prosecutor and not a judge, and that the statutory grounds for review are narrow, are open to criticism. As under the previous Diplock process, where a non-jury court trying a terrorist offence convicts the accused, there is a right of appeal without leave of the Court of Appeal or a certificate from the judge of the trial court. A written judgment, stating the reasons for conviction, is also required as soon as reasonably practicable.

This aside, throughout the Troubles terrorist offences committed in England, Scotland, or Wales were tried by the regular criminal courts according to largely standard criminal procedure, a practice which has continued since 9/11. While the police charge suspects, the Crown Prosecution Service Special Crime and Counter Terrorism Division (CPS SCCTD) decides whether or not to prosecute and, in line with the Code for Crown Prosecutors, how to frame the indictment. Due to their sensitivity and importance, a Protocol on the Management of Terrorism Cases issued by the President of the Queen's Bench Division[54] seeks to ensure closer judicial management of the case, including service of documents and consultation with the police about security risks. Terrorism-related cases, all of which are tried by jury, are also listed before experienced judges in a special 'terrorism cases list'.

A stark difference between counterterrorist trials during the Troubles and those in mainland Britain today is the absence from the latter of any notorious

---

53 S. Greer, *Supergrasses: A Study in Anti-Terrorist Law Enforcement in Northern Ireland* (Clarendon Press, 1995).
54 www.hmcourts-service.gov.uk. cms. files. management_of_terrorism_cases.pdf.

miscarriages of justice. This does not necessarily mean that nobody has been wrongfully convicted. But no campaigns of the kind which eventually led to the quashing of the convictions of the Birmingham Six and Guildford Four – which, incidentally, occurred in the routine English criminal justice system not the Diplock process – have yet appeared.

Of the 1,247 defendants charged with terrorism-related activity under both counterterrorist and non-terrorist law between end of September 2001 and 2019, 1,057 (85 per cent) were prosecuted and 913 (86 per cent of those prosecuted) were convicted.[55] The majority of those arrested, charged, and convicted of a terrorist offence also defined themselves as British (60 per cent, 71 per cent, and 71 per cent respectively).[56]

Punishment and rehabilitation

According to a principle of sentencing and punishment enunciated in the pre-9/11 context, a terrorist dimension to any given offence compounds its gravity and entitles the court, when considering sentence, to 'punish, deter and incapacitate', and to regard rehabilitation as 'likely to play a minor (if any) part'.[57] However, there have been three important developments since. First, reflecting the changing nature of the terrorist threat, including increasing concern about the availability of potentially self-radicalizing extremist material online, comprehensive guidelines providing a detailed tariff for each terrorist offence came into effect for the first time in England and Wales on 27 April 2018.[58] The impact of harm and the degree of culpability plus aggravating and mitigating factors are among the issues considered. The second development relates to growing awareness of the risk of radicalization in prison, while the third concerns the importance of effective custodial de-radicalization and rehabilitation programmes.

In recent years fewer 'goal line clearances' (arrest and prosecution of well-developed plots shortly before activation), and more 'upstream diversions' involving the prosecution of preparatory and other ancillary offences, have resulted in a more diffuse population of terrorist offenders serving a wider range of prison sentences.[59] As of 30 September 2019, 28 prisoners were in custody on remand for terrorism-related offences and 196 in custody following conviction. Of those on remand, 11 (39 per cent) were white and 17 (61 per cent) non-white, while of those convicted 24 per cent were white and 76 per

---

55 Home Office, *Operation of Police Powers*, Table A.06c.
56 *Ibid.*, Tables A.12a, b, and c.
57 *R v Martin* (1999) 1 Cr App S 477, 480.
58 www.sentencingcouncil.org.uk/wp-content/uploads/Terrorism-Offences_Definitive-guideline_WEB.pdf.
59 R. Pickering, 'Terrorism, Extremism, Radicalization and the Offender Management System in England and Wales' in A. Silke (ed.), *Prisons, Terrorism and Extremism: Critical Issues in Management, Radicalization and Reform* (Routledge, 2014), pp. 161–2.

cent non-white.⁶⁰ Of the 224 persons in custody for terrorism-related offences (convicted and on remand), 77 per cent were Islamist, 17 per cent extreme right-wing, and six per cent other.⁶¹ Seventy-seven per cent self-declared as Muslim, ten per cent as Christian, and eight per cent as of no religion.⁶² While there have been steady increases in recent years in the number of terrorist prisoners embracing a range of ideologies, the number of jihadi prisoners slightly decreased from 187 in 2016–17 to 173 in 2018–19. The proportion of far-right prisoners has also steadily increased over the past three years, from 16 in 2016–17 to 38 in 2018–19.⁶³

Segregation

As with other aspects of the criminal justice response to terrorism in contemporary Britain, there is no special counterterrorist penal system as such. Apart from concerns about the radicalization of other prisoners, and challenges regarding rehabilitation, terrorist offenders experience substantially the same custodial and post-custodial regimes, including those relating to release on licence, as any other high security prisoner. As a result of the particular characteristics and dynamics of the conflict, those imprisoned for terrorist offences in Northern Ireland during the Troubles were segregated according to their paramilitary affiliation.

Some commentators continue to regard the risk of radicalization of other prisoners by those imprisoned in Britain for jihadi and far-right terrorist offences as negligible while others believe it to be more significant.⁶⁴ Terrorist inmates can be accommodated in High Security Units (HSUs), including at Belmarsh where 20 per cent are Muslim, compared with 12 per cent in UK prisons as a whole. But this tends to be related more to concerns about the risk of escape than inmate radicalization.⁶⁵ Often described as 'prisons within prisons' the 'intrusive and strict security procedures' which apply in HSUs nevertheless comply with human rights standards if they are proportionate to legitimate concerns about threats presented to the good order and discipline of the establishment.⁶⁶ Prison imams and other staff are required to compile Security Intelligence Reports (SIRs) about a given prison and its inmates. Although few of the 8,400 of those prepared in 2010 concerned radicalization, they are, nevertheless, regarded as the 'cornerstone' of British counterterrorist prison policy and are critical in determining whether or not any prisoner is transferred

---

60 Home Office, *Operation of Police Powers*, Table P.02.
61 Ibid., Table P.01.
62 Ibid., P.04.
63 Ibid., Tables A and P.01.
64 Pickering, 'Terrorism, Extremism, Radicalization', pp. 159–60.
65 C. Murray, '"To Punish, Deter and Incapacitate": Incarceration and Radicalization in UK Prisons after 9/11', in Silke (ed.), *Prisons, Terrorism and Extremism*, p. 23.
66 *R v Ahmed and Others* [2011] EWCA Crim 446.

to an HSU.⁶⁷ Regular reviews of cases also tend to result in transfer out of high security confinement and back to freer association with other inmates.⁶⁸

Those serving sentences for terrorism may also occasionally be segregated from other prisoners, but generally only for their own protection following high profile domestic terrorist incidents. As the domestic jihadi terrorist threat unfolded in Britain it was assumed that there was little risk that terrorist inmates would radicalize their fellow inmates. Not only were there comparatively few such prisoners, but there were also few, if any, other prisoners likely to share the political assumptions and communal allegiances which were integral to the Northern Irish conflict.⁶⁹ However, a segregation unit, with only a handful of occupants so far, has been established at HMP Frankland to keep Islamist inmates away from other 'vulnerable' prisoners.

Desistence and disengagement

Irrespective of the risk of inmate radicalization, since the mid-2000s the prison service has taken the challenge of deradicalizing terrorist prisoners very seriously, including by establishing an Extremist Prisoners Working Group in 2006. This undertakes psychological studies, explores the prospects of enhanced faith-based interventions, support and advice, and develops appropriate guidelines and training programmes.⁷⁰ In 2015 the Counter Extremism Strategy included a commitment to deliver a new de-radicalization programme aimed at changing the behaviour (desistence) and beliefs (disengagement or 'deradicalization') of those already involved in terrorist-related activity. This included prisoners and others further down the path towards radicalization than those for whom the Channel programme, discussed in the previous chapter, was designed.

With an initial pilot focussing on prisoners due to be released on licence, the Desistance and Disengagement Programme (DDP) was launched in October 2016⁷¹ and extended shortly thereafter to include the TPIM and TEO regimes (see following section). A wide spectrum of partners and agencies – including the Ministry of Justice, Police and Her Majesty's Prison and Probation Service, plus NGOs – deliver a range of tailored programmes and practical assistance in an attempt to tackle the drivers of radicalization and to provide the best means possible for those involved to disengage from terrorism and reintegrate safely back into society. This includes mentoring, psychological, theological, and ideological support and advice. However, unlike the *Prevent* strategy, the DDP, which runs alongside existing statutory risk assessment and management processes such as Multi-Agency Public Protection Arrangements (MAPPAs), is

---

67 Murray, 'To Punish, Deter and Incapacitate', pp. 23–4.
68 *Ibid.*, p. 24.
69 *Ibid.*, p. 22.
70 Pickering, 'Terrorism, Extremism, Radicalization', pp. 160–6.
71 Home Office News Team, *Factsheet: Desistance and Disengagement Programme*, 5 November 2019.

mandatory in certain cases.[72] Non-compliance potentially raises the possibility of prosecution for breach of conditions or prison recall. It is not, however, a substitute for criminal investigations into, or prosecution of, those who have committed terrorism offences at home or abroad. While it is not easy to measure the success of prisoner deradicalization, it is also difficult to argue that any and every attempt to do so is illegitimate and misconceived and should be abandoned.

Executive controls

As already indicated, it is widely accepted in liberal democracies including the UK that the optimal means of tackling terrorism is through the collection of intelligence which reaches a sufficiently probative standard to sustain criminal convictions. However, a dilemma arises when credible sources indicate that certain individuals pose a threat, but either the intelligence in question is not of a sufficiently probative standard to support prosecution, or the sources themselves might be gravely compromised if their role were to be exposed in a public trial. The challenge is compounded by the fact that effectively managing the risks posed by mass casualty suicide terrorism may require pre-emptive intervention. The far-from-perfect solution is to subject such suspects to various forms of administrative or executive control. Depending upon the circumstances, these may or may not be compatible with constitutionalism, the rule of law, and/or human rights. Three different kinds have been tried in Britain over the past few decades: indefinite detention without trial (internment), limitations upon freedom of movement and other liberties including house arrest (Control Orders and TPIMs), and restrictions upon travel into, and out of, the UK.

Indefinite detention without trial (internment)

Internment (indefinite detention without trial), a classic type of executive control, is permitted by Article 15 of the ECHR in times of war or public emergencies threatening the life of the nation where the exigencies strictly require it. From 1971 to 1975 it was used in Northern Ireland against some 600 internees and remained on the statute book until 1998. Introduced by the Unionist government as the IRA's campaign increased in intensity, it was targeted almost entirely against suspected republican terrorists. Nationalists, and others, objected to it on the grounds that the involvement of few loyalists made it discriminatory, the data upon which the initial roundup was based were highly unreliable and included many who were not involved in terrorism at all, and that it facilitated the mistreatment of a small sample of internees subjected to various kinds of sensory deprivation as an experiment in how to break

---

72 *Ibid.*

resistance to interrogation. The Strasbourg institutions eventually declared the internment regime, though not the mistreatment of the detainees in the sensory deprivation experiment, compatible with the ECHR.[73] But by this stage, convinced that internment was counterproductive and difficult to defend internationally, the British government had already prorogued the Stormont regime and decided to replace it with the 'Diplock process', to which reference has already been made.

The use of internment was revived post-9/11, albeit in a modified form, by Part IV of the Anti-terrorism, Crime and Security Act 2001.[74] Although the new regime applied, in principle, throughout the UK, in practice it operated only in England and Wales. It was also limited only to foreign terrorist suspects, who could not be prosecuted because the evidence against them did not meet the requisite standard, who did not want to leave the UK, and who could not be deported on account of the risk of torture and other ill-treatment if repatriated to their countries of origin.

The detention process began with the Secretary of State certifying that he/she suspected that a named person was a terrorist and that he/she reasonably believed their presence in the UK posed a threat to national security. The detainee could appeal against this decision to the Special Immigration Appeals Commission (SIAC) staffed by a senior judge, an Immigration Appeal Tribunal member, and a third member generally from a security background. Security-vetted 'special advocates' were appointed to represent the appellant's interests. Both they and their clients were excluded from the proceedings on national security grounds. SIAC was also required to conduct regular reviews of the cases of those detained. Both the Judicial Committee of the House of Lords and the ECtHR held, in the 'Belmarsh case', that the UK was entitled to derogate from the right of detainees to be brought promptly before a judicial authority and to regard the post-9/11 terrorist threat as constituting 'a public emergency threatening the life of the nation'. It was also found that the detention-without-trial regime was discriminatory, since it only applied to foreign nationals, when some British nationals domiciled in the UK also presented a similar threat, and was disproportionate since other less draconian measures could have been applied instead.[75]

Lasting from 2001–5, and by sharp contrast with the scale of its Northern Irish predecessor, 17 detention orders were issued, over half of them in December 2001.[76] By February 2005 two of the subjects had 'voluntarily departed' from the UK, two had certificates against them revoked, one was released on bail by the SIAC and one had been granted bail in principle, subject to discussion of

---

73 *Ireland v United Kingdom* (1979–80) 2 EHRR 25.
74 C. Walker, *Blackstone's Guide to the Anti-Terrorism Legislation* (Oxford University Press, 2002), ch. 8.
75 *A (FC) and Others (FC) (Appellants) v Secretary of State for the Home Department (Respondent)* [2004] UKHL 56; *A v United Kingdom*, ECtHR, judgment of 19 February 2009.
76 Walker, *Anti-Terrorism Legislation 2014*, p. 244.

the conditions. As the Prevention of Terrorism Bill 2005 made its way through Parliament, ten of the remaining detainees were released from detention on bail, and, once new legislation had been passed, made subject to control orders (see following section).[77]

House arrest and other restrictions

In December 2004, following the judgment of the House of Lords in the Belmarsh case, the Prevention of Terrorism Act 2005 replaced the detention-without-trial regime with 'control orders', capable of being imposed by the Secretary of State and applying to UK citizens as well as other nationals. In addition to house arrest, a given regime typically included night-time curfews, the prohibition of, or restriction upon, the possession or use of specified articles particularly computers and phones which facilitate communication, limited access to specified services such as banking facilities, restrictions on movement, association, and place of residence, obligations to comply with searches and checks, and requirements regarding the provision of information to the police. However, a derogation from the ECHR was not required since, in principle, liberty was restricted rather than suspended. In a series of cases the UK courts held that, although control orders did not inherently violate the ECHR, excessive conditions did.[78] Over the six or so years in which control orders were available, there were never more than about a dozen in use at any given time.[79]

However, following the May 2010 general election which led to a Conservative/Liberal Democrat coalition government, control orders were themselves replaced by Terrorism Prevention and Investigation Measures (TPIMs) by an Act of the same name.[80] Like their predecessors, TPIMs are also 'primarily disruptive and ... preventive' executive measures 'within the context of investigation',[81] designed to curtail the activities of individuals suspected of involvement in terrorism where relevant intelligence does not meet the criminal standard of proof. While curfew powers are limited to night-time, the Secretary of State may also restrict the possession or use of electronic devices and regulate their use by others residing with the TPIM subject. The standard of proof was raised from 'reasonable suspicion' for control orders to 'reasonable belief' in the TPIMS Act 2011, and then to 'a balance of probabilities' in the Counter-Terrorism and Security Act 2015. While TPIMs did not initially include a requirement to relocate, this has been reversed by the

---

77 House of Commons Constitutional Affairs Committee, *The Operation of the Special Immigration Appeals Commission (SIAC) and the Use of Special Advocates*, Seventh Report of Session 2004–05, Volume 1 Report, together with formal minutes, HC 323-I, 3 April 2005, para. 30.
78 C. Walker, *Terrorism and the Law* (Oxford University Press, 2011), ch. 7.
79 D. Anderson QC (Independent Reviewer of Terrorism Legislation), *Control Orders in 2011: Final Report of the Independent Reviewer of the Prevention of Terrorism Act 2005*, March 2012, para. 4.5.
80 Walker, *Anti-Terrorism Legislation 2014*, ch. 7.
81 *Hansard*, Public Bill Committee, col. 109 (June 23, 2011), James Brokenshire.

Counter-Terrorism and Border Security Act 2019. However, the person to whom a TPIM applies must be allowed to possess and use a landline telephone, a computer providing fixed line access to the internet, and a mobile phone which cannot access the internet. Restrictions upon association or communication are also limited to specified persons, or those meeting certain requirements, such as living outside the UK. Subject to an allowance of one nominated account with a bank or building society, the Secretary of State can also restrict the use of, or access to, specific financial services.

'Enhanced TPIMs', issued in times of emergency, may include requirements to relocate for a specified period not necessarily confined to 'overnight', not to leave a specified geographical area, plus restrictions or total prohibitions on the possession or use of electronic communications devices, on financial services, and, with certain exceptions, upon association or communication with anyone else or certain specified people. During the life of any given TPIM, the possibility of prosecution also remains open. As a result, a subject's conduct is kept under police review throughout a TPIM term, hitherto but no longer limited to a maximum of two years renewable upon evidence of fresh terrorism-related activity committed during this period. The Secretary of State is also required to keep under review whether any given person should continue to be subject to a TPIM and whether the terms imposed remain necessary and are being met. The obligation for quarterly quantitative ministerial reports to Parliament about control orders is retained for the TPIM regime, as is the requirement that the legislation be renewed after five years. However, annual parliamentary reviews, to which control orders were subject, have been abandoned on the grounds that they had become largely pointless principally on account of their limited use. For example, as of 31 May 2018, only eight were in force.[82]

Travel restrictions

As the Syrian civil war developed from 2011 onwards, many countries in Europe and around the world became increasingly concerned about their own citizens travelling there to fight, or to support those doing so, and also about the risk of 'blow back' if and when they returned home. These worries intensified as ISIS/DAESH conquered large swathes of both Syria and Iraq in 2014 and set up their own 'Caliphate'.[83] From 2014–18, for example, more than 900 individuals of national security concern to the UK, of whom approximately 40 per cent have since returned home and a further 20 per

---

82 HM Government, *Transparency Report 2018: Disruptive and Investigatory Powers*, Cm 9609, July 2018, p. 23.
83 See ch. 2.

cent were killed whilst abroad, joined this particular jihad.[84] On 29 August 2014, the Joint Terrorism Analysis Centre was sufficiently concerned to raise the UK national terrorist threat level from 'substantial' to 'severe'. And on 24 September 2014, UN Security Council Resolution 2178 enjoined member states to combat foreign terrorist fighters and to counter violent extremism.

As already indicated in the previous chapter, in the spring of 2015 the UK Parliament passed the Counter-Terrorism and Security Act (CTSA). As the Explanatory Notes put it, the preceding Bill had four main objectives: to 'disrupt the ability of people to travel abroad to fight such as in Syria and Iraq', to 'control their return to the UK', 'to enhance operational capabilities to monitor and control the actions of those in the UK who pose a threat', and to 'help combat the underlying ideology that supports terrorism'. Part I of the Act is designed to prevent 'foreign terrorist fighters' from travelling abroad, and to manage those with British citizenship seeking to return home.[85]

Different arrangements now exist for outgoing and incoming suspects. As far as the former are concerned, section 1 and Schedule 1 of the CTSA empower the police, at ports or the border, to require production of, and to search for, inspect, seize, and temporarily retain travel documents (ie passports and tickets) where they have reasonable grounds to suspect the person in question intends to leave the UK in connection with terrorism-related activity abroad.[86] The suspect must be informed of the suspicion – typically triggered by prior intelligence or observation at the scene – but not the grounds. For these purposes, travel between Great Britain and Northern Ireland, the land border between Northern Ireland and the Republic of Ireland, and the Channel Tunnel rail link, are all covered, though only if the suspected purpose of such travel is involvement in terrorism outside the UK. While no additional power is provided to detain such suspects, those unwilling to cooperate may be held under Schedule 7 of the Terrorism Act 2000 as discussed in Chapter 4.

In order to retain any travel document, a constable must, as soon as possible, seek authorization from a senior police officer of at least the rank of superintendent.[87] Authority may be granted on the same reasonable grounds that triggered the initial suspicion but, otherwise, the travel document must be returned unless other independent legal action, such as immigration or criminal proceedings, intervene. A further review must be conducted after 72 hours by a police officer of at least the rank of chief superintendent, and the chief constable must also be notified. Where authority is granted, travel documents

---

84 V. Dodd, 'Isis Commanders "Liaised with Plotters Planning to Attack UK in Past Year"', *The Guardian*, 24 December 2016; Speech by the then-Home Secretary, Theresa May, to the Center for Strategic and International Studies, Washington, DC, 16 February 2016, www.gov.uk/government/speeches/home-secretary-international-action-needed-to-tackle-terrorism.

85 J. Blackbourn and C. Walker, 'Interdiction and Indoctrination: The Counter-Terrorism and Security Act 2015', *Modern Law Review*, (2016) 79, 840–70.

86 Ibid., pp. 845–9.

87 Ibid., pp. 846–9.

may be retained for up to 14 days in order to facilitate consideration of cancelling the passport, charging with an offence, or making an executive order such as a TPIM. A police superintendent can apply to a judge for a further extension. If, without regard to the merits of the case, the judge is satisfied that the investigation is being conducted diligently and expeditiously, this can be granted for up to a total of 30 days. The suspect must be given an opportunity to make oral or written representations. But they, and their representative, may be excluded from any part of the hearing if one or more of a number of specified reasons applies. These include the prevention and/or prosecution of acts of terrorism and the protection of national security. Suspects whose travel documents are retained may be provided with welfare support. After 30 days, and in the absence of other independent legal proceedings, the travel documents must be returned. The legislation also provides some limited restrictions against repeated use against the same individual.

These powers are open to criticism on several grounds.[88] First, since other pre-existing measures have already been applied to interdict many would-be outgoing foreign terrorist fighters, the CTSA powers plug a relatively insignificant gap in the law. Second, since retention of travel documents constitutes an interference with, and a potential violation of, the right to respect for private and family life, the courts should be able to intervene much sooner. Indeed, the lack of provision for judicial intervention during the first 14 days is at odds with comparable arrangements under the Anti-Terrorism, Crime and Security Act 2001 which requires the police to seek judicial approval within 48 hours if they wish to retain cash seized at a port for longer. Third, even after 14 days, a court can only review the process not the merits of the decision to retain travel documents. Fourth, such judicial proceedings may be conducted in closed session without a special advocate scheme or a requirement for a minimum degree of disclosure. Finally, while there are no powers to deal with a determined extremist prepared to wait until the 30-day period elapses, the courts have, nevertheless, turned to other legal powers, particularly wardship orders, to stop would-be foreign terrorist fighters under 18 leaving for the Middle East. More rarely, care orders may be used where parents are suspected of grooming their teenage children for this purpose.[89] Conditions imposed may include electronic tagging, removal of passports, all-port alerts, injunctions against removing the children in question from the jurisdiction and requiring them to live at a specified address, monitoring both parents and children by unannounced visits from local authority officials, regular reporting to the police or local authority, and swearing on the Qur'an that the order will be observed.

In order to control the return of British nationals suspected of having been involved in terrorism abroad, the CTSA established a Temporary Exclusion

---

88 Ibid., pp. 847–9.
89 *Tower Hamlets v B* [2015] EWHC 2491 (Fam); [2016] EWHC 1707 (Fam).

Order (TEO) regime.⁹⁰ This is, however, a type of regulated re-entry and residence rather than a revival of the regime which applied from 1974–98 during the Troubles. The latter resulted in 'exclusion orders' being issued by the Home Secretary to a total of some 500 terrorist suspects preventing them from entering mainland Britain or expelling them to Northern Ireland or the Republic of Ireland,⁹¹ arrangements which lapsed in 1998 as the peace process began. They were finally abolished in 2000 as part of the Terrorism Act 2000 reforms.

The CTSA regime authorizes the Secretary of State to impose a TEO provided he/she reasonably suspects that the individual, who has a right of abode in the UK is, or has been, involved in terrorism outside the jurisdiction, reasonably considers that it is necessary to impose a TEO to protect the public in the UK from the risk of terrorism, and reasonably believes the individual was outside the UK when the order was imposed. As with TPIMs, unless revoked sooner, TEOs apply for two years from the date when notice has been served. However, by contrast with TPIMs, subsequent TEOs can be issued without any new evidence being required.

TEOs invalidate any British passport held by the subject and permit the seizure of foreign passports. In any case, as already indicated, the prime purpose of the TEO regime is not exclusion as such but managed return. Unless the Secretary of State previously required the individual concerned to be interviewed and they failed to comply, permits to re-enter the UK under specified conditions, including the timeframe and travel arrangements, must, therefore, be granted upon application. A travel document must also be issued to a British national being deported by a foreign state or when it is deemed expedient to do so when, for example, the life of the person abroad may be in peril or they are at risk of ill treatment.

In considering a request for permission, the court, which may include advisers and may proceed without notice or without allowing the subject to be present, applies judicial review principles, particularly the negative criterion that the decision is not 'obviously flawed'. Provided the right to fair trial under Article 6 ECHR is not violated, closed hearings and the briefing of special advocates are permitted. If the suspect has already returned to the UK, they may also apply for 'statutory judicial review' independent of the 'not obviously flawed' criterion. The Secretary of State may also appeal against the court's decision, but only on a matter of law.

Having received training and indoctrination and expanded their network of terrorist contacts, many of the individuals presenting the greatest danger to the UK remain overseas and are deemed to continue to pose significant challenges for the security and intelligence agencies, and for law enforcement, both at home and abroad. However, having been investigated on their return,

---

90 Blackbourn and Walker, 'Counter-Terrorism and Security Act 2015', pp. 843–56.
91 Prevention of Terrorism Acts 1974–89 ('PTAs').

a significant proportion has been assessed as no longer presenting a risk to national security. In June 2018 the government noted that most of those arriving back in Britain in the previous two years had been women with young children.[92] Since 2015, around 100 children have also been safeguarded by the courts from being taken to Middle Eastern conflict zones.[93] Many others are likely to be suffering from post-traumatic stress, which if not properly addressed, may impact negatively upon their future well-being and behaviour. Some may meet statutory thresholds for social care. Having been born in ISIS/DAESH controlled territory, babies are likely to have received less than adequate health and social care. In order to ensure their needs and risks are appropriately addressed, the Home Office and the Department for Education have been working with local authorities and civil society organizations to ensure support is available to local authorities dealing with returning families. This includes ensuring that responsible adults are involved in care and upbringing, plus providing suitable advocates to act in the children's best interests where necessary.

The relationship between the TEO regime and full-blown TPIMs is, however, unclear. Although TEOs are civil law instruments, not uncommon in the security field, non-compliance invites the imposition of criminal law sanctions. Since the management of returnees does not end at the border, 'TPIM-lite' obligations can be imposed after return, including reporting to and notifying the police about residence, plus attending appointments including for de-radicalization, and discussions about education and/or housing.

It is difficult to deny that controlling the departure and managing the return of those suspected of intending to become, or having been, involved in terrorism overseas, are worthwhile objectives. The TEO regime provides, for example, a proportionate response to those suspected of 'terrorism related activity' such as supporting those who have acted as housewives rather than having engaged in fighting itself. Some may argue that this constitutes 'Islamophobic net-widening'. But disruption to travel is not loss of liberty. Many anguished Muslim parents have also begged the authorities to intervene to stop their offspring becoming cannon fodder in the killing fields of the Middle East.

However, several practical difficulties may stand in the way of effective delivery.[94] First, detection can be complex and challenging. Foreign terrorist fighters have learned that booking a flight home via Turkey risks giving the game away. More elaborate return routes have, therefore, been devised, though not always with success. Second, the main policy objection to TEOs is that they disincentivize return and thereby encourage the adoption of terrorism as a long-term lifestyle. This may encourage those fighting abroad to continue exacerbating foreign conflicts, obtaining further experience in terrorism,

---

92 HM Government, *CONTEST 2018*, para. 172.
93 *Ibid.*, para. 169.
94 Blackbourn and Walker, 'Counter-Terrorism and Security Act 2015'.

becoming further alienated from the UK, increasing their interest in instigating terrorist attacks in Britain from abroad, and posing a greater risk if and when they do finally arrive home. Third, since it may be said to amount to dumping undesirables on other states, the current policy may clash with the international duty to cooperate to address the common threat. Finally, subjecting the decision to issue a TEO to more effective independent judicial review would be welcome, not only for its own sake, but also for the contribution it might make to legitimizing it.

A scheme akin to the loss or theft of a passport, without the language of 'exclusion' or 'permission to return', might, therefore, have better prospects. So, for example, with foreign agencies properly notified, a warrant to return could be issued but without the original passport being confiscated. It is also unclear whether the TEO regime is consistent with international law, a difficulty likely to be further complicated if citizenship is cancelled. For example, effectively preventing return may breach the positive obligations arising from Articles 2, 3, 5, and 8 ECHR. Article 12(2) of the UN International Covenant on Civil and Political Rights also provides that 'Everyone shall be free to leave any country, including his own'. According to paragraph (3), any restrictions must be 'provided by law, … necessary to protect national security, public order (*ordre public*), public health or morals or the rights and freedoms of others, and … (be) … consistent with the other rights recognized in the present Covenant'. Paragraph (4) stipulates that: 'No one shall be arbitrarily deprived of the right to enter his own country'.

Although no legal proof is provided and no hearing or review is offered, exclusion lasts for two years. Nevertheless, according to the UN Human Rights Committee there are few, if any, circumstances in which deprivation of the right to enter one's own country could be reasonable.[95] It has also held that, by stripping a person of nationality or by expelling them to a third country, a State party must not arbitrarily prevent them from returning to their home state. Nor is it clear that the threat posed by those subject to a TEO would amount to an exceptional circumstance.

On the other side of the debate, it can be argued that those who have chosen to become the armed enemies of their home state should be formally regarded as traitors with all the legal and other implications this implies.[96] However, although the offence of treason is no longer subject to the death penalty in the UK and has been largely superseded by other offences its revival against the jihadi threat would be far from unproblematic, not least because of the danger that such a charge might be worn as 'a badge of honour'. Another alternative – designating, subject to valid exceptions, certain parts of the world off-limits to UK citizens – has also been enacted by the Counter-Terrorism and Border Security Act 2019.

---

[95] General Comment 27, Freedom of movement (article 12), 110 para. 21.
[96] 'Treason Charge Idea Considered for UK Jihadists', BBC News, 17 October 2014.

Cancelling British citizenship

Cancelling British citizenship by exercise of the Royal Prerogative is another way in which those deemed a security risk may be prevented from returning to Britain. But, since it is contrary to international law for a state to revoke anyone's citizenship if this would leave them stateless, this can only lawfully apply to those entitled to the citizenship of more than one country. Complications however arise, as in the Shamima Begum case, where it is unclear if another nationality is in fact available. The ECtHR recently unanimously held that stripping a dual national of one of their nationalities, after a prison sentence for a terrorist offence had been served, does not violate Article 8 ECHR, the right to respect for private and family life, home, and correspondence.[97] However, it is not clear if the same result would be reached in the absence of conviction. The power to deprive a dual national of their British citizenship, including for suspected involvement in terrorism, was used 14 times in 2016, 104 times in 2017, and 21 times in 2018.[98]

Conclusion

The *Pursue* agenda, much of which predates the formal enunciation of the 'four Ps', is the most legally complex of CONTEST's components. It is, therefore, not surprising that it has had the most sustained attention from lawyers, judges, and legal commentators with the public debate tending to focus upon secret surveillance, pre-trial detention, and executive controls. The 'securitized Muslim community thesis' is made less stridently in these contexts than in others. But there is no reliable evidence that it is any truer here. The majority of those arrested, charged, prosecuted, convicted, and imprisoned in Britain for terrorism-related offences over the past few years have been young, male, non-white, British Muslims, facts which simply reflect the chief characteristics of the dominant terrorist threat. While there is, nevertheless, scope for fine-tuning in some areas, relevant law and policy already largely comply with constitutionalism, democracy, human rights, and the maintenance of public confidence and community cohesion.

The view taken here is that, notwithstanding definitional difficulties, 'terrorism-related conduct' should be criminalized as it is by UK law, including all the ancillary offences, even though it may be difficult in specific cases to distinguish sharply between innocent, but ill-advised, conduct from that which is genuinely terrorism-related. The simple fact is that the criminal law is inescapably full of such distinctions and the best that can be hoped for in this, as in other contexts, is that offences are defined by legislators and courts with as much precision as possible, that there are adequate and effective defences, and

---

97 *Ghoumid and Others v France*, App. Nos. 52273/16, 52285/16, 52290/16, 52294/16, and 52302/16.
98 J. Hall QC, *The Terrorism Acts in 2018: Report of the Independent Reviewer of Terrorism Legislation on the Operation of the Terrorism Acts 2000 and 2006*, March 2020, para. 1.15.

that the prosecution is genuinely required to prove guilt beyond reasonable doubt in fair trials. Until credible evidence is presented to the contrary, there is no reason to believe this is not true of terrorist offences in Britain.

The key to effective counterterrorism in all liberal democracies lies in the effective gathering and processing of intelligence coupled with the responsible management of the terrorism-related risks it discloses. Constitutionalism, the rule of law, and human rights must of course be respected and community cohesion and public confidence in law and public policy maintained. It is with respect to these dimensions that some of the sharpest public debates about the *Pursue* agenda have arisen. But these would be much better informed if the following were more widely appreciated – provided it is regulated by appropriate institutions, processes, and norms, the gathering of intelligence, including through secret surveillance, is not inherently inconsistent with any legitimate requirement, including human rights.

In an attempt to arrive at an appropriate balance between rights, on the one hand, and crime and security-related intelligence gathering on the other, the UK has had a decades-long history of negotiation with the Strasbourg institutions. The fundamental challenge for both sides has been to arrive at a shared understanding which ensures that relevant law, bureaucracies, and processes are capable of responding to developments in information technology, such as the encryption of messaging and information, while at the same time adequately complying with personal freedoms, particularly privacy. The key to striking an appropriate balance has been found in four core elements: precision-engineered legal instruments which reduce the risk of arbitrary targeting to a minimum; entrusting decisions regarding secret surveillance to senior officers in law enforcement and security agencies; subjecting relevant bureaucratic systems, but not individual decisions, to effective scrutiny by independent commissions and parliament; and enabling aggrieved applicants to bring complaints about alleged rights violations to a specialist tribunal.

Regular independent review has also ensured that counterterrorist powers of arrest and detention are now broadly compliant with the ECHR. There may be scope for some further fine-tuning concerning, for example, limiting arrest to 48 hours in the initial seven-day period before judicial approval, and then for no more than 14 days. There is also a case for a presumption that detainees will be present at judicial approval hearings, and if not, that special advocates are appointed. But there are no credible grounds for believing that arrest and detention facilitate 'the securitization of the Muslim community' or are in systematic violation of human rights. As in other contexts, it is simply a consequence of the inescapable logic of demography that, if the principal terrorist threat facing Britain is from jihadis, no non-Muslim will be legitimately or lawfully suspected of, or prosecuted for, involvement in this kind of terrorism. The position will, of course, be quite different with respect to other types of terrorism which currently have a much lower profile.

With the Diplock courts mothballed, and guidelines for prosecutors and judges now provided, there are no significant problems with counterterrorist prosecutions and trials either. A case can, however, be made for the admissibility of intercept evidence at trial, that more resources should be devoted to the Desistance and Disengagement Programme, and that participating in it to a satisfactory degree should be a compulsory requirement for all terrorist releases on licence.

Probably the greatest public controversy relating to *Pursue*, also difficult to disentangle from the other 'three Ps', concerns non-judicial executive measures. Internment is off the agenda for the foreseeable future, with its return contingent, at the very least, upon a significant deterioration in the security situation. It is also clear that the courts will not regard TPIMs as violations of human rights provided the terms are not excessive. Current restrictions upon travel out of the UK are also difficult to contest in principle. However, managed return presents some unresolved challenges, particularly regarding the potential prosecution of returnees and the conditions under which British citizens with dual nationality are, and should be, deprived of their UK citizenship where there are good grounds for suspecting that they have participated in terrorism abroad.

7 Threats, responses, and challenges

Introduction

This chapter seeks to summarize the core conclusions of the preceding parts of this study, to weave them into a coherent whole, and to identify possible and desirable future pathways for countering domestic terrorism in Britain. It should be acknowledged, at the outset, however, that although the distinction between threats, on the one hand, and responses and challenges, on the other, is relatively clear, the difference between responses and challenges is less so.

Threats

The UK faces a serious, though not an existential, threat from three principal types of domestic terrorism. Though deadly, the risks presented by dissident Irish republicanism, both in Northern Ireland and in mainland Britain, are currently a pale reflection of those posed by its predecessors at the height of the Troubles. The problem of far-right terrorism has been growing as a result of both 9/11 and the world-wide rise of right-wing populism. But there can be no doubt that the jihadi threat is currently by far the most significant. Its increased global profile since the end of the 20th century is inextricably linked to the slow-burn modern political crisis of Islam. Gaining momentum since the 18th century, this has deepened in reaction to the decline, collapse, and dismemberment of the Ottoman empire, and subsequent events. However, although jihadi terrorism, both in Britain and elsewhere, is unlikely to involve non-Muslims, its relationship with the Islamic faith is not straightforward. For a start, its goals and activities appeal to and motivate only a tiny fragment of the global Ummah and are also greatly complicated, and often compromised, by complex tribal, sectarian, national, and other conflicts, including competition between Saudi Arabia and Iran for hegemony in the Middle East and further afield. These have pitted jihadis against each other as much, if not more, than the common cause has united them, and Muslims in general, against everyone else.

The threat from jihadi terrorism in Britain is, therefore, essentially a local manifestation of a global problem galvanized and focused rather than having been caused by specific national social, political, and religious factors. Although a sense of alienation, grievance, and injustice is common to all jihadis at home and abroad, Islamist terrorism in Britain cannot be adequately explained simply in terms of a reaction by Muslims to domestic material disadvantage, racism, and/or anti-Muslim prejudice, real though these may be for many. In other words, the deeper and wider social context has, at most, provided the environment for the cultivation of the threat rather than having given rise to it.

And while the UK's long, continuing, and controversial involvement in 'Muslim lands' has given Islamism a powerful, though distorted, anti-British focus, this cannot credibly be regarded as having caused domestic British jihadi terrorism either. For a start, the UK's foreign policy is much too complex and multi-dimensional, even with respect to Muslim-majority states, to be credibly described as anti-Muslim. Nor can jihadi terrorism at home and abroad be plausibly regarded as 'anti-imperialist' or 'anti-colonialist'. It is rather 'alt-imperialist' in the sense that it seeks to replace western influence and involvement in the Middle East, the core of the Muslim world, with a revived Islamic empire, and a particularly brutal one at that.

Responses

While the 'four Ps' of the UK's CONTEST strategy may be more memorable than other less alliterative alternatives, arguably, they do not clearly distinguish functions or objectives as clearly as they might. *Prepare* is, for example, the only one with no preventive element. And, although they were not so formally distinguished by Troubles-related counterterrorist law and policy, the core elements were, nevertheless, covered in some shape or form. Nor is it always entirely clear to which stream a particular policy or legal regime, such as stop and search, belongs. However, one of the key differences between the Troubles and contemporary contexts concerns the decisive shift in official thinking from attempting to 'hold the ring' until a political settlement is found, to managing contemporary risks in order to maximize public resilience. This has required a correspondingly enhanced emphasis upon preparation, protection, and prevention, coupled with familiar criminal justice responses involving criminalization and punishment, plus a suite of executive measures.

Building resilience by preparing, protecting, and preventing

The key ingredient in effective preparation, protection, and prevention lies in the gathering of intelligence and acting upon it responsibly, legally, and effectively. While relevant technology has become vastly more sophisticated over the past 50 years or so, the sources – places, people, their communications, and their belongings – remain largely the same. Provided it is effectively regulated by appropriate institutions, processes, and norms, the gathering of intelligence, including by secret surveillance, can be justified in a state and society committed to democracy, human rights, the rule of law, and cosmopolitan community cohesion. The fundamental challenge is to enable relevant law, bureaucracies, and processes to respond effectively to developments in information technology, particularly the encryption of messaging and information, while at the same time requiring them to comply adequately with personal freedoms, particularly privacy. Four core elements are required: precision-engineered legal instruments which reduce the risk of arbitrary targeting to a minimum; entrusting relevant decisions with implications for human rights to senior officers in law enforcement and security agencies; subjecting relevant bureaucratic systems, though not individual decisions, to effective scrutiny by independent commissions and Parliament; and enabling aggrieved applicants to bring complaints about alleged rights violations to a specialist tribunal.

Compliance with these criteria enables official policies, for example, universal compulsory baggage checks at airports, to be legitimized even though they may apply to, and therefore 'securitize', society at large, or at least significant sections of it such as the air travelling public. But they will also inescapably impact more upon those individuals, locations, and groups from which specific risks credibly derive, than they do upon others. Seeking to prevent dissident Irish republican, jihadi, and far-right terrorism in the UK will, therefore, involve focusing security attention upon those communities, associations, and networks from which, according to reliable intelligence, each of these types of terrorism originates: respectively nationalist/republican ones, mostly in Northern Ireland; predominantly non-white Muslim ones, mostly in Britain; and non-Muslim, white ones mostly in Britain. But, providing this is proportionate to risk, it will fall far short of systematically officially 'securitizing, criminalizing, stigmatizing, or victimizing' the 'Irish', 'Muslims', or 'non-Muslim, non-Irish British whites' in Britain as a whole.

The *Prepare* and *Protect* streams of CONTEST provide not only valid, but essential, elements in countering domestic terrorism of all kinds in Britain. They have, however, been developed without organizational structures comparable to those provided for *Prevent* and *Pursue*. Success in *Protect* is officially conceived in terms of identifying vulnerabilities to terrorist attack, reducing these to an acceptable level, effectively sharing official priorities with the private sector and the international community, where possible acting together to address them, and ensuring the disruptive effects and costs of protective security are proportionate to risk. Nevertheless, how these elements are calibrated and who is responsible for auditing them, remain unclear. The *Protect* stream also suffers from further difficulties. Although relationships have been maintained between relevant corporate sectors and central government, levels of engagement with localities are poor. Local and national accountability are also generally weak. And while there have been improvements in recent years, the activities of some agencies have been criticized for not being sufficiently transparent. Parliament has also been less than attentive in maintaining oversight, and the Independent Reviewer of Terrorism Legislation has no jurisdiction over much of the *Protect* agenda. As a result, the setting of priorities concerning what is protected, and the devotion of public resources to them, remains obscure.

General prevention in Troubles-related counterterrorism was focused primarily upon the deterrent effect of criminalization and punishment. But suicide bombing has undermined this in the post-9/11 era. More concerted policies of 'counter-radicalization' and 'de-radicalization' have, therefore, been required. Underscoring that countering terrorism is a responsibility shared by state and society, the *Prevent* programme has an indispensable role to play. It is not inherently incompatible with democracy, human rights, or the rule of law, and there is no credible evidence that it has been systematically implemented in such a manner either. While the contribution it may make to counterterrorism is difficult, if not impossible, accurately to measure, there is no evidence that it is having a significantly counterproductive effect. Demands for it to be scrapped are based, at best, on myth, misinformation, misconception, misrepresentation, and muddled thinking. There is also a deafening silence from the anti-*Prevent* movement about how jihadi terrorism could and should be prevented in a manner which would avoid the charge that the 'Muslim community' has been 'unfairly securitized', how right-wing terrorism could and should be prevented without a similar complaint arising about its effect upon non-Muslim whites, and why de-radicalization initiatives may be appropriate in the custodial context but not otherwise.

Nevertheless, *Prevent* would benefit from the disclosure of much more information about how the strategy operates in practice, ideally provided by independent and scientifically credible studies. Several modifications would also be welcome including, for example, greater transparency about operating criteria (particularly the obscure but increasingly significant 'mixed, unclear or unstable ideology' category), performance indicators, and outcomes. There is also a strong case for enhanced legal clarity and accountability, and either the appointment of a regular specific independent reviewer, or the expansion of the mandate of the current Independent Reviewer of Terrorism Legislation to include *Prevent*.

While it is appropriate for liberal democracies to outlaw those religious and secular ideologies which promote violence and hatred, the same is not so obviously true of official attempts to counter, and to encourage others to counter, 'non-violent extremism'. Allied to the huge problem of defining what this term means, the right to freedom of expression – integral to pluralism, tolerance, and broadmindedness – includes the right to express 'extreme' non-violent opinions even if they offend, shock, and disturb. The more the *Prevent* programme is formally structured and clarified, arguably the less scope there is for an official campaign against non-violent extremism. By the same token, the greater the official commitment to countering extremism, the less scope there may be for *Prevent*. A major challenge on the counterterrorist preventive front should, therefore, involve demarcating more clearly between these two, otherwise legitimate, programmes than is currently the case.

Punishment and rehabilitation

Domestic terrorism in liberal democracy involves conduct and activities which invite responses from the criminal justice system. These include the framing of specific terrorist offences, the arrest and detention of suspects, the charging, prosecution, and trial of defendants, and the sentencing of those found guilty. However, a particular challenge in this context concerns how an appropriate balance should be struck between criminalization and punishment, on the one hand, and rehabilitation on the other. Notwithstanding definitional difficulties, it is unconvincing to argue that 'terrorism-related conduct', in its varied forms, should not be criminalized in UK law. This includes all current ancillary offences even though it may be difficult, in specific cases, to distinguish between innocent but ill-advised conduct from that which is genuinely terrorism-related. The simple fact is that the criminal law is inescapably full of such distinctions. The best that can be hoped for in any relevant context is that offences are defined by legislators and courts with as much precision as possible, that there are adequate and effective defences, and that the prosecution is genuinely required to prove guilt beyond reasonable doubt in fair trials. There is no reason to believe this is, or should be, less true of terrorist than other offences.

Broadly speaking counterterrorist powers of arrest and detention are now also as compliant with the ECHR as it is reasonable to expect them to be. While there may be scope for some fine-tuning, there are no grounds for believing that they have such systematic defects that they have, for example, facilitated the 'securitization' of any minority community. If the principal terrorist threats facing Britain come from certain specific communities, associations, or networks, as they undeniably do, this is likely to be reflected throughout criminal justice statistics as a matter of demographics rather than official prejudice. A case can be made for the admissibility of intercept evidence in criminal (particularly terrorism) trials. The Desistance and Disengagement Programme (DDP) could also be better resourced and satisfactory participation in the DDP could, and arguably should, be a compulsory element in all terrorist releases from prison on licence. Otherwise there are no significant systemic problems with counterterrorist prosecutions, trials, or punishment.

Probably the greatest public controversy relating to the *Pursue* agenda, also difficult to disentangle from the other 'three Ps', concerns the rights-compliance of non-judicial counterterrorist executive measures. With internment now off the agenda for the foreseeable future, and its return contingent at the very least upon a significant deterioration in the security situation, the courts have signalled that they will not regard TPIMs as violations of human rights provided the specific terms are not excessive. Current restrictions upon travel out of the UK can also be justified, as can the managed return of those reasonably suspected of having participated in terrorism abroad. However, the latter presents some unresolved issues, particularly regarding potential prosecution and the conditions under which British citizens with dual nationality are, and should be, deprived of their UK citizenship.

Challenges

The two greatest generic challenges facing counterterrorism in the UK are ensuring that the implementation of relevant law and policy is transparent, accountable, complies with legality and rights, and that it is properly understood and that its social impact is effectively managed.

Accountability, legality, and human rights

As Chapter 1 indicated, over the past few decades the delivery of public policy of all kinds has been subject to more effective democratic accountability than before. As a result, awareness of the importance of the rule of law and respect for human rights in the design and delivery of counterterrorist measures has increased in state and society. The courts have, in particular, become pivotal in determining what is and is not permissible on the counterterrorist front. While international human rights law, especially the ECHR, provide frameworks within which the issues can be structured and publicly defensible choices made, there is, however, no perfect or objectively valid equilibrium between human rights and counterterrorist measures.

In counterterrorist, and all other, contexts, the question of what counts as legitimate restriction and impermissible violation of human rights is legally structured in the first instance by the distinction between 'non-derogable' and 'derogable' rights. The former can never be lawfully suspended by way of 'derogation' (an official notice of suspension from a specific international human rights regime on the part of a given state party), nor are most subject to any express restriction for any reason, including counterterrorism. However, these rights comprise a very limited category. For example, under the ECHR, only the following are included – not being: tortured, inhumanly or degradingly treated or punished; held in slavery or servitude; subject to the retrospective criminalization of conduct, or to a heavier sentence than that prescribed at the time; killed, except as a result of lawful execution, lawful act of war, or where no more force than absolutely necessary was used to defend someone from unlawful violence, to effect a lawful arrest or to prevent the escape of a person lawfully detained, or lawfully to quell a riot or insurrection.

All other human rights can be restricted or limited in one of two ways. Because they are 'derogable' they can be suspended across the board providing this is strictly necessary in a war or public emergency threatening the life of the nation. But liberal democracies rarely find this necessary for counterterrorist purposes. This is because derogable rights are also typically subject to express exceptions – including, for example, the interests of national security and the prevention of disorder or crime – which can be successfully invoked in various contexts, including counterterrorism, providing various tests, such as compliance with the rule of law, democratic necessity, and proportionality, are observed. Where this is the case, the rights in question are said to have been 'restricted', 'limited', or 'interfered with', without necessarily having been 'violated' or 'breached'. For example, secret surveillance by the state constitutes an interference with, or a restriction upon, the right to respect for private and family life, home, and correspondence as provided by Article 8 ECHR. But it can, nevertheless, be justified if the principle of legality is satisfied and it is necessary and proportionate in a democratic society for the purpose of national security, to protect the rights and freedoms of others, and/or in pursuit of certain other specified public interests. In the final analysis it is down to the courts to decide whether, if contested, any given restriction upon, or the formal suspension of, any right by way of derogation is excessive and therefore amounts to a violation.

Several other subtle, but important, distinctions in addition to that between 'interference' and 'violation' often get lost in debates about whether or not a given feature of counterterrorist law and policy is, or is not, compatible with human rights. One is between 'formal' and 'substantive' violations, the latter of which may also lie on a spectrum between 'very serious' and 'relatively trivial'. Prima facie, any use of torture will, for example, constitute an extremely serious formal and substantive violation of the right not to be tortured. By contrast, the unlawful eavesdropping on email correspondence by the security services, which is only discovered by chance and which causes no other loss or harm, is a much less serious formal violation of the right to privacy. This does not mean that it should be officially ignored. But, since the victim will have experienced no loss or suffering, disciplining the officials and the agency concerned provides the primary justification for condemnation and sanctioning.

For two main reasons the courts have not been particularly closely involved in the management of *Prepare* or *Protect*. First, the tension between liberty and security is arguably less acute here than with respect to *Pursue*. Second, initiatives in these largely technical-bureaucratic domains tend to impact less visibly on potentially litigious individuals than upon corporate constituencies which are likely either to have been consulted by government in advance or, if not, to be largely unconcerned about it as long as their material interests are not adversely affected. Most of the relevant infrastructure is owned by the private sector. As a result, the willingness to share commercially sensitive information becomes crucial, as does the effectiveness of sectoral regulators. However, although the corporate sector shares an interest with government in effectively combatting terrorism, it tends to privilege accountability to shareholders over accountability to customers which, in turn, affects transparency and modes of cooperation with the state.

The most rights-contentious element of *Protect* concerns the exercise, without subject-specific reasonable suspicion, of stop and search street and port powers. However, the view that the relevant provisions were, and are, inherently Islamophobic, or have been and continue to be operated in a systematically Islamophobic manner, is unsustainable because there is, as yet, no reliable evidence that this was or is the case. The same cannot so readily be said about alleged racial bias. But it should be noted that, in an attempt to eliminate possible abuses of this kind, government and Parliament have tightened relevant provisions. Provided they operate within a framework governed by intelligence assessments, they are exercised respectfully within strict time limits and not in a repetitive manner against the same subjects without very good reason, it is difficult to deny that random powers to stop and search, without subject-specific reasonable suspicion, are necessary and legitimate to tackle jihadi and other forms of terrorism in Britain. Given the ethnic profile of those likely to be involved in the former, it is also statistically inevitable that such provisions will impact more upon non-whites than whites. But of itself this does not make them inherently racist, or systematically racist in application. In any case, as a result of recent legislative amendment, it is difficult to see how the balance could be struck more appropriately without unacceptably detrimental consequences for one side of this delicate balance or the other.

Of the 'four Ps', the *Pursue* agenda is also the most legally complex. It is, therefore, not surprising that it has received the most sustained attention from lawyers, judges, and legal commentators. The wider public debate has tended to focus upon arrest, pre-trial detention, and executive controls rather upon prosecution, trial, and punishment. But there is no reliable evidence that the relevant law is excessively permissive or that it has contributed to the construction of a 'securitized Muslim community'.

State and society

Nobody could seriously doubt that, in any liberal democracy, effectively addressing the challenge of terrorism requires an active state-society partnership with appropriate responsibilities negotiated in an atmosphere of mutual trust and compromise. An essential ingredient is effective, 'distortion-free', communication. But this is difficult to achieve for the following principal reasons. Although the scale of the threat is often exaggerated, acts of terrorism, and terrorist campaigns in particular, dramatically and visibly rupture the safety normally expected in public spaces and in public life. Nevertheless, although both in Britain and worldwide, terrorism kills and injures significantly fewer than a host of other dangers, including accidents on the roads and in the home, it poses a considerable threat to public institutions, systems, and processes.

However, when a serious terrorist incident occurs, governments come under pressure from the media and others to be seen to respond, typically by passing legislation which inevitably alters the delicate balance between security and liberty in favour of the former. But, as already indicated, providing certain principles, particularly proportionality, are observed, this is not inconsistent with commitments to democracy, the rule of law, and human rights. Since the Human Rights Act 1998, draft legislation in the UK has been subject to multiple human rights audits in Whitehall and Parliament, and by NGOs. Needless to say, the version which eventually appears on the statute book will also depend upon the balance of power between governing and opposition parties in Parliament. It is, therefore, very unlikely to please everyone.

Particularly controversial draft legislation may stimulate demands for amendment which may survive as campaigns for repeal once the final version has been passed. Some contributions to relevant debates are responsible, measured, and carefully reasoned, while others are not. And this is where the challenge to distortion-free communication, mutual trust, and cooperation between state and society arises. Controversial legislation is vulnerable to caricature and misrepresentation, particularly by those who already believe that 'the state', or 'the system', is 'racist', 'Islamophobic', or irredeemably hostile to equality, fairness, and justice more generally. These then echo round the siloes and echo-chambers of affiliates and fellow travellers and are repeated, including on social media, by many who never bother to question the accuracy of the misinformation they have so uncritically imbibed. The campaign against *Prevent* is a classic case in point. It is doubtful, for example, if any, of the long list of academics and others who signed the denunciatory letters to the press in 2015 and 2016, when the *Prevent* duty was passed, had taken the trouble to read the legislation itself or the hundreds of pages of supporting official documents describing how it works and its limits.

As already indicated, it is, of course, impossible to 'please all of the people all of the time'. Nevertheless, the principal challenge is to ensure that all perspectives, apart from those involving hate speech and the encouragement of terrorism, are included in open and respectful dialogue and that a critical mass does not distort and dominate the debate with unchallenged mythologizing. Optimally, criticism of any allegedly flawed, unjust, unfair, or oppressive law or policy should be accompanied, either by an explanation of why no law or policy of the kind is required, or by clearly articulated alternatives. This is conspicuously absent from the radical critiques of CONTEST, especially *Prevent*.

It is also appropriate for a liberal democracy to outlaw those ideologies (religious and secular) which promote violence and hatred. But the same is not so obviously true of official attempts to counter, and to encourage others to counter, non-violent extremism. To begin with there are huge problems in defining what 'non-violent extremism' means. The right to freedom of expression – integral to pluralism, tolerance, and broadmindedness – also includes the right to express 'extreme' non-violent opinions even if they offend, shock, and disturb. Arguably, instead of distinguishing between 'British values' and 'extremism', as counterterrorist and counterextremism policy currently do, a distinction should instead be drawn between 'humane' and 'inhumane', or between 'life-affirming' and 'life-denying' ideologies, the latter of which can be violent or non-violent. In a democratic society committed to human rights, the rule of law, and pluralism, it is perfectly legitimate to criticize laws and policies for allegedly falling short of these values. But it is difficult to imagine any genuinely humane or life-affirming ideology which contests, or seeks to undermine, these values themselves.

Unlike conflict/securitization approaches, the reflexive alternatives discussed in Chapter 1 recognize that a particularly vital contribution to counterterrorism can, and must, be made by Muslims in Britain themselves. This is not because they are collectively 'to blame' for jihadi terrorism, but because they are much better placed than anyone else to contest and to resist the distortion and debasement of their faith by jihadis. This implies that, in seeking to counter all forms of domestic terrorism, the principal contribution of society and the state should be to support and encourage those interpretations of all faiths and ideologies which are life-affirming, tolerant, and non-violent, and to discourage those which are not. Inter-communal and inter-faith dialogue are essential. The broad features of the Northern Irish model of reconciliation may, in principle, be applicable to other conflicts elsewhere in the world. But the fact that it arose, and continues to thrive, in a context where the protagonists share much in common suggests that greater challenges may arise in applying it where these conditions do not obtain. How intercommunal and interfaith dialogue should be delivered and promoted with respect to Muslim and non-Muslim communities in Britain is a matter for further, inclusive debate.

Conclusion

Domestic British counterterrorist law and policy have exhibited complex continuities and discontinuities over the past few decades with multidimensional and fluid effects across many relevant landscapes. There is no prospect of either negotiated political or definitive security solutions to any of the principal current domestic terrorist threats at the national level. The only credible goals are, therefore, for state and society to maintain public resilience, to address all forms of injustice, discrimination, and prejudice together, and to frame counterterrorist law and policy in a spirit of mutual trust and shared responsibility. This has several implications for both state and society.

For the state it should first involve greater public recognition of the fact that, while terrorism threatens life, limb, public institutions, and processes, our 'way of life' is not currently endangered. The state's principal responsibilities are, instead, to manage two competing sets of risk – on the one hand, those posed by the need to ensure that relevant law and policy are as efficacious and efficient as possible in protecting society, preventing terrorism, and dealing with those engaged in it. On the other hand, it is also vital to respect human rights, democracy, the rule of law, and the legitimate interests and needs of liberal cosmopolitan society in order, amongst other things, to avoid alienating minority communities whose active support is vital. Public bodies must also ensure that their own activities are as transparent and accountable, and that communication with society is as effective and distortion-free, as possible.

Second, in order to discourage Islamophobia, and to de-couple Islamic extremism from peaceful mainstream Islam to which the vast majority of Muslims in Britain subscribe, a much greater official effort needs to be made to explain publicly the differences between the latter and two other interpretations of the faith which are highly marginal both in this country and across the globe: Islamism (the aspiration that all states should be governed by Islam) which only the most deluded could possibly think has any prospect in contemporary Britain, and jihadi terrorism (engaging in violent conflict with state and society in an attempt to impose political and cultural Islamization) to which even fewer in Britain are committed. More energy also needs to be expended in addressing and minimizing the sense of official victimization on the part of some, or even many, Muslims, whether or not this corresponds with the 'objective' reality. Third, there must be greater public recognition of the valuable contribution Muslims make to society and public life in Britain, not least, to counterterrorism itself.

As for society at large, it is vital that critics of any aspect of counterterrorist law and policy should refrain from denouncing it as 'Islamophobic', 'racist', or a violation of human rights until they can provide reliable evidence that it has any or all of these characteristics. If such perspectives are to be taken seriously, viable alternatives with greater legitimacy must also be identified. The failure of the Labour Party to win the 2019 general election has also made it highly unlikely that any aspect of CONTEST, especially *Prevent*, will be abandoned in the foreseeable future. And even if Labour were to win the next general election, it is inconceivable that its current leader, former DPP, Sir Keir Starmer, would be as hostile to *Prevent*, or to any of the core features of CONTEST, as the rejectionist critics. The current official and unofficial reviews of *Prevent* might prompt some tinkering at the margins of the programme. But it, and the entire edifice of counterterrorist law and policy, are likely to remain largely intact for the foreseeable future. And so they should.

Finally, the principal relevant social responsibilities we all share include refraining from participating in, supporting, encouraging, advocating, or celebrating terrorism, contributing to maintaining cosmopolitan community cohesion, and engaging constructively, if critically, with relevant law and policy, particularly on the preventive front. There is plenty of room for debate about which responsibilities should be framed as legal obligations as well as with specifics and consequences. But there is no place in the mature debate for sterile denunciation and condemnation, which typically rest upon prejudice and myth, much less for the kind of boycott and 'resistance' some advocate. Those who call for the latter, and who denounce as 'government stooges' those Muslims who willingly cooperate with official counterterrorism, should be robustly challenged. The focus for all serious contributions should instead be upon the more subtle question of whether the blurred line between legitimate and illegitimate official responses has been crossed, a matter upon which reasonable people equally committed to the same goals and core humane and democratic values may reasonably disagree. It has been the intention of this study to contribute positively to such debates. It is up to others to determine whether or not this has been achieved.

Appendix A
Fatal terrorist incidents in the UK, 2005–20[1]

Date	Location	Type of attack	Casualties	Type of terrorism
7 July 2005	London	Suicide bombings	56 killed (including bombers), 700+ injured	UKJ
30 June 2007	Glasgow	Attempted suicide bomber	1 bomber died from injuries, 5 injured	UKJ
7 March 2009	Massereene	Shooting	2 soldiers killed, 2 others injured	IR/G
9 March 2009	Craigavon	Shooting	1 police officer killed	IR/G
28 May 2010	Belfast	Shooting	1 killed	UL/G
2 April 2011	Omagh	Bomb	1 police officer killed	IR/G
1 November 2012	Craigavon	Shooting	1 prison officer killed	IR/G
29 April 2013	Birmingham	Stabbing/bombing	1 killed	XRW
22 May 2013	London	Stabbing	1 killed/decapitation	UKJ
4 March 2016	Belfast	Bomb	1 prison officer killed	IR/G
16 June 2016	Birstall	Stabbing	1 killed	XRW
22 March 2017	Westminster	Vehicle & knife	6 killed (including attacker), 40+ injured	UKJ
22 May 2017	Manchester	Suicide bombing	23 killed (including attacker), 130+ injured	UKJ
3 June 2017	London Bridge	Vehicle & knife	11 killed (including 3 attackers), 40+ injured	UKJ
19 June 2017	Finsbury Park London	Vehicle	1 killed, 11 injured	XRW
4 March 2018	Salisbury	Poisoning (Novichok nerve agent)	1 killed, 3 injured	Russian officials
4 December 2018	Belfast	Shooting	1 killed	IR/G
29 November 2019	London	Stabbing	2 killed, 3 wounded	UKJ
20 June 2020	Reading	Stabbing	3 killed, 3 wounded	UKJ

Total killed: 115 (UK-wide)
107 (mainland Britain)

Appendix A

Annual average fatalities (15 years, July 2005 to July 2020)

    7.7 (UK-wide)
    7.1 (mainland Britain)

UKJ = UK jihadi: 103 (96% of fatalities in mainland Britain, 90% in UK)
IR/G = Irish republican/gangster: 7
UL/G = Ulster loyalist/gangster: 1
XRW = Extreme right wing (Britain): 3
Russian officials: 1

Note

1 Does not include use of firearms and explosives in riots.

Appendix B
Chronology of key events, 1997–2020

1 May 1997	'New' Labour wins UK general election with biggest Commons majority ever (179 seats) beginning 13 years of Labour government.
23 February 1998	*Al-Quds al-Arabi*, an Arabic newspaper published in London, prints the text of a *Declaration of the World Islamic Front for Jihad against the Jews and the Crusaders*, signed by Osama bin Laden and the leaders of four other militant groups, which becomes the iconic testament of jihadi terrorist grievances and ideology.
10 April 1998	Good Friday/Belfast Agreement heralds end to the 30-year armed conflict ('the Troubles') in Northern Ireland laying foundations for power-sharing devolved government.
15 August 1998	Main Street in Omagh, Co. Tyrone, Northern Ireland, devastated by bombs planted by dissident republican terrorist group the Real IRA. Twenty-nine people (including a woman pregnant with twins) are killed and some 220 injured, making it the deadliest single incident of the Troubles.
9 November 1998	UK Human Rights Act 1998 passed, coming fully into force on 2 October 2000. Amongst other things, the Act requires draft legislation to be screened for compliance with the European Convention on Human Rights (ECHR) and creates a statutory obligation upon public authorities to act in accordance with the ECHR.
20 July 2000	Terrorism Act 2000 – containing provisions relating to, amongst other things, offences, property and funds, investigations, powers of arrest, entry, search, questioning, seizure and detention, proscribed organizations, port and border controls – consolidates

	piecemeal counterterrorist legislation passed during the Troubles.
28 July 2000	Regulation of Investigatory Powers Act 2000 passed. Empowers certain public bodies, for the purpose of counterterrorism and the policing of other types of crime, to carry out surveillance and investigation, including the interception of communications, to conduct mass surveillance of communications in transit, to monitor internet activities, and to demand from internet service providers secret access to a customer's communications and cooperation in conducting surveillance. Establishes an Investigatory Powers Tribunal, the Security Service Tribunal, and the Intelligence Services Tribunal. The Investigatory Powers Tribunal hears complaints about any conduct or alleged infringement of human rights by, or on behalf of, MI5, SIS, and GCHQ, and provides opportunities for redress to anyone concerned that they may have been a victim of unlawful use of covert investigative techniques by a public authority.
9 September 2001	'9/11'. Four aircraft, hijacked by 19 Al Qaeda terrorists, are deliberately crashed into the twin towers of World Trade Centre, New York, and the Pentagon, Washington, DC. A fifth is brought down by its passengers to avert greater loss of life. 2,996 people are killed (including hijackers), 25,000 are injured, and at least $10 billion of damage to infrastructure and property is caused.
16/20 September 2001	US President, George W Bush, inaugurates 'War on Terrorism' (16 September) and 'War on Terror' (20 September), signalling a military and security response to 9/11, Al Qaeda, and its allies, including the Taliban regime in Afghanistan which facilitated the 9/11 attacks. Neither term was endorsed by the Pentagon, the US military/security establishment, the UK, or other states.
28 September 2001	Unanimous UN Security Council Resolution 1373 calls upon states to prevent and suppress the financing of terrorism.
7 October 2001	United States leads a UN-sponsored international invasion of Afghanistan, including the UK, to depose the Taliban government.
14 December 2001	Anti-terrorism Crime and Security Act 2001 passed. Includes, amongst other things, provisions for indefinite detention without trial, deportation of foreign

	nationals suspected of terrorism, and freezing of suspected terrorist funds. Adds 'religiously aggravated' to 'racially aggravated' offences.
Early 2003	Inauguration of UK's official counterterrorist framework, CONTEST, centred around the 'four Ps' – *Protect, Prepare, Prevent,* and *Pursue.*
20 March 2003	US coalition (including UK) invades Iraq, without UN authorization, to dismantle presumed weapons of mass destruction (which are never found) as the peace settlement imposed at the end of the Gulf War in 1991 fragments.
18 November 2004	Civil Contingencies Act 2004 repeals the Emergency Powers Act 1920 and the Emergency Powers Act (Northern Ireland) 1926 and imposes a number of duties on specified bodies regarding, amongst other things, assessing the risk of emergencies and maintaining plans for responding to them.
16 December 2004	In *A v Secretary of State for the Home Department* the Judicial Committee of the House of Lords (since renamed the Supreme Court of the UK) holds that the power to detain foreign nationals indefinitely without trial, provided by the Anti-terrorism Crime and Security Act 2001, is discriminatory and disproportionate and contravenes the ECHR.
11 March 2005	Prevention of Terrorism Act 2005 passed. Detention-without-trial regime replaced with 'control orders' capable of being imposed by the Secretary of State upon both UK citizens and nationals of other countries.
16 May 2005	Council of Europe proclaims Convention on the Prevention of Terrorism, and Council of Europe Convention on Laundering, Search, Seizure and Confiscation of the Proceeds from Crime and on the Financing of Terrorism.
7 July 2005	'7/7': jihadi suicide terrorist bomb attacks on London transport system kill 52 and injure 700.
21 July 2005	Four attempted bomb attacks by Islamist extremists disrupt part of London's public transport system. Devices fail to explode but one minor injury is caused by detonator. A fifth bomber dumps his without attempting to set it off.
22 July 2005	Jean Charles de Menezes, a Brazilian living in London, is shot dead by armed police officers at Stockwell station on the London Underground, having been wrongly identified as one of the fugitives involved in the previous day's failed attempted bombings.

6 October 2005	Home Office, *Preventing Extremism Together: Places of Worship* report published.
8 March 2006	Judicial Committee of the House of Lords (since renamed the Supreme Court of the UK) unanimously decides that, provided stops and searches in the street are not based on racial profiling alone, the 'random' power provided by section 44 Terrorism Act 2000 complies with ECHR.
30 March 2006	Terrorism Act 2006 passed. Drafted in the aftermath of 7/7, it extends powers of proscription, detention for questioning (up to a total of 28 days), and search and seizure, and creates new offences, including those relating to preparation, encouragement, attending training, dissemination of publications, possession of items, etc., relating to terrorism.
July 2006	CONTEST strategy publicly launched.
24 May 2007	Justice and Security (Northern Ireland) Act 2007 passed. Among other things it provides special arrangements to protect jurors in all trials by ensuring greater anonymity and fuller checks in their selection, while preserving the possibility of non-jury trial in highly exceptional circumstances.
9 July 2007	Muktar Said Ibrahim (29), Yasin Hassan Omar (26), Ramzi Mohammed (25), and Hussain Osman (28) convicted of conspiracy to murder in connection with attempted bombings on London transport system on 21 July 2005. Sentenced to life imprisonment with recommended 40-year terms.
28 November 2008	Counter Terrorism Act 2008 passed. Includes offences relating to publication of information about, eg police officers and members of armed forces likely to be useful for terrorism, lifts prohibition on post-charge questioning, provides for seizure of assets of convicted terrorists and taking of fingerprints and DNA evidence of subjects of control orders, establishes register for monitoring those convicted of terrorist offences, and alters rules on use of intercept evidence.
12 January 2010	The European Court of Human Rights rules that the 'random' street stop and search power provided by section 44 Terrorism Act 2000 violates the right to respect for private life under Article 8 of the ECHR.
8 April 2010	Equality Act 2010 consolidates existing equality-related legislation and seeks to protect people against discrimination, harassment, or victimization in employment, and as users of private and public services, with respect to nine protected characteristics:

	age, disability, gender reassignment, marriage and civil partnership, pregnancy and maternity, race, religion or belief, sex, and sexual orientation.
6 May 2010	UK general election ends 13 years of Labour governments and brings Conservative/Liberal Democrat coalition to power.
16 December 2010	Terrorist Asset Freezing Act 2010 passed, imposing financial restrictions upon those suspected of involvement in terrorism.
2 May 2011	Osama bin Laden, leader of Al Qaeda, killed with others by US special forces in a night raid on his compound in Abbottabad, Pakistan.
June 2011	Publication of official review of *Prevent*.
14 December 2011	Terrorism Prevention and Investigation Measures Act 2011 replaces control orders with TPIMs ('control orders light').
1 May 2012	Protection of Freedoms Act 2012 amends 'suspicion-less' street stop and search power provided by sections 44–47 of the Terrorism Act 2000.
21 May 2012	NATO-member countries endorse an exit strategy for all 130,000 combat troops, but not advisers and trainers, from Afghanistan by end December 2014.
23 May 2013	US President Barack Obama announces formal end to 'Global War on Terror', indicating US military and intelligence agencies will focus on specific networks determined to destroy the United States.
7 July 2013	In accordance with a Memorandum of Understanding, radical Islamist preacher, Abu Qatada, deported from UK to Jordan where he is later tried and acquitted of terrorist offences.
27 August 2013	Police Firearms Training Centre under construction in Portishead near Bristol burns to the ground in an arson attack claimed by the anarchist group Angry Foxes Cell.
December 2013	Tackling Radicalisation and Extremism Taskforce established in the Cabinet Office following the murder of Lee Rigby.
13 March 2014	Anti-social Behaviour, Crime and Policing Act 2014 passed, consolidating and expanding law enforcement powers to address anti-social behaviour, and to replace Anti-Social Behaviour Orders with Criminal Behaviour Orders.
24 September 2014	UN Security Council Resolution 2178 enjoins member states to combat foreign terrorist fighters and to counter violent extremism.
31 December 2014	NATO withdraws combat troops from Afghanistan. Total coalition fatalities: 3,502 (US: 2,400; UK: 456).

12 February 2015	Counter-Terrorism and Security Act 2015 passed covering a range of issues including the '*Prevent* duty', seizure of passports, temporary exclusion from the UK, TPIMs, aviation, shipping, and rail security, plus other miscellaneous matters.
7 May 2015	Conservative Party wins UK general election with a majority of 12 seats.
22 July 2015	In *Beghal (Appellant) v Director of Public Prosecutions (Respondent)* Supreme Court of the UK rules that stop and search powers provided by Schedule 7 Terrorism Act 2000, as amended, are human rights compliant.
16 March 2016	Charities (Protection and Social Investment) Act 2016 provides stronger powers for registered mosques, madrassas, and other institutions.
14 April 2016	European Parliament approves PNR directive 2016/681 obliging airlines to collect passenger data and pass it on to EU member states.
16 June 2016	Jo Cox, Labour MP for Batley and Spen, dies from gunshot and multiple stab wounds in Birstall, West Yorkshire.
23 June 2016	UK votes in a referendum to leave the EU.
22 August 2016	Publication by Home Office of policy paper *Islamist extremism in prisons, probation and youth justice: An overview of, and government response to, the review into Islamist extremism in prisons, probation and youth justice*.
6 September 2016	Anjem Choudary, radical Muslim preacher, agitator, and leader of al-Muhajiroun, is sentenced to five years and six months in prison following conviction for inviting others to support the proscribed organization ISIS/DAESH. He is released automatically on licence in October 2018.
October 2016	Desistance and Disengagement Programme, a de-radicalization initiative for prisoners, launched.
23 November 2016	Thomas Alexander Mair, a 53-year-old gardener with far-right views, who killed Jo Cox MP because of her liberal views about the EU and immigration, was found guilty of murder and other related offences and sentenced to whole life term of imprisonment.
29 November 2016	Investigatory Powers Act 2016 passed. Contains provisions concerning investigatory powers and national security including interception of communications, interference with equipment, and the acquisition and retention of communications data, bulk personal datasets, and other information. Establishes the Investigatory Powers Commissioner to provide independent oversight of the use of investigatory powers

	by intelligence agencies, police forces, and other public authorities.
16 December 2016	British neo-Nazi terrorist movement, *National Action*, banned under the Terrorism Act 2000, the first far-right group to be proscribed since the Second World War.
31 January 2017	Police and Crime Act 2017 passed, amongst other things, granting the police the legal power to enter premises to seize passports cancelled under the Royal Prerogative in relation to national security.
March 2017	Cross-Government Victims of Terrorism Unit established to liaise with local authorities, the police, regional and national organizations, to ensure that those affected by terrorist attacks, including victims, witnesses, and bereaved families, receive quick, effective, and coordinated support.
22 March 2017	Jihadi vehicle and knife attack kills six (including attacker) and injures over 40 in Westminster, London.
27 April 2017	Criminal Finances Act 2017 passed. Establishes office of Counter-Terrorism Financial Investigator and gives law enforcement agencies and partners new powers to investigate and disrupt terrorist financing, money laundering, and criminal finance.
22 May 2017	Jihadi suicide bombing kills 23 (including attacker) and injures over 130 at pop concert in Manchester Arena.
3 June 2017	Jihadi vehicle and knife attack kills 11 (including three attackers) and injures over 40 at London Bridge.
8 June 2017	UK general election deprives Conservative Party of overall majority and forces Prime Minister Theresa May to rely on Northern Ireland's Democratic Unionist Party to remain in office.
19 June 2017	Darren Osborne drives a van into pedestrians assembled outside the Muslim Welfare House, Finsbury Park, London, one of whom, who had collapsed earlier and was receiving first aid, died at the scene.
January 2018	Commission for Countering Extremism established under leadership of Sara Khan.
1 February 2018	Finsbury Park mosque attacker, Darren Osborne, found guilty of terrorism-related murder and attempted murder and sentenced to life imprisonment.
7 March 2018	Paul Golding and Jayda Fransen, leader and deputy leader of *Britain First*, are imprisoned for religiously aggravated harassment. Golding had previously been convicted of offences linked to far-right activity and had served two short prison sentences in 2016 and 2017.

8 March 2018	In *Salman Butt v Secretary of State for the Home Department* High Court rejects a complaint that including complainant's name on an official list of 'extremists', mistakenly made public, violated his right to freedom of expression.
14 March 2018	Facebook removes accounts of British far-right movement *Britain First*, and those of its leading members.
26 April 2018	UK High Court rules that the Investigatory Powers Act violates EU law by permitting the storage of and access to internet data without adequate safeguards.
23 May 2018	Sanctions and Anti-Money Laundering Act 2018, amongst other things, provides a framework for the detection, investigation, and prevention of money laundering and terrorist financing. Where appropriate, permits sanctions, including but not confined to counter-terrorism, currently implemented through the UN and EU, to take effect in the UK.
31 October 2018	Data Retention and Acquisition Regulations 2018 come into force limiting access to communications data to serious crime and requiring authorities to consult the independent Investigatory Powers Commissioner before requesting data.
End 2018 to beginning 2019	Appearance of mysterious drones grounds 1,000 flights, affecting some 140,000 passengers at Gatwick during the Christmas period 2018, and more briefly at Heathrow in early 2019. Both airports invest in military-style anti-drone technology.
12 February 2019	Counter-Terrorism and Border Security Act 2019, amongst other things, extends and clarifies a number of existing terrorist offences, increases sentences for serious terrorist offences, improves post-release police management of those having served relevant custodial sentences, and strengthens national border defences against activities of hostile states.
28 February 2019	In *Beghal v United Kingdom* European Court of Human Rights condemns port stop and search powers provided by Schedule 7 of Terrorism Act 2000 (prior to amendment) for not being sufficiently circumscribed and for lacking sufficient safeguards against abuse.

26–27 October 2019	Abu Bakr Al-Baghdadi, self-proclaimed Caliph of ISIS/DAESH Caliphate in eastern Syria and western Iraq, killed in Syria by US forces.
12 December 2019	Conservative Party wins UK general election with 80-seat majority.
1 January 2020	UK leaves EU and transition phase commences.
31 December 2020	Transition phase of UK's departure from EU ends.

Index

accountability 193–195
Accountability and Data Returns (ADRs) 130
ACPO *see* Association of Chief Police Officers (ACPO)
administration: institutional discrimination 67; justice 172; law, public 9; local 52
agency/agencies: foreign security 167; intelligence and law enforcement 161; law enforcement and security 80, 89, 154, 165, 186, 190, 207; military and intelligence 205; police and intelligence 161; security and intelligence 182
ahkam al-jihad 40
Al Afghani 32, 35–36
al-Aqsa Mosque 44
al Banna, Hassan 36
al-Mawdudi, Mawlana 36
al-Muhajiroun 83
Al-Qaeda: 9/11 attack 35, 47, 202; bin Laden, Osama 205; company headquarters 47; Salafi-Jihadism 42–7; War on Terror 202
al-Quds al-Arabi 43
al-Salam Faraj, Muhammad Abd 43
Al Shabaab 42
al-Wahhab, Abd 35
al-wala'wa-l-bara 43
Anderson, David 7–8
Angry Brigade 50
antecedents 57; of contemporary jihadi terrorism 24; Irish 163
anti-discrimination laws 68
anti-globalization activists 50
anti-multiculturalism 58
anti-Muslim/ anti-Islam 76, 135–139; British foreign policy 75; comments 58; discrimination 67–70, 79; grounds 71; politics 57; prejudice 58, 69–72, 79, 140, 189

anti-*Prevent*: movement 135–141, 144, 199; scholarship 149
anti-Semitic/Semitism 58, 131
Anti-social Behaviour, Crime and Policing Act 2014 90, 147, 205
Anti-Social Behaviour Orders (ASBOs) 84
anti-social elements 55
Anti-Terrorism Crime and Security Act 2001 99, 161, 165, 177, 202, 203
anti-western-imperialism 47
Armed Response Vehicles (ARVs) 108
arrest 166–170; European warrant 19; house 95, 176, 178–179
ARVs *see* Armed Response Vehicles (ARVs)
ASBOs *see* Anti-Social Behaviour Orders (ASBOs)
Association of Chief Police Officers (ACPO) 121; Allied Matters unit 8
asylum 93–96; seekers 63
Ataturk, Kemal 37
Atomic Weapons Establishment 108
aviation security 89–90; Act 1982 89

baradari 62
Bedouin tribal organization 31
Belfast/Good Friday Agreement 1998 55
Biological Security Strategy 99
blood sacrifice 74
Boko Haram 42, 46
border security 89–90
Bosnian conflict 79
Brexit 18–20
British domestic terrorism 3–5; continuity and discontinuity in 5–11; far-left 50; far-right 56–60; jihadi 61–85
British citizenship cancellation of 185
British Transport Police (BTP) 108
BTP *see* British Transport Police (BTP)
Buddhism 29
Bush, George W. 46

Carry ('No Fly') scheme 89
CBRN attack *see* chemical, biological, radiological, or nuclear attack
Centre for the Protection of the National Infrastructure (CPNI) 97
CFA *see* Criminal Finances Act 2017 (CFA)
Charities (Protection and Social Investment) Act 2016 206
chemical, biological, radiological, or nuclear (CBRN) attack 105
Civil Authorities (Special Powers) Act 1922 52
Civil Contingencies Act 2004 104, 106, 203
Civil Nuclear Constabulary (CNC) 99
CNC *see* Civil Nuclear Constabulary (CNC)
CNI *see* Critical National Infrastructure (CNI)
cohesion: community 13, 16–17, 116, 135, 151, 185–190, 198; social 16, 144
colour-based racism 79–80
Commission for Countering Extremism 147
Common Foreign and Security Policy 19
Common Travel Area (CTA) 89
Commonwealth Immigration Act 1968 62
Communication Service Providers (CSPs) 162
community/communities: active interfaith groups 17; anti-social behaviour 17; civic participation 17; cohesive 16; festivals 17; ghettoization 17; hate crime 17; impermeable social segregation 17; integrated 16; international 88; Irish 163; Muslim 26, 85; prejudiced conduct 17; securitized 17; Ummah 26; violence 17
conflict/securitization models 15–17
constitutionalism 14
CONTEST 11–12; *see also Protect, Prepare, Prevent, Pursue*
contingent discrimination 67
Continuity IRA 55
Council of Europe 19
countering non-violent extremism 144–149
counter-radicalization 53, 112
Counter Terrorism Act 2008 97, 101, 169, 204
Counter Terrorism and Security Act (CTSA): 2015 7, 118–119, 178, 180, 206; 2019 91, 157, 179, 184, 208
Counter Terrorism Command (CTC) of Metropolitan Police 8

Counter Terrorism Intelligence Units (CTIUs) 8
counterterrorism/terrorist: continuity and discontinuity in British domestic 5–11; criminal investigations 163–170; criminalization 52; law and policy 10; national digital exploitation service 8; non-statutory police network 8; normalization 52; official 3; police primacy 52; Senior National Coordinator for 8; surveillance 159; Ulsterization 52
Counter Terrorist Specialist Firearms Officers (CTSFOs) 107
covenant of security 76, 84
Covid-19 pandemic 20–21
CPNI *see* Centre for the Protection of the National Infrastructure (CPNI)
CPS SCCTD *see* Crown Prosecution Service Special Crime and Counter Terrorism Division (CPS SCCTD)
Criminal Finances Act 2017 (CFA) 165, 207
Criminal Injuries Compensation Act 1995 109
criminalization 52: *Pursue* 154–158; terrorism 7
Criminal Justice Act 2003 167
Critical National Infrastructure (CNI) 97–98
crowded places 100–101
Crown Prosecution Service Special Crime and Counter Terrorism Division (CPS SCCTD) 172
CSPs *see* Communication Service Providers (CSPs)
CTA *see* Common Travel Area (CTA)
CTC *see* Counter Terrorism Command (CTC)
CTIUs *see* Counter Terrorism Intelligence Units (CTIUs)
CTSA *see* Counter Terrorism and Security Act (CTSA)
CTSFOs *see* Counter Terrorist Specialist Firearms Officers (CTSFOs)
Cyber Security Operations Centre 97

Data Protection Act 1998 133
Data Retention and Investigatory Powers Act 2014 161
daughter communities 62
Da'wah 82–83
DCLG *see* Department for Communities and Local Government (DCLG)
death cult 74

212 Index

declaration of incompatibility 10
Defence Science and Technology
  Laboratory 108
Dehlawi, Shah Waliullah 64
Department for Communities and Local
  Government (DCLG) 115
de-radicalization 7, 11, 22, 112; anti-
  Prevent movement 149; Channel
  cases 123; diversion-by-persuasion
  113; *Prevent* strategy 112; prison 117;
  programmes 84, 141, 143, 173, 175;
  rehabilitation 113, 116
Derogation 10
desh pardesh 62
Desistance and Disengagement Programme
  (DDP) 175–176
de-territorialization 81
Dhu-al-Hijjah 32
Diplock courts 2, 171–172
discrimination 67; anti-Muslim 67–70, 79;
  contingent 67; direct 67, 69; individual
  67; institutional 67; objective 67;
  official 67; perception of 67; racial 92;
  systematic 67
dissident Irish republican terrorism:
  grievances 54; mobilization 54–56;
  modus operandi 54–56
drone crisis 90

EAU *see* Extremism Analysis Unit (EAU)
ECHR *see* European Convention on
  Human Rights (ECHR)
ECJ *see* European Court of Justice (ECJ)
ECtHR *see* European Court of Human
  Rights (ECtHR)
EDL *see* English Defence League (EDL)
Education Reform Act 1988 120
EHRC *see* Equality and Human Rights
  Commission (EHRC)
Emergency Powers Act 1920 106, 203
Emergency Powers Act (Northern Ireland)
  1926 106, 203
Energy Act 2004 99
English Defence League (EDL) 57–59
Equality Act 2010 68, 91, 104, 120,
  142, 204
Equality and Human Rights Commission
  (EHRC) 142
European Arrest Warrant 19
European Convention on Human Rights
  (ECHR) 9–10; Article 8(2) 102; Article
  10 120, 133, 148–149; Article 14 68;
  Article 15 11, 176

European Convention on the Prevention
  of Terrorism 2005 2
European Court of Human Rights
  (ECtHR) 9–10, 67, 92, 102,
  148–149, 166
European Court of Justice (ECJ) 161
Explosive Substances Act 1883 157, 169
Extremism Analysis Unit (EAU) 132
Extremism Community Trigger 146

far-right terrorism 56–60, 188
fascism 37, 58
FASS programme *see* Future Aviation
  Security Solutions (FASS) programme
fatal terrorist incidents 199–200
fatwa 77, 44
Financing of Terrorism 19
Firearms Acts 1968 and 1997 98
First Indian War of Independence 35
Five Pillars of Islam 32
foreign security agencies 167
Franklin, Benjamin 9
Future Aviation Security Solutions (FASS)
  programme 90

GCHQ *see* Government Communications
  Headquarters (GCHQ)
glorifying terrorism 155
Gnosticism 28
Good Friday/Belfast Agreement 1998 20,
  24, 51, 54, 115
Government Communications
  Headquarters (GCHQ) 97
Gulf War 45

hadith 65
hajj 32
hakimiyya 43
halaqahs 82
Harakat-ul-Mujahideen 77
Hibernophobia 163
Hijra 25
Hisbah 82
Hizb ut-Tahrir 77
HM Inspectorate of Constabulary and Fire
  & Rescue Services 72
Home Office Extremism Analysis Unit 132
homophobia 70
Hostile Vehicle Mitigation 101
house arrest 95, 176, 178–179
House of Commons Home Affairs
  Committee 90
HRA *see* Human Rights Act 1998 (HRA)

human rights 193–5; compliant 7, 10, 92, 111; derogation 11; international 10; Joint Parliamentary Committee 10, 128; liberty and security 9; man-made law 33; organization 57–8; *Prevent* threat to/violation of 139–43; systematic violation 46; *see also* European Convention on Human Rights (ECHR); European Court of Human Rights (ECtHR)
Human Rights Act 1998 (HRA) 8, 9, 91, 195, 201
human rights organization 57–58
Hussein, Saddam 45

ICAO *see* International Civil Aviation Organization (ICAO)
ijma 39
ijtihad 39
'illa 39
immigration 93–6; Commonwealth Immigration Acts 62; Immigration Appeal Tribunal 177; independent legal action 180; Muslim 61–3; Pakistani 62; Special Immigration Appeals Commission 177
Immigration, Asylum and Nationality Act 2006 93–94
imperial absolutism 27
Independent Reviewer of Terrorism Legislation 7, 117
individual discrimination 67
Initial Operational Response (IOR) 107
institutional discrimination 67
intelligence 6–7; based police power 104; information and 158–162; and law enforcement agencies 161; official surveillance and 159
International Civil Aviation Organization (ICAO) 89
internet threats 97
internment 176–178
investigation 163–70
Investigatory Powers Act 2016 159, 161, 162, 206
Investigatory Powers Commissioner's Office (IPCO) 162
IOR *see* Initial Operational Response (IOR)
IPCO *see* Investigatory Powers Commissioner's Office (IPCO)
Irish National Liberation Army 55
Irish Volunteers 55
ISIS/DAESH 42, 46, 47, 81–82, 118

Islam/Islamist/Islamism: Day of Judgement 41; education 33; enemies of 43; extremism 78, 144–146; Five Pillars 32; governance 43; history 24–30; *ijma* 39; *ijtihad* 39; *'illa* 39; just and holy war traditions 38–42; *kalam* 39; man-made law 33; *maslaha* 39; non-violent extremism 34, 145–149; noxious absences 33; *qiyas* 39; Qur'an 30; scholars 27; *shabah* 39; Sufism 28; Sunnis and Shias 28–29, 64; *taqlid* 39; terrorism 23; traditionalism 32; vicious presences 33; violent extremism 34
Islamophobia 18, 69–72; *see also* anti-Muslim/ anti-Islamic
izzat 62

Jaish-e-Mohammed 77
Jam'iat Ihyaa Minhaaj Al-Sunnah (JIMAS) 77
JESIPs *see* Joint Emergency Services Interoperability Principles (JESIPs)
jihad/jihadi/jihadism: anti-Muslim discrimination and 67–69; anti-Muslim racism, prejudice 69–72; demographics 63–65; holy and just war traditions in Islam 38–42; insurgent movement ISIS/DAESH 21; Islam and Islamism 30–38; Islamic history 24–30; Islamophobia 69–72; Muslim immigration 61–3; Muslim material disadvantage 65–66; non terrorists 59; Salafi-Jihadism 42–47; of sword 82; terrorism 24, 155; violent 23
JIMAS *see* Jam'iat Ihyaa Minhaaj Al-Sunnah (JIMAS)
JMLIT *see* Joint Money Laundering Intelligence Taskforce (JMLIT)
Joint Counter Terrorism Oversight Group 8
Joint Emergency Services Interoperability Principles (JESIPs) 105, 107
Joint Money Laundering Intelligence Taskforce (JMLIT) 165
Joint Parliamentary Committee on Human Rights 10, 128
Joint Security and Resilience Centre (JSaRC) 100
JSaRC *see* Joint Security and Resilience Centre (JSaRC)
Justice and Home Affairs 19
Justice and Security (Northern Ireland) Act 2007 172, 204

214 Index

kalam 39
Kelsay, J. 26, 40
Kenny, M. 81–85

law enforcement and security agencies 80, 89, 154, 165, 186, 190, 207
legal/human rights environment 147–149
legality test 133
LGBT+ people 58
liberty 9–11
literalism 32
Local Resilience Forums (LRFs) 105
London Bridge attack 108
Londonistan 79
LRFs *see* Local Resilience Forums (LRFs)
Lyrical Terrorist 157

Manchester Arena attack 61
Manufacture and Storage of Explosives Regulations 2005 99
maslaha 39
materials of concern 98–100
Memoranda of Understanding (MoU) 95
micro aggressions 69
military and intelligence agencies 205
military-style anti-drone technology 208
Ministry of Defence Police Act 1987 97
Ministry of Housing, Communities and Local Government 118
misogyny 69
MoU *see* Memoranda of Understanding (MoU)
Multi-Agency Public Protection Arrangements (MAPPAs) 175–176
Muslim: communities in Britain 63, 116, 137; immigration 61–63; lands 25, 33, 42, 75–76; law-abiding 58; material disadvantage 65–66; non-Muslim 33, 70–71; non-white 70; patrols 147; secularism and modernization 37; self-declaration 65; true 33; white 70; *see also* Islam/Islamist/Islamism
Muslim Parliament 77

NaCTSO *see* National Counter Terrorism Security Office (NaCTSO)
National Counter-Terrorism Exercise Programme 109; and emergency services 107
National Counter Terrorism Security Office (NaCTSO) 98
National Counter Terrorist Exercise Programmes 105

National Crime Agency's National Cyber Crime Unit 97
National Digital Exploitation Service (NDES) 8
National Offender Extremism Management Unit 116
National Police Chiefs Council (NPCC) 98, 117
National Risk Assessment (NRA) 105
National Security Risk Assessment (NSRA) 105
NDES *see* National Digital Exploitation Service (NDES)
neo-Nazism 58
New IRA 55
9/11 attack 35, 47, 202; anti-Soviet war 76; British domestic jihadi terrorism 3–4; CONTEST 11; counter-radicalization 7; counterterrorist intelligence 159; Critical National Infrastructure 97; de-radicalization 7; domestic counterterrorist 1, 7; EU counterterrorist activity 19; European Arrest Warrant 19; far-right terrorism 188; fatal bomb attack 46; imprisonment 156; internment 177; jihadi terrorism 113; national security 93; non-statutory police counterterrorism network 8; public emergency threaten 177; punishment and rehabilitation 173; securitized community 159; suicide attacks 22, 191; Terrorism Act 2000 8; transnational counterterrorist policy 18; war on terror 46
No Fly scheme 89
non-derogable rights 10–11
non-political crime 93–94
non-refoulment 95
non-statutory police counterterrorism network 8
non-violent extremism 34, 122, 127, 133–134, 145–149
no-platforming 127
Northern Ireland (Emergency Provisions) Act 1973 2, 171
NPCC *see* National Police Chiefs Council (NPCC)
NRA *see* National Risk Assessment (NRA)
NSRA *see* National Security Risk Assessment (NSRA)

objective discrimination 67
obsessive-compulsive tendency 74
Office for Students (OfS) 130–131

Office of Cyber Security and Information Assurance 97
official discrimination 67
Operation TEMPERER 106
Ouseley, Mr Justice 133

Pakistani immigrants 81
pentiti process 113
perception of discrimination 67
PHE *see* Public Health England (PHE)
poison gas as offensive weapon 74
Police and Crime Act: 2009 89; 2017 165, 207
police and intelligence agencies 161
Police and Judicial Cooperation in Criminal Matters 19
Police Counter Terrorism Board 8
Police Firearms Training Centre 50
Police Services Agreement 89
Policing and Crime Act 2009 89
Pool Reinsurance Company (Pool Re) 100
Prepare: adequate capacity 105–108; resilience 108–109
Prevent: in action 120–125; Counter Terrorism and Security Act 2015 118–119; domestic background 114–118; duty 119–120; in health sector 125; in higher education 127–134; international background 112–114; policy implications of scrapping 143–145; politics of 134–135; public debate 143; in schools 125–127; threat to/violation of human rights 139–143; toxic and anti-Muslim 135–139
Prevention of Terrorism Act 2005 19, 178, 203
Protect: asylum 93–96; border and aviation security 89–90; counterterrorist stop and search at ports 90–92, and on streets 101–105; critical national infrastructure 97–98; crowded places 100–101; immigration 93–96; transport systems 96; unauthorized usage 98–100
Protection of Freedoms Act 2012 103, 205
Provisional IRA 55
PSED *see* Public Sector Equality Duty (PSED)
Public Health England (PHE) 108
Public Sector Equality Duty (PSED) 120
punishment 173–176, 192
Pursue: criminalization 154–158; executive controls 176–185; information and intelligence 158–162; investigation 163–170; prosecution and trial 171–173;

punishment 173–176; rehabilitation 173–176

qisas 43
qiyas 39
Qur'an 30
Quraysh 26

racism 18, 69, 92; colour-based 79–80
Radiological and Nuclear (RN) deterrence and detection 99
RAG *see* Risk Advisory Groups (RAG)
rationalism 32
Real IRA 55
reasonable excuse 157
reciprocal radicalization 59
reflexive approach 15–16, 15–17
reformism 14
Refugee Convention 1951 Article 1F 93; Article 33 (2) 94
Regulation of Investigatory Powers Act 2000 (RIPA) 134, 159, 160–162, 171
rehabilitation 173–176, 192
reign of terror 1
Reinsurance (Acts of Terrorism) Act 1993 109
religious prejudice 71
Republican Action Against Drugs 55
resilience 11; Capabilities Programme 109; risk 12–13
right wing: extremism 122; radicalization 124; terrorism 155
RIPA *see* Regulation of Investigatory Powers Act 2000 (RIPA)
Risk Advisory Groups (RAG) 89
Rowley, Mark 60
Royal Prerogative 13
Run, Hide, Tell campaign 105
Rushdie, Salman 76–77

safe space campaigns 127
salaf 35
Salafi/Salafism 24, 42–47, 79
salat 32
Sanctions and Anti-Money Laundering Act 2018 165, 208
Satanic Verses 76–7
sawm 32
Secretary of State for Transport and the Civil Aviation 89
Security: 9–11, 17, 76, 196; aviation 89–90; border 89–90; CNI 97–98; community 139, 140, 159; covenant of 76, 84; Cyber Security Operations

Centre 97; and intelligence agencies 182; JSaRC 100; MDP 97; Police Services Agreement 89; Sector Security and Resilience Plans 89–90; of society 15; stop and search at ports 90-92 and on streets 101–105; threats 95; vetted advocates 95
Security Executive Groups (SEG) 89
Security Industry Authority 100
Security Service Act 1989 97
'See it. Say it. Sorted.' campaigns 108
SEG *see* Security Executive Groups (SEG)
segregation 17, 47, 67, 174–5; gender 131–2
self-radicalization 78
Senior National Coordinator for Counter Terrorism 8
Sepoy Mutiny 1857 35
Serious Organised Crime Agency 98
7/7 attack 102; bombers 62; domestic threat 114; Lindsay, Germaine 79; Siddique Khan, Mohammed 62, 73, 78, 80; Tanweer, Shehzad 80; Terrorism Act 2006, 204
shabah 39
shahadah 32, 70
Sharia 31–32
Shias 28–29
Sinai, N. 41
Special Immigration Appeals Commission (SIAC) 177
stop and search at ports 90-92 and on streets 101–105
street-based anti-Islamic politics 57
Sufism 28–29
sunnah 28
Sunnis 28–29, 64
systematic discrimination 67

Tabligh Jamaat 35
takfir 43
Tanweer, Shehzad 80
taqlid 39
tatarrus 43
tawhid 43
Tell MAMA 71–72
Terrorism Act 2000 50, 155, 201, 206–8; arrest, charge, and detention 166; continuity 8; counterterrorist legislation 154; stop and search at ports 90 and on streets 101–105; investigation 153; prosecution and trial 171; section 41 170; section 44 204; section 58 157
Terrorism Act 2006 99, 157, 161
Terrorism Prevention and Investigation Measures (TPIMs) Act 2011 178, 205

terrorism/terrorist: anarchist 2; anti-colonialist 2; British domestic 3–5; counter-radicalization 7; criminalization 7; de-radicalization 7; dissident Irish republican 51–56; far-right 56–60; financing of 19, 165; glorifying 155; Islamist 23; Lyrical Terrorist 157; miscellaneous 4; new left/right 2; non-jihadi 59; non-state 2–3; religious 2; right wing 155; state 3; street-based anti-Islamic politics 57; tier one threat 106; training 155; treaty on Prevention of 19; Troubles-based 3, 54–55; *see also* 7/7, 9/11; jihad/jihadi/jihadism; violence
Terrorist Asset Freezing Act 2010 205
Threats 188
tit-for-tat retaliation 43
TPIMs *see* Terrorism Prevention and Investigation Measures (TPIMs)
transphobia 70
transport systems 96
travel restrictions 179–184
trivial anti-social activities 161
the Troubles 3, 24, 54; counterterrorism and 191

Ulster Defence Association and Ulster Volunteer Force 52
Ulsterization 52
ultra-nationalism 58
Ummah 26
universal human emancipation 50
UN Refugee Convention 1951 93
UN Security Council resolutions (UNSCR) 1373 19; 2309 and 2396

vicious circle radicalization 59
vicious presences 33
Victims of Terrorism Unit (VTU) 109
violence: blood-curdling endorsements 41; extremism 114; far left and far right 50; human rights 139–143; Islamic extremism 23, 34; jihadism 23, 42
VTU *see* Victims of Terrorism Unit (VTU)

Wahhabism 35
wars of succession/apostasy *(riddah)* 27
weaponized suicide 54
Wilkinson, P. 29, 32–34

xenophobia 58, 70

zakat 32

Printed in the United States
by Baker & Taylor Publisher Services